Alternatives to Prison

Sage Contemporary Criminology

Series editors

John Lea • Roger Matthews • Jock Young
Centre for Criminology, Middlesex Polytechnic

Geoffrey Pearson
Goldsmiths' College London

Sage Contemporary Criminology draws on the best of current work in criminology and socio-legal studies, both in Britain and internationally, to provide lecturers, students and policy-makers with the latest research on the functioning of the criminal justice and legal systems. Individual titles will cover a wide span of issues such as new developments in informal justice; changing forms of policing and crime prevention; the impact of crime in the inner city; and the role of the legal system in relation to social divisions by gender and race. Throughout, the series will relate theoretical problems in the social analysis of deviancy and social control to the practical and policy-related issues in criminology and law.

Already published

Jeanne Gregory, *Sex, Race and the Law: Legislating for Equality*
John Pitts, *The Politics of Juvenile Crime*
Roger Matthews (ed.), *Informal Justice?*
Roger Matthews (ed.), *Privatizing Criminal Justice*
Nigel South, *Policing for Profit: The Private Security Sector*

Alternatives to Prison

Punishment, Custody and the Community

Antony A. Vass

⑤ SAGE Publications
London • Newbury Park • New Delhi

SAGE Publications Ltd
28 Banner Street
London EC1Y 8QE

SAGE Publications Inc
2111 West Hillcrest Drive
Newbury Park, California 91320

SAGE Publications India Pvt Ltd
32, M-Block Market
Greater Kailash – I
New Delhi 110 048

British Library Cataloguing in Publication data

Vass, Antony A.
     Alternatives to prison. — (Sage contemporary criminology)
     1. Prison reform
     I. Title
     364.68

     ISBN 0-8039-8263-1
     ISBN 0-8039-8264-X pbk

Library of Congress catalog card number 90-061472

Typeset by AKM Associates (UK) Ltd, Southall, London
Printed in Great Britain by Billing and Sons Ltd, Worcester

Contents

For Artemis and Andonis

. . . I will light a candle for you
and keep it burning in the night
and pray that you are alright.

Candles (Chris Rea)

Acknowledgements

As always when writing a book, the author depends on many sources, both primary and secondary. But there are also those people who help in a number of ways and contribute to a book's ideas, even its completion. These are the people who constitute in many respects the 'significant other' and who deserve recognition. In this case, my significant others are, first, Geoffrey Pearson. I am indebted to him for his comments and advice in general. He may not realise it, but he has been supportive, both formally and informally. Indeed, informally, our occasional social gatherings in the college bar have been significant in terms of the book's 'development'. At the end of often long, sometimes exhausting and difficult days, the experience of having a friendly chat with colleagues over a drink can be quite educational. It is often said that the best education takes place away from classrooms. It is true. Some of the ideas here, though mine and raised by me in the first instance in the course of conversation or writing, were sharpened and informed further by Geoff's witty style and fast observations.

Secondly, there are those colleagues who may not say much but whose influences can be quite real nonetheless. Jock Young is a prime example. His academic influences on me go back a long way, starting in the early 1970s and continuing to the present day. But he also has a talent for staying quiet for long and uninterrupted periods and thus allowing others, like me, to talk endlessly. His modesty and supportive responses plus his humour have always been qualities which I admired in him. Roger Matthews for his reading of the manuscript. I am still awaiting his comments! I guess his silence must imply a meaningful message about what the book says. But I would not like to ponder on that. I would rather let the reader reach a conclusion on this matter. Stephen Barr, Vivienne Dunlop, Susan Haberis and Sally Green at Sage whose advice and encouragement have contributed to the completion of the book. Gillian Stern, at Sage, and the anonymous 'readers' of the manuscript whose formidable comments have helped to improve the text. Alan Weston and Hertfordshire Probation Service for supplying me with data on the Cedar Hall day centre (Chapter 6). Ken Menzies whose writings on community service in the Canadian context, personal communications, and our joint research and publications on the administration and enforcement of the order helped me to develop a comparative perspective about practices in Canada and this country. Guardian Newspapers Ltd for giving me permission to reproduce Table 1. Warner Chappell Music Ltd for granting me permission to reproduce lyrics from Chris Rea's *Candles*, © Magnet Music Ltd.

Special thanks are due to my two sons, Andreas and Nicholas, for their valuable information and guidance, based on their inside knowledge of the activities and whereabouts of 'Batman', 'Spiderman' and 'Snow White'. 'Batman's' assistance was called for in an article I wrote for *Social Work Today*, 'Tagging: Spiderman looks at the web of electronic tags' based on ideas from this book. 'Snow White' makes a brief appearance in Chapter 7. Mind you, their assistance did not come cheap. They demanded a 'tenner' each before parting with information!

Finally, I would like to thank those few people, my intimate circle, for being there when I need them most, and whose presence gives me a purpose and a reason for just being 'me'. Their love and affection have had the effect of pushing me out of bouts of lethargy and helping me to ride a few storms — who hasn't any troubles anyway. However, my troubles got just a bit more complicated when I lost a whole chapter of this book: a disc suddenly decided to end its useful life in a rather abrupt and premature manner. It took with it all my precious data. Second copy? What second copy? I kept none. My immediate solution was a strong (very strong) desire to throw, literally, my information technology in the deep end of the fish pond and return to my old Imperial 66. Then I remembered that I had disposed of it in part exchange for more information technology. The last thing I wanted to do at that stage was to rewrite a chapter from scratch and complete a book on alternatives to prison. My 'intimate circle' was instrumental in regenerating my interest. It helped me to regain my composure, and enabled me to complete the project.

Preface

This book is about attempts to 'punish' offenders in the community instead of sending them to prison. It is a critical appraisal of alternatives to custody.

Historically, alternatives have been shown to have little influence in controlling the expansion of the prison institution — either in physical or human terms. Indeed there is some evidence which tentatively concludes that alternatives may assist the prison establishment to expand and proliferate. The book explores and critically evaluates this thesis and finds it convincing in some respects but quite unconvincing in others. However, irrespective of the state of knowledge on the subject, I suggest that alternatives do have a positive side and a useful role to play in the criminal justice system. I argue that with careful policy, alternatives to custody can be used as a powerful antidote to the supremacy of the prison. But they cannot be expected to resolve the prison crisis which, as I demonstrate, is essentially a *policy crisis*. A reduction in the rate of incarceration and the prison population, a resolution of the dilemma of what the task of alternatives (among other matters) should be, and what role they play in the criminal justice process, cannot be achieved unless there is a coherent criminal justice policy to guide and organise activity.

Before I briefly describe the subject-matter of the book, it is important that I should state my own ideological standpoint. I believe that prisons are bad: that there are better, more acceptable ways of punishing and controlling offenders than sending them to prison. Community alternatives — whether one calls them alternatives to custody, or supervision, or punishment in the community — provide a reasonable and, as will be shown, equally 'effective' way of administering penalties against people who commit criminal offences. In a sense, I am making a moral judgement here. The moral issue is that alternatives are a more desirable approach to punishing offenders, if that is what it is all about, than locking them up in conditions which are an affront to a society which calls itself 'civilised'.

Having stated that personal preference and viewpoint, I must add that the existence of that value does not prevent me from being critical of alternatives to custody and policies of 'diversion'. Although I subscribe to such a policy, I remain sceptical. I have yet to be convinced that those penal measures do not lead, when left unchecked, to serious and very undesirable consequences. They may be desirable on moral grounds but they do have, when looked at in a detached and analytical manner, serious flaws, and they exhibit real risks. For instance, that they may not be so humane after all; that they may not be so cheap; that they may not be so effective in reducing recidivism; that they may not always be real alternatives to prison but alternatives to other non-custodial penal measures; and as said earlier, that instead of challenging custodial institutions they may encourage their existence and perhaps even their expansion.

In recognising and allowing the above personal value, on the one hand, and a strong dose of scepticism on the other to coexist, has created a balance whose result is a book which, I believe, offers a fairly detached analysis and appraisal of prisons, community penal measures and policy.

The book draws together many diverse findings concerning the viability and rationale as well as problems of such penal measures. It offers, where possible, results and findings emanating from research in the field. For obvious reasons (availability of information, for instance) these findings relate in the main to England and Wales (hereafter, 'England'). However, where it is relevant and viable to offer ideas and findings emanating from research outside England, the book retains and sustains a comparative focus stretching to other countries, mainly European states, Canada and the USA.

Chapter 1 is the historical backcloth against which the rest of the book can be understood. It offers a brief historical account of the development of the prison institution, its recurrent crises, and the development of alternatives.

Chapter 2 builds on the general context offered by Chapter 1 by focusing on current concerns about prisons, their rising populations, sentencing policy, costs and other related matters. It gives an up-to-date account and analysis of the reasons for the prison crisis in the 1980s and suggests that, far from being challenged, the prison is expanding at an alarming rate.

Chapter 3 looks closely and in detail at the debates concerning prisons and alternatives to custody. It identifies and discusses a set of core theoretical and empirical issues which need to be addressed in any debate about prisons and their alternatives. The analysis of the debates helps to separate rhetoric from reality, and puts the arguments about the relationship between prisons and alternatives in perspective.

Chapter 4 develops the argument one step further by critically examining claims that alternatives, instead of challenging custodial establishments, tend to promote further expansion within and outside institutions: that they widen the net of social control and surveillance.

Chapter 5 builds on the preceding discussion by arguing that alternatives cannot be adequately understood or measured in relation to their 'effectiveness' as prison substitutes unless the analysis is allowed to depart from a mere preoccupation with crude 'outcomes' to focusing instead on an appreciation of the part played by 'process' in creating or sustaining those results. This chapter is a case study offering a direct, albeit brief, account of the way in which the community service order (which is regarded as an alternative to custody) is enforced as a 'process of tolerance'. That is to say, how supervising officers, in their efforts to exercise authority over offenders and make their work manageable, downgrade the formal rules of conduct by inventing and resorting to their own flexible means of control — as opposed to the more authoritative, legal codes of practice. This process of accommodation and negotiation of conflict or violations of requirements (that is, the exercise of 'tolerance') shields many offenders from re-entering the criminal justice system as defaulters of their order and enhances their chances of successfully discharging their obligations to the courts.

Chapter 6 offers a second example of an alternative to custody and its relationship to prison — probation day centres. In this case, the workings of this fairly recent and largely unexplored area are examined and serious questions are raised about the way in which this penal measure is used as an alternative to custody, particularly in respect of women and individuals from ethnic minority groups. The chapter addresses and questions the role played by the magistracy and judiciary in reducing or enhancing the status of community penal measures as alternatives to custody.

Chapter 7 draws together the basic findings and themes of the book. It looks at current policy in England in some detail, including plans for the privatisation of parts of the criminal justice system. It suggests what possible implications such policy may have, and offers tentative recommendations of how to strengthen the powers of existing alternatives to act as reliable and, in a sense, 'true' alternatives. The chapter concludes that alternatives on their own cannot achieve a great deal unless they are backed by a determined and concerted criminal justice policy whose genuine objective should be to control and deplete the incarceration process. In that sense, in the last chapter, I return to the political and moral issue: what a government *can* do as opposed to what it is currently doing or intending to do; what it *could* do; what it *should* do; and maybe what it *ought* to do.

The final chapter, therefore, raises the question of whether a government's (any government's) moral and ideological stance can endow it with enough courage to exercise the political will to set in motion a chain of events which could alter — for good — the current but depressingly singular map of human warehouses.

Antony A. Vass
Middlesex Polytechnic

1 The prison crisis and alternatives to custody: A brief history

'Alternatives to custody' refer to a wide assortment of tasks, sentences and dispositions. There is no single definition of what they are, for it appears that in general terms anything which involves crime prevention, and punishment or control *outside* custodial establishments, is deposited in the 'community' category and thus can be legitimately defined as an 'alternative'. In this sense, alternatives to custody can include many diverse activities in the criminal justice system: not just sentencing choices following conviction, but also pre-trial decisions and even broader policies of preventing risk groups, such as juveniles, from even experiencing formal justice and control. Examples of such 'community programmes' or alternatives to custody in their more confused and general form include: neighbourhood crime prevention schemes; bail; police cautioning; intermediate treatment projects for juveniles; probation orders (with or without special requirements); fines and fixed penalties; conditional discharge orders; tracking schemes; tagging; supervision orders with special requirements; suspended sentences; parole; deferred sentences; compensation orders; binding over; attendance centre orders; suspended sentence supervision orders; and community service orders.

All of these, and more, have been variously described as 'community-based penal measures'; 'community-based dispositions'; 'community care programmes'; 'community corrections'; 'community correctional programmes'; 'non-custodial penal measures'; 'diversionary penal measures'; 'decarceration'; 'deinstitutionalisation'; 'humane punishment'; 'supervision in the community'; or more recently, since the early 1980s, 'punishment in the community'. All such concepts, irrespective of tone and ambiguity, have been used, at some point, as synonyms or substitutes for each other as though anything which denotes some small notion of 'community' within which penal services and penalties are administered should make sense and be applicable on a universal scale. This more general and equivocal meaning of alternatives to custody, though successfully housing as an umbrella term a variety of activities in the penal system, is limited in its usefulness as an analytical tool. It is quite problematic both in conceptual as well as practical terms: as it means 'all things to all people', it has little value as a heuristic device in understanding prisons, prison crises, and attempts to control their expanding populations by designating or using specific community penal measures as 'alternatives'.

In order to avoid such confusion and the umbrella term of alternatives to custody, I treat alternatives as those penalties which are administered following a conviction for a criminal offence; and whose availability and use by courts — explicitly or implicitly — renders them officially (that is, in terms of legislation) or unofficially (that is, in the absence of clear legal terms of reference) as alternatives to custody. In short, alternatives to custody *are those penalties which, following conviction and sentence, allow an offender to spend part or all of his or her sentence in the community and outside prison establishments*. In this sense, even parole and remission of sentence (which refer to executive powers or means in attempting to reduce the prison population) fall within this category. Under this definition there are three types of alternatives to custody at work. One type is those sentences (such as the community service order, suspended sentence, attendance sentence orders, and probation with conditions) which are designated as substitutes for a prison sentence; a second type is those sentences which are not specifically designated as substitutes (which fall under the general banner of 'non-custodial penal measures', such as a probation order without conditions) but which may be, and are increasingly being used or promoted as alternatives to custody; and a third type — such as parole and remission of sentence — which reduces the term of a custodial sentence by offering an 'alternative' (early release of an offender to the community and, where parole is concerned, subject to supervision and to possible recall to serve the remainder of the custodial sentence). In this book reference is made to all three types of alternatives though the emphasis is on sanctions which require offenders to be supervised by designated officials (for example probation officers) in the community; and in the course of that supervision that they are expected to comply with specific and general requirements as stated by courts and applied by supervising officers. In that sense, although information and evaluations are offered with regard to examples of such alternatives in the context of the whole book, in the final chapters I shift the emphasis from the general to the specific to offer an analysis and a discussion of two examples of alternatives to custody (community service and probation day centres); and to provide detailed accounts of the workings of those alternatives.

Finally, in this introductory section, and before I offer a brief historical account of the prison, its crisis, and the development of alternatives to custody in order to set the social context and the backcloth against which current debates and developments can be understood, there is one further qualification which needs to be made. The terms 'prison' and 'custody' are used interchangeably in this text. Unless otherwise stated, where 'prison' is referred to, it is used in its general sense (involving the incarceration of both juveniles and adults) and as such it is the equivalent of 'custody'. However, though I refer to both juveniles and adults in the more general discussion and debates about alternatives, in the more specific parts of the book which deal with examples of alternatives to custody the discussion and the emphasis is on adults.

The quest for alternatives

In order to understand alternatives to custody in a contemporary sense and appreciate attempts which are currently made by governments to expand such alternatives and to contain prison populations, it is necessary to dwell on the historical precedents which led to the emergence of alternatives and the prison institution (for detailed accounts see Bailey, 1981; Cohen, 1985; Foucault, 1977; Garland, 1985; Ignatieff, 1978, 1983; Rothman, 1971; Scull, 1977; Vass, 1984: 6–41).

It is easy for any researcher to package history into square, polished and well-labelled compartments as though everything fits into a pattern; that everything — from means to ends — follows a well-planned and engineered routine which becomes pervasive and inescapable. I wish to avoid that impression by stating the obvious. What follows is a very sketchy and perhaps slightly distorted image of a long and highly complex historical process of development and social relationships. It is a combination of historical snapshots which, like any snapshots, manage to portray not the whole but parts which have been captured by a pointed lens. Although useful and perhaps reliable as accounts, they are nonetheless incomplete and the reader who is interested in this historical backcloth should consult other textbooks. The purpose here is merely to offer a brief glimpse of history in order to use it as a foundation and build on it a detailed analysis of the contemporary scene with regard to prisons and alternatives to custody.

Ball et al. (1988: 22) argue that, historically, alternatives to custody in their proper sense form a new 'fourth phase in the development of European–North American punitive policy'. They build on Rusche's (1980) analysis which identifies three distinct phases in the development of criminal sanctions: a period which used the body as the object of severe punishment; the decline of this approach by the eighteenth century and the search for other more refined measures; and the emergence of the prison and other sanctions in the nineteenth century (which have been amplified in the twentieth century). They suggest that a fourth phase characterised by a distinct reaction against prisons and custodial penalties has in general emerged in the last 40 years or so, but especially since the 1960s. Although it is true that a distinct *shift* towards alternatives is a contemporary phenomenon, the phenomenon itself is not new. First, the present-day legislative framework and profile of the sentencing process and its available penal options, including alternatives to custody, has its roots in the middle or latter part of the nineteenth century (Thomas, 1979). Secondly, in terms of historical relevance and connection, one may suggest that in the history of criminal law there have been processes, if not actual efforts and programmes, to offer 'alternatives' at different and earlier periods. For instance, under the procedural rules of the sixteenth, seventeenth, and eighteenth centuries, release of an offender from capital punishment often amounted to de facto diversion (European Committee on Crime Prevention, 1980).

Until the seventeenth century, criminal sanctions were mainly corporal, capital, financial and compensatory. Transportation was also added, and remained in force until the nineteenth century. The English prison until the early eighteenth century served as a bridging service rather than as a distinct form of control for the containment and punishment of felons. Its purpose was primarily to house civil and criminal debtors or offenders awaiting trial; and acted as a holding agency, a sort of reserve, for people awaiting corporal or capital punishment or expecting transportation to the colonies.

Though that early version of the contemporary prison institution was embryonically assuming a more specific role in the criminal justice process, one could identify in the period between the sixteenth and eighteenth centuries the emergence and availability of several diverse programmes in the methods of containment and confinement: the Bridewell, the workhouses, the reformatories for young offenders, transportation and impressment among others. These measures not only extended the scope of available sanctions but also served certain national needs relevant to the period: economic stringencies; colonial needs; alleviating the pressure on the authorities emanating from overcrowded gaols; and offering opportunities for finding soldiers and sailors for service abroad (Radzinowicz, 1968).

Much of the push towards alternatives was concerned with attempts to cut public spending. They were seen as part of an economic and social drive to control the ever-expanding burden of the 'poor'. Thus for example, in the sixteenth century, there was a drive to police the poor and much of criminal law was directed against the 'idle' classes. In 1553 the introduction of the first British 'House of Correction' at Bridewell to deal with vagabonds and petty offenders marked the start of a series of attempts to use hard work as a means of reforming people's characters; reducing, deterring or stamping out idleness; and instilling a measure of self-help and reliance. This particular aspect was further exemplified by the Elizabethan Vagabonds Act 1597 which listed classes of disreputable characters liable to impressment. Under the Act, idle people, rogues, sturdy beggars and vagabonds (boys or men) could be liable for enlistment in the army or navy as an alternative to spending time in goal, or receiving corporal or capital punishment.

The condition of impressment as a regular statutory penal sanction for the enlistment of people sentenced to death, transportation, or imprisonment was particularly relevant in the eighteenth century following the gradual curtailment and eventual abolition of transportation to the colonies and plantations. For example, the significance of impressment as an alternative penal sanction was made abundantly clear in the wake of hostilities with the American colonies. The hostilities put an end to the process of transporting disreputable characters there and alternative 'dumping grounds' (such as Australia) soon proved to be as problematic. The inability to export unwanted individuals created two specific problems at the time and in subsequent years. First, gaols were becoming increasingly overcrowded with convicts under sentence of transportation. Secondly, there was an urgent need for more recruits to expand the armed forces and to contribute to the war effort. As there was great reluctance at the time to invest in penitentiaries (on economic and political grounds) as a way out of the dilemma, new sanctions were engineered as credible alternatives. These alternatives were based on a refinement of the workhouse principle and hard labour. In terms of the latter, the control of convicts took the form of an initial period in hard labour, followed by a period of employment in association on public works. As to the workhouse principle, the authorities aimed at punishing paupers and economising on the rate of relief to the poor by making relief conditional on entering the workhouse and supporting themselves by hard work. This idea of controlling costs and using the principle of work as a sanction continued to occupy an important role among penal alternatives until the early part of the nineteenth century when its importance was once again redefined and revived by the introduction of new experiments in their regimes. Further, the same idea of hard work as a useful penalty in both controlling offenders and making them pay something back to the community has been a familiar notion throughout the last few decades and in the main since the 1970s following the introduction of the community service order.

Although such measures did much to expand and refine the scope of containment and the choices available in dealing with 'undesirables', they were not very effective in either controlling or stemming the growing problem of overcrowded gaols. More serious, they could not satisfy the national need for labour to assist in the war effort. In effect, together with the introduction and refinement of other alternatives, the condition of impressment (by pardoning criminals on condition of enlistment) was an impressive move to establish a penal alternative which could happily reconcile various ideological needs and practical necessities of the time. These included a reduction of pressure in gaols by turning them into recruiting depots; the provision of labour for the services; banishing criminals, the poor, or innocent bystanders — 'the dregs of the population' — to sea or to foreign lands as 'civil power men' whose highest honour, they were told, was to die gracefully for their country; applying penalties while at the same time instilling in the offender a sense of responsibility and personal worth; and, finally, finding a way of reducing the importance of the death penalty which began to be seen by that stage as a brutal and inhumane method of punishment.

As at present, the search for alternatives in the latter part of the eighteenth century and first half of the nineteenth century was dictated by political and economic considerations concerning the ability of the state to sustain, under the Poor Laws, an ever-increasing population of paupers, beggars and petty offenders. Thus, Parliamentary Committees considered that 'the cost of poor relief was so heavy, and had increased so rapidly, that it would soon become greater than the country could bear' (Radzinowicz, 1968: 61). Such pronouncements could almost be a text taken out of present concerns about the escalating costs of public expenditure and attempts to curtail spending; and calls for cheaper alternatives to prison in dealing with offenders (Home Office, 1988c). In addition to such financial concerns and the need to exercise economic stringency and self-help, the period also witnessed an increase in social arrest in rural areas, crime in the cities and the development of more organised and systematised methods of thieving (McIntosh, 1971). These changing patterns of crime and social unrest were seen by the authorities as subversive, 'lawless' behaviour directed against government, law-abiding citizens, and property (Nicholls, 1898: 282–3). As a result of these developments, changes in legislation to combat crime and lawless behaviour were in fact a direct attempt to expand and sharpen the means of control to deal with those who were considered to be the 'dangerous classes', the idle, and the 'hooligan' elements which worked against the 'good British way of life'; and constituted a direct threat to the legitimacy and powers of the state (Pearson, 1983). As Garland puts it, 'the overall effect of this amounted to a loosely organised, but none the less distinctive disciplinary strategy aimed towards the poor' (Garland, 1985: 41). For instance, the Poor Law Amendment Act 1934 aimed at easing the burden of rising poor rates through a process of demoralisation by making unlawful any relief to able-bodied persons outside the workhouse. Once more the workhouse was promoted as a 'spartan' institution designed to deter all but the genuinely needy and deserving poor (Stephenson, 1979).

Expansion of the prison

It is in this period that one witnesses the rapid expansion of the prison institution and its transformation into the core of all available sanctions. The changing pattern of crime, crime control, and civil disobedience (when the available sanctions were either discontinued or regarded as incapable of coping with the changing times and context of the period) called for something more robust, which could meet those needs. The prison fitted that expectation. By the middle of the nineteenth century the prison was firmly established as the bastion of the criminal justice system by changing its character from a mere depot for recruits, people awaiting trial or sentence and transportation, to an authoritative and organised penal institution for the containment and discipline of criminals; and which symbolised a new epoch of 'the philosophy of authority and the exercise of class power in general' (Ignatieff, 1983: 77; see also Foucault, 1977; Garland, 1985; Ignatieff, 1978; Rothman, 1971). In many respects, the emergence of the prison as a major penal sanction could be attributed not just to the social, economic and political needs of the period, but also to the rise and fall of those *alternatives* which were initially designed to control offenders by diverting them from gaol, corporal and capital punishment. For instance, the importance of transportation met with almost total disaster when its efficacy was questioned. By 1852, the authorities were left with 3000 convicts a year sentenced to transportation but with nowhere to go (cf. Tomlinson, 1981), thus creating a 'surplus' population of inmates. On a broader scale, the introduction and subsequent decline of impressment, the limited scope of workhouses in containing large numbers of different types of people regarded as being dangerous and unproductive and their social inutility, were important precipitants for the emergence of the prison as a real and powerful *substitute*, which in turn developed into the main panoply of the state. It is interesting to note that as in the case of the alternatives and their refined intentions, the prison was presented as a unique opportunity to reform, contain and deter its inmate populations as well as acting as a form of general deterrence to outsiders.

However, the attraction and expansion of the prison and the overhaul of the legal process in the middle and latter part of the nineteenth century did not remain inviolate from investigation and criticism (see for instance Cox, 1877; Mayhew and Binney, 1862). It was not until the early twentieth century that important attempts to challenge the hegemony of the prison were made by introducing penal changes which aimed at the diversion of offenders to supervision in the community. Examples of these penal changes included the Probation of Offenders Act 1907 which gave a statutory basis for the supervision of offenders in the community. This had its roots in the common law practice of the nineteenth century whereby offenders could be released from prison on condition that they kept the peace and came up for judgment if called upon. The Prevention of Crime Act 1908 expanded the provisions for the promotion of control programmes for young offenders which began in the middle of the nineteenth century. However, as at present, expansion of controls in the community were also accompanied by a similar expansion in custodial methods of disposition. Cases in point were the Children and Young Persons Act 1933 and the Criminal Justice Act 1948 which extended the scope of controls further still. In particular, the latter introduced, among other measures, corrective training and detention for young offenders. The introduction of the detention centre order had the avowed intention of administering a short sharp shock to 'young thugs' and sensitising them to their personal responsibilities in society.

The rise of welfare

The inauguration of the National Health Service in 1948, and the reorganisation of the social and economic fabric in relation to social insurance and allied social services, offered an era of optimism and an expansion of services in ameliorating deprivation, unequal opportunity, poor housing, lack of educational opportunity and unemployment. Invested into these programmes was also the notion that the amelioration of social and economic disadvantage would reduce the incidence of crime. Although the crime rate was not halted in those years, it did remain relatively stable. The daily average (adult) population in penal establishments varied from about 17 800 in 1900, to about 11 000 in the mid-1920s and, after the Second World War, to just over 20 000 in 1950. Thus although there was a fairly sharp rise in the prison population after the war, that rise was not so severe as it first appears, as the increase had taken place over a considerable length of time. In that sense, there was an expressed euphoria about the benefits accrued from social and economic reconstruction which led to the belief that the available penal sanctions were both adequate and useful in controlling crime (Advisory Council on the Treatment of Offenders, 1957).

The euphoria was short-lived. In the late 1950s the social and economic climate began to alter. The benefits of the welfare state in alleviating social problems were difficult to gauge, particularly in the face of a sharp increase in the crime rate and reception of offenders into custody. Between 1948 and 1953 the number of adults found guilty of indictable offences hovered around the 100 000 mark for each relevant year. But whereas in 1955 there were just over 100 000 people found guilty of indictable offences, by 1958 the number rose to 150 000. By 1963, in just eight years, the proportion of offenders found guilty of similar offences per head of the population was more than double the 1955 level. By 1969, the number reached over 250 000. This increase in the crime rate (and it must be remembered that it only constituted those convicted and not the larger figure of indictable offences known to the police to have been committed) had obvious repercussions for the prison population, leading to the re-emergence of the problem of overcrowding and disillusionment with existing measures in containing the crime rate. Between 1950 and 1955 the daily average prison population varied slightly and remained close to 20 000. By 1960, it reached 27 000. Seven years later, the daily average prison population was the highest ever recorded at 35 000. In 1970, after a small drop in 1968, the prison population rose to its 1967 peak and beyond. This grim picture, and the escalating cost of maintaining a failing institution, undermined the philosophy of containment and the practical capacity of the prison establishment to punish and deter adequately. There was renewed scepticism about the rehabilitative effects of incarceration and the appropriateness of existing non-custodial penal measures — mainly the fine, the probation order and the discharge order — to contain the situation. Hence the search, in the late 1960s and early 1970s, for additional alternatives, particularly in the form of the suspended sentence and community service by offenders.

In addition to the fear of social consequences (the fear of a 'social catastrophe' and the total collapse of the prison establishment), there were also severe economic and political considerations at play in the renewed interest in the promotion of alternatives to custody. The welfare state's increased share of the national product at a time of worsening economic climate brought a barrage of criticisms in the late 1960s about waste, weakening of the moral fibre, abdication of personal responsibility, and encouragement of idleness. Consequently, this early phase of an ideology which, in the 1980s, has come to be associated with the policies of the New Right, explained personal, social and economic disorder, crime and lack of civic duty on a dependency, or 'living off the state', culture (cf. Boyson, 1971; Joseph, 1972). This was the time when the state was accused of creating a society of 'broiler hens': an 'evil state' which creates an irresponsible society where no one cares or because the state takes from 'the energetic, successful and thrifty to give to the idle, the failures and the feckless' (Boyson, 1971: 1–9). The critique of the welfare state by a conservative ideology was neither left unanswered by counter-critics (see for instance Donnison, 1975; Holman, 1973; Townsend, 1970) nor was it an original venture relevant to the 1970s. As I have already indicated, in the nineteenth century similar criticisms were levelled against the Poor Laws. Equally relevant, the same situation was a consistent feature of social policy in the late 1970s and has continued to be so in the 1980s. In all instances, criticisms and plans to alter the face of the state and its services centred on issues of personal and social responsibility; economic stringencies; discouragement of dependency and idleness; self-help and the liberation of the individual from the state's web, and therefore the realisation of 'real' freedom; and the reduction of criminal activity as a function of those goals.

Community care and the rise of alternatives

Despite the ideological disagreements concerning the merits or defects of welfare policies, there was, nonetheless, a general agreement about the assumed benefits of self-help, 'community care' and 'participation', and in diverting clients, offenders, or other groups in need, from institutions to community methods of treatment and control. It is not a coincidence, therefore, that the disagreements about the status of the welfare state were matched by agreement and a strong revival of the spirit of 'community'. The Mental Health Act 1959 introduced the principle of community care in the case of mental health services. This, in many respects, led the way to the emergence of community work in the 1960s as a distinct method of combating social problems and social deprivation. The 1968 Seebohm Report furthered the romanticism and ideology of community care by suggesting that it reduced stigma and allowed reintegration; gave a sense of well-being; and acted, at the same time, as a social control apparatus (Home Office, 1968: paras. 492, 476, 477). In 1969, the Home Office's much-trumpeted Community Development Project was launched (later to collapse under the weight of failure and political critique) for the purpose of combating social deprivation and related issues such as crime and delinquency in inner cities and selected neighbourhoods.

Although much of the ideology and general practice of community work were later to come under criticism (see for instance Baldock, 1974; Jones and Mayo, 1974; Plant, 1974; Vass, 1979), they succeeded in creating a new momentum for the expansion of services and in guiding new initiatives in social and penal policy, with an emphasis on treatment or containment in the community; 'patch' work in the 1980s as explored by the Barclay Report (Working Party, 1982); new initiatives in community care (Griffiths, 1988); new alternatives to custody since the late 1960s which include the power to suspend sentences of imprisonment; binding over; parole; probation hostels; day training centres (and later just day centres), attendance centre orders, community service, 'curfews' (a variant of house arrest) and current plans to introduce, in addition to amendments to existing alternatives, such as community service, new forms of alternatives. For example, the introduction of electronic tagging of offenders and the introduction of a new supervision and restriction order, an intensive probation programme, which may include some or all of the following at one and the same time: compensation to the victim; community service; residence at a hostel or other approved place; prescribed activities at a day centre or elsewhere; curfew or house arrest in general; and restrictions on mobility (cf. Home Office, 1988c).

Many of those measures (for example tagging and intensive probation) have been in operation in the USA since the early 1980s. For instance, the new proposed supervision and restriction order is a variant — almost a replica — of intensive probation supervision (IPS) programmes which exist in New York, Florida, Texas, Georgia, Massachusetts, New Jersey, Illinois and Ohio — all modelled after Georgia's original programme which was implemented in 1982. As an alternative to custody, the Georgia IPS includes the following requirements, among others: five face-to-face contacts per week between supervising officer and offender; 132 hours of community service; house arrest; mandatory employment; weekly check of local arrest records; routine and unannounced alcohol and drug testing (Petersilia, 1988: 171–2). Although these developments may not be entirely novel, they add, nonetheless, to the existing plethora of alternatives to custody.

The post-community service era, since 1972, has been characterised by increased government activity in restricting public expenditure and saving resources. Thus one more reason for the proliferation of alternatives to custody in the 1970s is not a re-worked but convenient excuse, that prison establishments are overcrowded and are an affront to civilisation, brutal, and ineffective in controlling the crime rate and recidivism; or that alternatives reduce stigma and are more humane methods of punishment. As in the past, in the late 1970s and throughout the 1980s policy has been guided by the dictum 'cut public expenditure and prosper'. Hence the emphasis on justifying anything which appears to cut costs and save money for the Treasury tends to receive uncritical support even by people who promote the 'get tough with thugs and the idle' approach. Of course, this political and economic expediency must be put within the social context of the prison establishment and its crisis: the continuing escalation of prison crowding and (as I shall show in the next chapter) the uninterrupted *expansion*, not reduction, of public expenditure on prisons. In 1972, there were nearly 265 000 adult offenders convicted for indictable offences. In 1978, there were over 328 000. By 1980, the convictions had reached over 456 000. In March 1980, the prison population stood at over 44 000. In July 1981, it rose to over 45 000 (for current trends, see the next chapter). In retrospect, by the late 1970s to the present date the available sanctions were thought to be inadequate in containing the complexity of the rising crime rate, in saving resources, and in preventing the 'overcrowded cattle-pens' from an impending catastrophe. The resultant lacuna (what to do with criminals, how to exercise economic stringency, how to ration resources, what new 'initiatives' or effective penal measures should be invented) has now been filled with calls for stiffer community penal measures which should be guided by an overt expression of punishment and deterrence. This policy is a shift in emphasis towards a new hard line against the criminal — through credible package deals which act as alternatives to custody with a 'sting'. This shift of emphasis from what one could loosely call a mixture of rehabilitative and control tasks to a more overt expression of a classical philosophy of punishment and deterrence is not merely advocated by government. Indeed even before the phrase 'punishment in the community' was coined in official pronouncements (Home Office, 1988c), there was already a gathering momentum in the probation service (cf. Griffiths, 1982; see counter-arguments by Lacey et al., 1983; Vass, 1982a) calling for 'containment' and 'punishment' to become the 'unambiguous objective of probation'. This objective of punishment, as in the judicial system of mid-eighteenth-century England, reasserts itself as the only conceivable means to ensuring the continuance of orderly society. Punishment should be administered along an axis of progressive provision of pain (not just to the body through rough and hard work for the community but also restrictions on mobility and free time — 'leisure'); and to be effective, it ought to be prompt and inevitable. 'Destructive' and 'anti-social' elements in the community should receive their just deserts. This thrust towards an overt expression of punishment in the community has reached such fervour that the following public remarks by the then Deputy Chairman of the Police Federation on the task of the police in dealing with offenders and socially disobedient subjects could well epitomise the philosophy behind the new directions in penal policy (quoted in Langdon, 1982: 26): 'In every urban area there is a large minority of people who are not fit for salvage. They hate every form of authority . . . The only way in which the police can protect society is quite frankly, by harassing these people so that they are too afraid to commit crime.'

Conclusion

One may suggest that the first major common element of the changes which have been introduced since the 1960s is that the mitigation between punishment and rehabilitation is achieved by the idea of imposing 'leisure controls' through close surveillance. With the exception of the suspended sentence of imprisonment, the fine and discharge orders, the rest of the main alternatives to custody centre on the aim of administering punishment through the principle of deprivation of leisure and the close supervision of offenders by designated community supervising officers. This control of mobility and free time backed by the background sanction of imprisonment, and enforced by supervising officers (such as probation officers), is part-time custody of a different kind (Vass, 1982a: 790). There is an immediate sanction embedded in such penal measures which requires offenders to spend some of their time under supervision as a condition of sentence. While under supervision offenders are then subjected to a compulsory application of what are regarded as worthwhile creative activities and constructive deeds for the benefit of their personal development or that of the community at large. If the contract is not honoured a second set of sanctions becomes activated to render those offenders responsible for their actions and failures and to remind them of their legal and standing obligations to comply with requirements or, in the extreme, to call the contract null and void and deal with defaulters by way of incarceration or other alternative sanctions. This new set of sanctions — a higher order of things — constitutes the second common element of alternatives to custody. The deprivation of leisure (liberty) for a temporary period; the expectation that they will contribute to and participate in manual or recreational tasks which are assumed to develop offenders' sense of and belongingness to 'community'; the re-emergence of 'community' as a convenient moral partner which guides and assists offenders to assume and subscribe to a personal and social culture of responsibility which in turn acts as a cleansing solution that helps in the purification process of body and soul; and the suspended threat of imprisonment (which may be activated in case of failure), are part and parcel of the philosophy of punishment through the administration of alternatives to custody. It is, in effect, a policy of 'constraints', 'privations', 'obligations' and 'prohibitions'. It is, as Foucault (1977: 11) would put it, a policy of 'suspended rights': 'Physical pain, the pain of the body itself, is no longer the constituent element of the penalty. From being an art of unbearable sensations punishment has become an economy of suspended rights.'

This policy of suspended rights allows a convenient interchange-ability between different sanctions (that is, they can be exchanged for each other, thus allowing a multiple assortment of penalties at any one time in the state's disposal), and offers immense opportunities for further expansion either through amendments, or new innovations.

From the brief historical account offered and more detailed accounts elsewhere (see for instance Pease, 1980; Young, 1979; Vass, 1984: 6–41 for an analysis of the possible factors which led to the emergence of community service by offenders in 1972), it is obvious that the enactment of penal policy does not take place in a vacuum. From the Bridewell, the workhouses, the hulks, transportation, impressment to prison and beyond, the social forces behind the expansion of controls show a remarkable affinity: what to do with criminals; how to avert the social consequences of a rising crime rate and the escalating pressure on the prison institution as a result of overcrowding; a need for governments of all political colours to be seen as doing something about the 'social evil' of crime; increasing the choice and range of sanctions for the benefit of the courts; satisfying national and local needs which are often smothered in ideological invective — increasing penalties and 'getting tough', cheaper alter-natives, reparation, drawing the balance between punishment and rehabilitation, and so on; and the need for sanctions which are flexible enough to permit a convenient interchangeability between different modes of control under different conditions and circumstances prevailing at the time. In addition, there is nothing really new about contemporary community penal measures. Old and new penal sanctions always appear to share similar objectives and have relatively similar backgrounds. New measures are like new models of motorcars. As long as they are new they offer, for a temporary period, some novel excitement. We look after them, care for them and polish them with some pride, and ceremonially display them for others to see and envy. When the ageing process sets in, they begin to lose their lustre. Occasionally they let us down, the ride gets less comfortable, and our pride in their efficiency and reliability withers away. What do we do then? We usually search for an alternative motorcar. We consider our finances. We compare options — what make, what model, to what end. The outcome of that decision-making process is always justified out of expediency. That our choice is a *better* alternative; in shape, glamour, specification, performance, refinement, mechanical layouts which offer a pinch of innovation and sophistication and new assurances about reliability and durability, and low maintenance costs. We convince ourselves that it offers *value for money*. In short, we tell ourselves and others, we can, once again, depend on it. The process remains the same, car after car. The same with the criminal justice system. Penal options come and go. In particular, 'alternatives' — old with new — may coexist for a while but in the long term they join the scrapyard of the criminal justice process; and more 'up-market', 'innovative' and 'desirable' penal measures spring up to take their place. They may look different and their 'mechanical' (operational) layouts may have a higher degree of sophistication, but they are essentially clones of previous models.

The characteristic aspect, therefore, of this process of change and diversity is that it is only the shape of sanctions which undergoes a metamorphosis, not their substance. There may be an expansion in the number or type of alternatives to custody but they appear to have their roots in previous models from the past; and more significantly, and as we shall see later in this book, they appear to have little effect on the prison establishment. Mannheim (1939: 45) observed that this should be expected. For, as he argued, new penal measures evolve out of an existing structure, and the bastion of that structure in contemporary notions of crime and justice is the prison. In effect, the existence of the prison establishment is almost a prerequisite for the invention and evolution of new penal measures. There is at the abstract level an uneasy relationship, a common bond, between prison and alternatives. Imprisonment acts as a preparatory and necessary stage for the development and application of new sanctions. New penal sanctions — in the absence of a determined official policy to restrict a parallel expansion in the imposition of custodial sentences — become supportive and maintain the prison system. Either way, without the sustainment (and almost inevitably the expansion) of the prison establishment, measures which are enacted to contradict that establishment are meaningless and devoid of substance or credibility. Thus, the argument goes, as long as the prison system remains important and the foundation on which the apparatus of the criminal justice system is administered and organised, it can only get stronger and bigger by deriving its *raison d'être* from an expansion of community alternatives. It remains with us because it is needed. It acts as a nasty reminder that the violation of terms of reference — as in the case of alternatives — may force the criminal justice system to exercise threat by twirling and swishing the sword of Damocles. So when offenders are invested with the 'trust' of staying out of further trouble by being given non-custodial penal measures, and are expected to conform to the requirements of that trust, the prison, it is believed, becomes a good reminder of the inviolability of the rules. N. Morris (1965: 279), summarises this reciprocity between alternative sanctions and custodial sentences in these terms: 'Prison may not follow corporal and capital punishment and transportation into desuetude, for within the term "prison" great development is possible. In the late eighteenth and early nineteenth centuries the prison changed its character and it will change again. Prison walls will not entirely disappear. As a background sanction, supporting alternative punishments, the prison may long be required.'

As I shall show later, there is much evidence from many countries, especially England, the USA and Canada which supports that link. There are, of course, serious exceptions. For example, it has been argued that Australia and the Netherlands have managed to break this cycle of escalation by effectively reducing their incarcerated population (cf. Biles, 1983: Doleschall, 1977; Downes, 1982; Morrison, 1985; Smith, 1984). However, there are more recent data which suggest that, even in those countries, there has been in recent years a gradual increase in the rate of incarceration (see Chapter 2). If the claims are true, the findings do not necessarily contradict the reciprocal relationship which exists between alternatives and prison, for other factors come into play to negate that relationship — for instance, government and judicial policy, as in the Netherlands, to keep length of sentences short (cf. Downes, 1988; Fitzmaurice and Pease, 1982; Junger-Tas, 1986a, 1986b). Overall, the general trend is akin to the above prophetic vision and there appears to be both an escalation in the use of alternatives *and* custodial sentences. However, there is a qualification which needs to be made about this relationship. The assumed connection between alternatives and custodial institutions has a serious flaw. If accepted as a truism, it encourages the present expansion of various sanctions — including custodial — without allowing a serious attempt to bring prisons under control. It can lead, in many respects, to benign neglect and a sense of fatalism. In turn a self-fulfilling prophecy may emerge: the prison is not expendable; alternatives can only be possible if threat is applied in that they are linked to the background sanction of imprisonment (cf. Vass, 1984: 59–84 for evidence on this); so prisons are needed in order to justify more humane programmes; but more humane programmes must have a 'sting' — that of the background sanction of imprisonment, and so on. This rationalisation, if not tautology, works on the same principle, as every student of psychology will recognise, of the self-proclaimed prophet who predicted the end of the world and called on believers to join him in prayer so that they could be spared the coming cataclysm. But like the cataclysm which failed to take place because, as the prophet proudly explained later, the world had been saved because of the impressive faith of his small group of believers, so can the continued existence of the prison be blamed on the proliferation of other penal measures and as a confirmation of the prison establishment's permanence. As I have suggested above, and the point will receive close attention later, there may be other factors at play. If a linear relationship between two social events exists, irrespective of how closely related, it does not necessarily make an association. Nonetheless, for the purposes of exploring the position of the prison and that of alternatives, the gist of the problem, for the time being, is not that the prison system still exists or that it continues as a necessary sanction which gives relevance and credence to other penal measures. Rather, the gist of the matter, for our purposes, is that the prison system in England, and many other western states, is not getting smaller. It is actually *expanding* and the belly of the beast is constantly being enlarged to absorb and process more and more people than ever before. But as has happened so often in its history, right from its inception, the prison is currently going through another 'crisis'.

This current crisis, as in the past, has to do with the same old-fashioned questions: what to do about the rising costs of imprisonment; what to do to relieve pressure inside and outside prisons (disturbances and fears of 'catastrophes'); how to cope with and preferably reduce overcrowding; how to control the escalating crime rate; and how to satisfy the law and order lobby that something is being done to confront the problem. As always, the answer to these crises is a fairly regular, simple and plain affair: more investment in prisons, hence more 'capacity expansion' (Austin and Krisberg, 1985); and a concurrent expansion in the methods of control and surveillance in the community. The next chapter deals with these issues. It concentrates on the state of prisons, their costs, populations, capacity, and the sentencing patterns of the courts. It offers an analysis of the prison 'crisis' as it is relevant to the political, economic and social climate of the 1980s and 1990s.

2 The prison crisis in the 1980s

Crisis? What crisis, one could be tempted to ask. And with good reason, because the prison establishment is thriving under extensive investment and a vast prison-building programme.

Capacity expansion and expenditure

In England, in terms of manpower services, there has been a vast increase in the recruitment of prison officers. Rutherford (1984) suggests that manpower services are part and parcel of an 'expansionist option' and points to how the expansion in all grades of prison officers outstrips the corresponding expansion in prison population (see also Morgan, 1982). Forty years ago, the ratio of inmates to prison officers was six to one; by 1987-8 it had come down to nearly two inmates per officer. Recruitment for 1987-8 was particularly buoyant. All areas of prison officer recruitment expanded partly through more investment in the service by the government, and partly through an increased interest — given the current economic climate and unemployment — by prospective applicants to join the prison service. There were 34 807 applications and of those who were successful (1604 men and 228 women, total 1832), 1664 were posted as prison officers. In 1987-8, after allowing for promotions and natural wastage, the number of main grade prison officers (grade VIII) increased by 1156 over 1986-7. In comparative terms, since 1983-4 there has been a 300 percent increase in prison officer recuitment (Home Office, 1988e: 37).

In terms of cash expenditure for 1987-8, including the construction of new prisons, this amounted to £775 million. In real terms, that figure represents a £40 million (5.4 percent) increase in expenditure in comparison to 1986-7. When 'on costs' (superannuation and rates) are included, the overall cost of the prison service in 1987-8 was nearly £900 million, an increase of about 6 percent over 1986-7 (Home Office, 1988e). When current expenditure is compared to expenditure since 1983-4 the annual investment is impressive. In 1983-4, the average inmate population in prison establishments was 43 500; the service cost, in real terms, was £782.7 million. By 1985-6, there were 46 600 inmates (excluding those in police cells) which represented more than a 7 percent increase in the incarcerated population. Equally, the costs increased to nearly £812 million, a rise of nearly 4 percent in real terms. By 1987–8, the prison population had risen to 48 600, an increase of nearly 12 percent since 1983–4; and an increase of over 4 percent since 1985–6. In terms of real costs, the £882.3 million which was spent on the prison establishment represented a nearly 13 percent rise in expenditure over 1983–4; and a nearly 9 percent rise over 1985–6 (Home Office, 1988e).

Since 1985 eight new prisons (at Wayland, Stocken, Thorn Cross, Full Stutton, Littlehey, Mount, Swaleside and Garth) have been opened and eighteen more are at present at various stages of their development. The accelerated prison-building programme, which was expected to provide 22 000 new places by 1990 (14 000 in new prisons and 8000 by additions to existing establishments, and without doubt all of them filled to bursting point even before completion) was recently given another boost. On 1 November 1988, the Chancellor of the Exchequer, in his annual autumn statement in the House of Commons on the state of the economy and forecast of overall spending in the next fiscal year, made one thing clear: a commitment to law and order and specifically the continuing expansion of the prison. When Treasury forecasts on the economy are taken into account — with a projected conservative estimate of the average rate of inflation to be around 5 percent — law and order (under the hat of 'Home Office and Legal Departments') will continue to be one of the most obvious beneficiaries with regard to public spending. Law and order will receive an increase of 10 percent in its budget which corresponds to a 5 percent rise in real terms for 1989–90. Public expenditure on law and order (comprising the Home Office and Legal Departments) has risen by nearly 300 percent since 1979. Table 2.1 shows the overall spending patterns and comparisons with other selected departments.

As can be observed, the Treasury's money will be spent, in the main, on the following in order of spending power: social security (£51 billion); health (£23.2 billion); defence (£20.1 billion); education (£19.6 billion); law and order (£8 billion); transport (£5.4 billion); agriculture (£2 billion); housing (£1.7 billion); other (£30.7 billion).

The Home Office will receive enough extra money, £290 million in 1989–90, and a further £430 million in 1990–91, principally for a further expansion in the prison-building programme. The extra money will enable the Home Office to build two more prisons (thus bringing the total number of new prisons under construction since the early 1980s to 28) which will provide 3000 more places by 1991–2, meaning that by that time the revised increased capacity of the prison-building programme to expand its inmate population will be over 25 000 new places. This, of course, is a conservative estimate, for it refers to the official certified normal accommodation (CNA) and not to the actual

Table 2.1   *Public spending plans for 1989–92 (in £ billions)*

Departments	1989–90	Rise over 1987–8 %	Rise in real terms over 1987–8 %	Real rise since 1979 %	Plans for 1990–91	Plans for 1991–2
Home Office	6.90	10	5	63	7.22	7.39
Legal Depts	1.08	12	7	233	1.17	1.24
Defence	20.12	4	−1	17	21.18	22.09
Foreign Office	0.77	3	−2	17	0.81	0.85
Overseas Aid	1.54	4	−1	−13	1.63	1.69
EC	1.97	107	100	20	1.95	1.58
Agriculture	1.95	5	−1	6	2.16	2.35
Trade/Industry	1.36	−20	−25	−68	1.34	1.16
Energy	0.25	—	—	—	0.51	0.62
Employment	4.02	−2	−8	64	3.96	3.96
Transport	5.36	11	7	−11	5.54	5.66
Housing	1.71	−17	−21	−79	2.04	2.38
Education	19.57	6	1	10	20.24	20.77
Arts/Libraries	0.98	—	—	29	1.01	1.05
DHSS:						
Health	23.16	7	1	37	24.38	25.39
Social Security	51.00	7	2	36	55.30	58.70
Scotland	8.97	3	−2	—	9.14	9.68
Wales	3.79	5	—	6	3.90	4.01
N.Ireland	5.47	6	—	11	5.69	5.91
Chancellor's Dept	4.08	11	6	23	4.28	4.49
Other	0.32	−11	−16	−63	0.34	0.35

(*Source*: *Guardian*, 2 November 1988)

prison population. If current trends continue with regard to the disjunction between CNA and actual prison population (Home Office, 1988e), the new places will contain at least 35 000 inmates by 1994. In addition to the new prisons, the money will be enough to expand further alternatives to custody by setting up 30 probation day centres (see Chapter 6); giving more bail hostels; and in recruiting 300 more police officers in provincial forces. The new money increases Home Office spending by £610 million to nearly £7000 million in 1989–90, and by £760 million to £7220 million in 1990–91. The projected total for 1991–2 is £7390 million (Cook, 1988a: 3).

A crisis of space and crowding: Contributory factors

The above expenditure and further expansion of the prison does not justify claims that the prison is in a crisis. Far from it. As an institution the prison never had it so good! Even the Victorian expansion of the prison system is beginning to look almost insignificant when compared to the development of the prison in the 1980s. So what is the crisis about? It has to do with *space* and *crowding*. The prison population on 31 March 1988 was 50 500 (including 1300 in police cells). This was about 1000 higher than the same time in the previous year. The average prison population in 1987–8 was 49 300 including an average of 700 prisoners — who were mainly on remand — held in police cells which, in comparison to the previous year, constituted a 4 percent increase in the prison population. These increases took place despite reductions in the immediate incarceration of juveniles and a reduction of 5 percent in the incarceration of young offenders aged 17 to 20. The number of juvenile offenders given custodial sentences has dropped by more than one-third since 1983, from 6800 in 1983 to 4000 in 1987. The number of custodial sentences passed on young adults, aged 17 to 20, increased from 23 100 in 1983 to 25 200 in 1985 but fell to 20 900 in 1987 (Home Office, 1987a, 1987b, 1988e, 1988f). It is not clear why there has been a reduction in custodial sentences for juveniles (and for young offenders if the present fall in custodial sentences continues) but a number of factors may be at work: for instance, demographic factors, that is a reduction in the proportion of juveniles and young people in the general population. Since the early 1980s there has been a drop in the proportion of young people in the general population in England. Similar social trends are being experienced in other countries, for instance the USA, West Germany, France and Italy. It is estimated that by 1995 there will be 30 percent fewer young people than at present, a situation which has begun to cause social concern in terms of the labour market as well as social services (Beavis, 1988; McRae, 1988). However, there may also be other reasons such as a reduction of immediate custodial sentences given by magistrates' courts. For instance, between 1985 and 1986 there was a fall of 25 percent in such sentences given in magistrates' courts (Home Office, 1987b: 7), which may in itself be related to changes in legislation under the Criminal Justice Act 1982 (which introduced restrictions on the imposition of custodial sentences on young offenders, for instance that custodial sentences should only be imposed for serious crimes; or where young offenders fail to respond to other non-custodial penal measures); provisions for the advance disclosure of the prosecution case from mid-1985; increased use of police cautioning; and the introduction of the Crown Prosecution Service in 1986 (Home Office, 1987b: 7).

Longer sentences and a parallel expansion of
alternatives to custody
The reduction in custodial sentences for juveniles, and in a restrictive sense for young offenders, belies the increased rate of incarceration for

those aged 21 and over, despite a fall of 5 percent in the number of recorded notifiable offences in 1987 in comparison to an annual increase of 6 percent between 1980 and 1986; the rise in the prison population with medium or long sentences which reflects (in contrast to magistrates' courts) the continuing high rate of receptions from the Crown Court; the continuing increase in the population of remand prisoners (tried or untried); and the great variations across the country in the use of custodial sentences by courts. In 1986, for instance, the increase in the population of remand prisoners pending trial or sentence was mainly due to an increase in the untried population. This averaged about 8500 compared to 8100 in 1985; and 7200 in 1984 (Home Office, 1987b). In 1987–8 the major growth in the prison population was in inmates serving long sentences — over four years for men and over three years for women (Home Office, 1988e). On average the number of individuals serving long sentences increased by 17 percent in 1987–8. This trend towards longer prison sentences has increased substantially over the past three years and consistently since the early 1980s. In 1983, longer-sentenced prisoners (four years and over) constituted 13 percent of the average composition of the prison population and this rose steadily to 19 percent in 1987–8 (Home Office, 1988e). In terms of numbers, in 1983 there were fewer than 6000 people given sentences of four years and over but by 1987–8 the numbers increased to over 9000, representing a 50 percent rise in such receptions. It is not just those receiving sentences of four years and over who are forcing the prison population up. In general, there has been a trend towards longer sentences across the board on people sentenced to medium or long sentences, that is 18 months or more (Home Office, 1987b). Thus, the trend towards longer sentences goes against the claim made by John Patten, the Home Office minister at the time, that longer sentences are directed only against violent crime and that they are 'a very welcome trend indeed. I hope these increasingly savage sentences will act as the yellow card for anyone tempted to commit a violent crime' (quoted in Cook, 1988b). The trend in sentencing goes against the minister's claim that such sentences do not contribute to overcrowding. Furthermore, it contradicts the government's claim that it is trying to tackle overcrowding by 'urging punishment in the community for many of those imprisoned for trivial offences' (Cook, 1988b). The composition of the prison population tells a different story. In 1987, 387 000 offenders were sentenced for indictable offences, 0.5 percent more than in 1986, and 430 000 for summary non-motoring offences, 3 percent less than in 1986. The fine, despite its decline in recent years, was imposed on 80 percent of offenders in 1987, mainly for summary offences. Absolute or conditional discharge orders were given to 95 000 offenders (of which

80 percent were conditional and the majority for indictable offences). This was an increase of about 6 percent over the previous year.

Community service orders were given to nearly 36 000 offenders compared to 35 000 in 1986 (an increase of nearly 3 percent). Probation orders were given to nearly 42 000 offenders compared to 40 000 in 1986 (an increase of about 5 percent). But behind these increases in the use of alternatives, the fact is that 74 000 offenders were sentenced to immediate custody for all types of offences in 1987, 1500 more than in 1986 and representing an increase of 2 percent. Of these, 48 000 were sentenced to immediate imprisonment; 18 500 to youth custody; and 8000 to detention centre orders.[1] Of these custodial sentences, nearly 4500 (6 percent) were for summary offences. In comparison to 1986, the average sentence length for all indictable offences for adult males increased by nearly a month at the Crown Court, from 18.3 to 19.2 months (Home Office, 1988f: 129). In fact, when the use of immediate imprisonment and alternatives to custody for those aged 21 and over is considered for the years 1977 to 1987 inclusive, the picture is far from encouraging. Imprisonment has steadily *increased* its share of the sentenced population as alternatives to custody, with the exception of the fine and fluctuations in the use of the suspended sentence, have done too. Indeed, in relation to male offenders aged 21 and over, though immediate custody has increased by 5 percent in comparison to 1977, the use of probation has increased by 3 percent; absolute or conditional discharge by less than 2 percent; the use of the suspended sentence of imprisonment declined between 1979 and 1984 (from its share of 13 to 11 percent respectively of indictable offences) and has remained since then at 12 percent of indictable offences; the same with partly suspended sentences (they dropped from just 2 percent of indictable offences in 1985 to 1 percent in 1987). The main alternative to custody which has kept pace with a corresponding increase in the use of immediate imprisonment has been the community service order. Since 1977 it has steadily moved from a mere 2 percent of sentences for indictable offences to 7 percent in 1987.

A similar picture exists for female offenders aged 21 and over. However, for female offenders there has been a steady increase in the use of absolute or conditional discharge orders (from 19 percent of sentences for indictable offences in 1977 to 26 percent in 1987); a rise in the use of probation orders, from 12 percent in 1977 to 18 percent of sentences for indictable offences in 1987; a rise in the use of the suspended sentence of imprisonment from 6 percent in 1977 to 8 percent in 1987 of sentences for indictable offences. But there has been little change in terms of the community service order. It has gradually moved up from a mere 1 percent in 1977 to 3 percent in 1987. Interestingly, the use of the fine on female offenders aged 21 and over has declined faster and at a disproportionate rate in comparison to males. Whereas there has been a drop in the use of the fine on males by approximately 14 percent between 1977 and 1987, for women this drop is about 22 percent. In terms of imprisonment, on the other hand, there has been a steady increase in its use against female offenders. In all, referring to those aged 21 and over, between 1977 and 1988 the prison establishment grew by nearly 11 600 male and 1000 female inmates. Although the number of females incarcerated is relatively small in comparison to males, the disproportionate increase in the use of incarceration for females is alarming. A comparison between 1977 and 1987 shows that the difference in the number of incarcerated males aged 21 and over represents an increase of 38 percent. For female offenders this increase represents a staggering 66 percent (Home Office, 1988f: Tables 7.12, 7.13).

Untried and unsentenced prisoners
The problem is not just that there has been a steady use of custodial sentences for the age group 21 and over; or that custodial sentences are getting longer; or that, with some exceptions, alternatives to custody are moving up in use almost in parallel with custodial sentences, without appearing to have any discernible effect on the prison establishment. There are also other rather disturbing developments. The untried and unsentenced population — those who are remanded in custody awaiting trial or sentence — is, as I have already indicated, on the increase. For instance, in 1986 the average male population of untried prisoners was 8210 and the number of days they spent in custody was 57. The average female population of untried prisoners was 320 and the average number of days spent in custody was 44. Of those who were convicted and remanded in custody awaiting sentence, the average male population was 1362, and the average number of days spent in custody was 33. For females, the average population was 70, and the average number of days in custody was 25. In 1987–8 there was an increase of 4 percent over the previous year in this sector of the prison population (Home Office, 1988e: 7).

Despite attempts to reduce the number of, and days spent in custody by, remand prisoners, their numbers have been rising since 1976 (the only exception being that of female convicted unsentenced prisoners who have experienced a slight drop in days in custody since 1982). However, it is important to recognise that the average days in prison conceal important variations, that is the range of days spent in custody is considerable. Thus, in 1986 up to 700 untried individuals served up to 12 months in custody before being tried and sentenced. One hundred individuals served more than 12 months in prison. Similar figures are applicable to 1987. On 30 June 1987, 9140 people were remanded in custody. Of these, 6300 stayed in custody up to three months; 2000 over three and up to six months; 750 over six months and up to 12 months; and 100 spent over 12 months in custody before trial or sentence (*NAPO News*, 1988a: 11). What is also relevant is the outcome following sentence. In 1986, 5 percent were found not guilty or not proceeded against; 30 percent were given non-custodial sentences or were freed on rising (that is, those who were sentenced to immediate custody of such length that it had already been served on remand); 13 percent of sentences were unknown; of the rest, 52 percent received custody (Home Office, 1987b). In 1987, of those remanded in custody, 4 percent were found not guilty or not proceeded against; 27 percent received non-custodial penal measures or were freed on rising; and 21 percent of sentences were unknown. The latest figures, referring to 30 September 1988 with regard to the population in prison establishments, show that there were 9869 people remanded in custody awaiting sentence or trial. This constituted 21 percent of the total, including non-criminal, prison population (*NAPO News*, 1989a: 18).

The rising proportion of ethnic minority groups
There appears to be a disproportionate representation of ethnic minority groups in custodial institutions which has steadily worsened since the early 1980s (cf. Home Office, 1987b; 1988f). On 30 June 1987, there were 50 270 people in prisons in England. Of those individuals, 7050 (14 percent) came from ethnic minorities. Well over 4000 of those prisoners (9.5 percent) were of Afro-Caribbean origin, who represent only 1 to 2 percent of the general population (*NAPO News*, 1989b: 8). In addition, in 1987 of the untried and unsentenced population of inmates, 14 percent were black males and 21 percent black females. Finally, people from ethnic minority groups appear to receive longer sentences. Of adults sentenced in 1986 to 18 months or more of imprisonment, 45 percent were whites; over 51 percent were of Afro-Caribbean origin; more than 68 percent were of Indian, Pakistani or Bangladeshi origin; 55 percent were of Chinese, Asian or mixed origin; and 66 percent were of unknown origin (Home Office, 1987b: Table 1.13).

These figures are worrying considering that ethnic minorities constitute 5 percent of the general population of England and Wales.

Disparities in sentencing
Another aspect of the sentencing process which contributes to the prison crisis of space and overcrowding are the great regional variations in the use and length of custodial sentences. In 1987, in magistrates' courts, the use of immediate custody varied between 4 percent in Northumbria and Dyfed–Powys and 9 percent in

Derbyshire, Devon and Cornwall, Greater Manchester, Lancashire and Sussex. Average sentence length varied from 2.1 months in Derbyshire to 3.7 months in Gloucestershire. At the Crown Court variations in the use of immediate custody for adults varied, for example, from 43 percent in Avon and Somerset to 67 percent in Essex. Between 1985 and 1987 the use of immediate custody fell by 7 percent in Avon and Somerset, Durham and Hertfordshire, whereas it rose by 11 percent in Northamptonshire (Home Office, 1988f: 141). Indeed, average sentences ranged from 14.2 months in Durham to 34.7 in Sussex. In terms of young offenders aged 17 to 20, in Nottinghamshire magistrates' courts sentenced to custody 9 percent of young offenders for offences involving burglary; Durham sentenced 29 percent for similar offences. Dyfed–Powys sentenced 2 percent of young offenders for violence against the person whereas, for similar offences, Cleveland sentenced 17 percent of young people to custody. In the Crown Court, Lincolnshire sentenced 50 percent of young offenders to custody for burglary; Essex, on the other hand, sent 85 percent of its young offenders to custody. In Gloucestershire, the Crown Court sent 20 percent of offenders to custody for offences relating to violence against the person, and in North Wales, the Crown Court sentenced 72 percent of such offenders to custody (*NAPO News*, 1988b: 4). All the government (quoted in Cook, 1988b) could say about such variations was: 'This concerns us because one would like people to be treated in a similar way wherever they are brought to trial . . . All we can do is try to influence matters by circulating the figures to the magistrates courts while the Lord Chancellor's department does the same for the crown courts.'

The extent of prison crowding and international comparisons

When all these matters affecting prison space and crowding are put together, the actual picture of conditions in prisons becomes quite stark. Prison overcrowding has worsened in the last decade, despite the provision of extra places. In 1977 the average daily population was 41 570 in a prison establishment which was designed for 37 520, giving nearly 11 percent overcrowding. In 1987, the average daily population had grown to 48 425 when the CNA was for 41 994, giving over 15 percent overcrowding. When those who could not be accommodated in prisons and were put in police cells (on a daily average of 537) are added to the figures, overcrowding increases to nearly 17 percent. Despite increases in space by opening new prisons, renovations in existing prisons, temporary measures by converting ex-army camps, or application of executive powers, by 31 March 1988 the prison population exceeded all available accommodation by 5500 (Home Office, 1988e: 8). In July 1987 the number of prisoners sharing cells designed for one inmate reached a peak, with 5091 people sharing three to a cell and 13 892 sharing two to a cell (Home Office, 1988e: 8). In order to cope with the growing population of unsentenced prisoners (for instance, in March 1988, 1500 prisoners mainly on remand were held in police cells), 1000 extra places were made available through 'tactical use of accommodation': by opening a new remand centre at Feltham and converting existing institutions — Campsfield House, Chelmsford and Hindley (Home Office, 1988e: 9). By 1987, in some of the ten most crowded prisons, demand for places (actual population) outstripped CNA by over 100 percent. For example, Leeds prison with 642 CNA had a population of 1345; Leicester prison with 204 CNA had 416 inmates; Lincoln prison with 359 CNA had 416 prisoners (cf. *Guardian*, 1988a).

The above issues, from an absolute expansion of the prison system in its capacity to contain more offenders (hence the rising cost) to the problems of space and overcrowding, appear to be features shared by other countries, notably the USA. Angelos and Jacobs (1985: 101) write that the problems of space, crowding and costs have created a crisis in prisons and jails to the point that 'prison and jail administrators, budget personnel, governors, and their staffs have been scrambling to cope with the need to reduce the number of detainees and prisoners and/or to increase the amount of available space'. According to the authors, expanding the prison is an impractical way of solving the crisis unless construction and expenditure are accompanied by reforms to prevent the prison population from 'swelling to fill the expanded capacity'. The costs of continuous expansion are prohibitive. For instance, the annual cost for keeping a prisoner in the USA is estimated to be in the range of $10 000 to $30 000, and 'would require an estimated $10–20 billion to bring existing facilities up to accepted standards of habitability' (Angelos and Jacobs, 1985: 117). Funke (1985: 87), looking at incarceration rates per 100 000 population, writes that in the USA in 1970, 'the number of persons incarcerated per 100 000 population was 96; by 1982 the rate had nearly doubled to 169 per 100 000 population. Average time served rose . . . from two to three years during that period.' Despite increased space made available, supply cannot meet demand for space. Thus, from 1972 to 1977 the prison establishment increased by more than 23 000 extra prison cells but the inmate population rose by 81 000. Between 1978 and 1980, 7000 more cells were added, but the prison population rose by 61 000 inmates. In 1981, 21 000 extra places were provided, but the population increased by

39 000. Funke (1985: 87) concludes: 'this lag has resulted in wide-spread prison crowding — in the typical prison, 1000 inmates crowded into space designed for 500, or, nationally, about 500 000 inmates occupying space designed for 350 000'.

In a similar vein, Austin and Krisberg (1985) confirm these developments by pointing out that in the fiscal years 1982 and 1983 $800 million was spent on expanding or improving prison capacity. An additional $2.2 billion was allocated for prison construction through bond issues or other methods of raising revenue. Direct fiscal outlays for the operation of prisons exceeded $5.5 billion in the fiscal year 1983 (Austin and Krisberg, 1985: 17). They also point out that the rate of incarceration in the USA has been climbing since 1974. The rate per 100 000 population has increased from 138 in 1980 to 179 in 1983, giving an upward trend of 30 percent. However, in actual prison numbers, from 1970 to 1982 the daily average prison population increased by 110 percent while the jail population showed an increase of 30 percent. Over the whole period, the prison population increased by 34 percent, which compares with a 25 percent increase in the supervision of offenders in the community under a probation order, and a 12 percent increase in offenders on parole. In short, the increase in the rate of incarceration was much higher than the increase in the use of alternatives to custody (Austin and Krisberg, 1985: 23). They also report a situation similar to the English experience with regard to the incarceration of juveniles: that between 1972 and 1982, in the USA, the rate of incarceration declined by 18 percent which they attribute to the declining proportion of young people in the general population. In general, official projections claimed that the incarcerated population in state and federal institutions would reach 566 170 and the projected increase in the rate of incarceration per 100 000 population would be 227 by 1990 (Austin and Krisberg, 1985: 18). However, by 1988 those projections were found to be very conservative, for the total prison population had reached nearly one million and the incarceration rate had shot up to 382 per 100,000 population (*NAPO News*, 1989c: 7). In contrast, in 1972 the rate of incarceration was 93 per 100 000 population. In 1981, this rose to 153. In 1984 the rate reached 188 (Bureau of Justice Statistics, 1985). By 1984, at least 29 states had formed task forces to address the problem of prison crowding (Evans Skovron, 1988: 183). In the same year, the top ten prison systems in the USA rated as follows by number of inmates: in California the prison system had 64 737 (incarceration rate 227); New York had 39 799 (incarceration rate 224); Texas, 38 595 (incarceration rate 227); Florida, 32 771 (incarceration rate 273); Michigan, 22 334 (incarceration rate 243); Ohio, 22 332 (incarceration rate 217); Illinois, 19 928 (incarceration rate 172); Georgia, 18 191 (incarceration rate

271); and North Carolina, 16 948 (incarceration rate 249). In comparative terms, between 1984 and 1988, in just four years, the national rate of incarceration had increased by a staggering 103 percent per 100 000 population. According to Evans Skovron (1988: 184), by 1984 overcrowding had become a national 'scandal', to the point that it led to legal repercussions in many states (among them New Jersey, Kentucky, Tennessee, Louisiana and Mississippi), which were forced to operate under court orders or consent decrees concerning crowding. In addition, a number of states have resorted to housing state inmates in local jails, thus exacerbating an already severe crowding problem. In sum, the rate of imprisonment is climbing in such a manner that it is estimated that, within ten years, the prison population in the USA, in both state and federal prisons, will double to nearly two million.

Allen and Simonsen (1986) argue that despite the pressure on the prison establishment the authorities in the USA, as in England, have followed old policies renovated with some new ideas. Thus, two main ways have been adopted in checking the growing prison crisis: building more prisons and expanding alternatives to custody. In 1984 there were 31 more state prisons and one more federal prison than in 1983. But the costs of this policy are well demonstrated by Cory and Gettinger (1984). They point out that on average a new prison space (cell) may exceed $80 000 and the yearly average cost of containing and keeping a prisoner exceeds $15 000. It is argued that it may even cost as much as $36 000 a year to keep a prisoner in a high security prison. Similarly, Evans Skovron (1988: 184) states:

> Prison crowding has resulted in great increases in expenditures for corrections. Expenditures have increased for both operating costs and construction of new facilities. Fiscal year 1984 operating budgets for state correctional systems increased by nearly $1.2 billion and approached a record $7.2 billion. More than 67 000 prison beds were added nationwide through renovation and construction from 1981 to 1983. The 1984 gain of 26 618 inmates implies a need to increase available beds nationally by 500 each week simply to accommodate new prisoners. In 1983, the 50 states reported capital expenditures greater than $780 million and bond issues and other financing mechanisms totaling nearly $1.2 billion to support prison capital improvements . . . In 1985, 35 states and the Federal Bureau of Prisons were involved in construction or planning approved construction totaling 61 975 beds.

She goes on to make a similar point to Austin and Krisberg (1985) that the principal factor for the rapid increase in the prison population has been an increase in the rate of admissions and thus incarceration. This rate far outstrips the gains made by alternatives to custody and there appears to be a determined and growing reliance on prison sentences as opposed to other sanctions (Evans Skovron, 1988: 185).

There is a suggestion that the prison population may, in due course, level off due to demographic factors — as in the case of notifiable offences which have shown a drop which could partly be explained by a declining youth population (Austin and Krisberg, 1985; Evans Skovron, 1988). Nonetheless, Austin and Krisberg argue that there is a sentencing pattern which may nullify that stabilisation process. They argue that if the current trend of incarcerating blacks at a higher rate than whites continues or worsens the estimated decrease in the prison population may not take place as the vacuum left would be filled by an increasing number of black inmates. They also suggest that other ethnic minority groups, for instance 'Hispanic males, who also have incarceration rates higher than white males and whose population is also expected to grow over the next few decades' (Austin and Krisberg, 1985: 25) may add to prison crowding. In fact, more recent figures suggest that that trend is already an established process. The rate of imprisonment for black prisoners is now six times the rate of imprisonment for whites per 100 000 population. It is suggested that by the turn of the century black people, even though they are a minority in the USA, will be a majority in prisons (*NAPO News*, 1989c: 7).

Of course, any comparisons with other countries may run the risk of decontextualising focus and impute unwarranted meanings and similarities to situations and circumstances which may have their own idiosyncratic social, political and economic characteristics. As Matthews (1987: 44, emphasis in original) rightly suggests, '*differentiation*' and not '*universality*' should be the emphasis. I would also add that data from different countries — including European states — are unlikely to be strictly comparable because the definitions of prisons, prisoners, and alternatives to custody may vary from country to country, reflecting different political decisions, and legal and administrative systems. However, despite the qualifications and differences which may exist among different states, the overall impression gained from examining trends on both sides of the Atlantic including England's European neighbours, is that the prison — whatever the definition — is expanding. This goes contrary to claims that some European states have managed to reduce their prison population quite substantially by a determined policy of offering alternatives (cf. Matthews, 1987: 44). In comparative terms, it is true that countries such as Italy, France and the Netherlands have successfully kept their incarcerated populations down. I think, though, that the comparisons and the claims made in favour of such European countries are somewhat flawed. For example, in terms of young offenders, it appears that states which have an upper age limit of 18 for the imprisonment of young offenders — Austria, Belgium, Italy and Switzerland — have very low proportions of young prisoners in their prison populations. In contrast, those countries — with the exception of Denmark and West Germany — which have an upper age limit of 21 for the imprisonment of young offenders have high or higher proportions of young people among their prison populations. Thus England ranks as the second highest among member states of the Council of Europe in terms of rates of incarceration for young people. Greece and Cyprus are top of the list (Council of Europe, 1987). When the overall prison population per 100 000 population in member states of the Council of Europe as on 1 February 1987 is considered, there appears to be a steady *increase* in the rate of incarceration in the Netherlands and France. The increase in the prison population has been taking place since 1983. In Italy, there was a steady increase between 1983 and 1985, and thereafter a decrease of 11 percent. With the exception of Italy then, in France and the Netherlands, though fewer people are imprisoned per 100 000 population than in England, recent increases in the rate of incarceration in those two states suggest that there is now a *proportionately higher* increase in their rate of incarceration than is the case in England. Table 2.2 indicates the rate of incarceration as reflected by the prison population per 100 000 population.

As can be seen (though bearing in mind the qualifications made earlier that such comparisons are riddled with difficulties) on 1 February 1987 the prison population, at 96 per 100 000 inhabitants in the United Kingdom, was the fourth highest incarceration rate compared to the other states. The Netherlands, though managing to keep incarceration rates low and rank seventeenth in the table, have experienced a 29 percent rise in the prison population between 1983 and 1987. In fact, the current situation in the Netherlands may defy or nullify earlier works (see for example Doleschall, 1977; Downes, 1982; Lijphart, 1975; Smith, 1984) which appear to compliment the Dutch for their 'tolerance'. Although that principle of 'tolerance' is now qualified and serious deficiencies are shown in the Dutch system (cf. Downes, 1988), there is still little appreciation of the fact that the reality of the Dutch system — particularly in relation to its prison population — is quite different from the outdated and rather simplistic accounts offered by those earlier studies. As De Haan (1987) suggests, even in the earlier studies there was a failure to realise that although the average length of prison sentences was reduced, prison sentences *increased* (hence implying a 'revolving door' policy) by 50 percent between 1950 and 1970. In the 1980s, criminal justice policy has 'taken an expansionist rather than a reductionist line' and the capacity of the prison in the Netherlands is 'being adapted currently to the growing demand': in 1985, the total capacity reached 4800 cells (as opposed to 3000 in 1975). Projections are not good either. Thus, 'it has been decided to make approximately 300 additional cells available every

Table 2.2   *Prison population per 100 000 inhabitants in member states of the Council of Europe on 1 February 1987*

Member state	1983	1984	1985	1986	1987	Ranking	Increase (%) February 1983 to February 1987
Austria	114	114	112	109	103	1	−10
Belgium	*	72	67	64	69	8	*
Cyprus	30	39	33	32	38	16	28
Denmark	63	70	68	69	69	8	10
France	68	74	80	81	89	5	31
W.Germany	103	104	100	92	84	7	−18
Greece	35	40	37	37	40	15	15
Iceland	35	32	34	36	37	17	5
Ireland	37	48	47	52	54	13	46
Italy	65	76	78	77	57	11	−11
Luxembourg	72	78	69	92	99	3	37
Malta	29	30	28	27	28	19	−5
Netherlands	28	31	34	35	37	17	29
Norway	52	48	51	51	50	14	−3
Portugal	53	69	87	96	85	6	60
Spain	60	38	51	61	67	10	11
Sweden	65	57	58	56	57	11	−12
Switzerland	58	62	68	*	*	*	*
Turkey	*	171	147	130	100	2	*
United Kingdom	91	88	90	94	96	4	6
England & Wales	87	86	88	92	94	*	8
Scotland	101	90	97	109	109	*	9
N.Ireland	162	156	135	125	121	*	−25

Source: Council of Europe (1987) and earlier issues. * Not available or not known.

year' (De Haan, 1987: 20). Furthermore, as Bottomley (1986) points out, the Netherlands are also moving towards longer prison sentences which may explain the rise in their prison population. For instance, the number of sentences of imprisonment of more than 12 months has risen from 3 to 12 percent since 1979 (Bottomley, 1986: 202–3). And as there has been an upsurge in the demand for prison accommodation, 'a large number of remand prisoners have had to be kept in police cells for part of the time — currently (1985) 250 per day, with an estimated annual total of more than 6500 persons' (Bottomley, 1986: 203). In comparison, the Nordic countries continue to do well. Sweden has managed to reduce the rate of incarceration by 12 percent; Norway has maintained a fairly stable population; whereas Denmark, with some fluctuation, has seen its prison population go up by 10 percent.

Overall, between February 1983 and February 1987, of the known percentage increase in 17 out of 20 member states, the prison population per 100 000 inhabitants *increased* in 11 of those states, setting, as said earlier, a general trend towards an expansion of the prison institution. In England the increase was 8 percent, which was substantially lower than in several European countries. However, what is notably different between England and most other countries is that whereas they are experiencing fluctuations (up or down), in England — with the exception of a short drop in 1984 — there has been an *upward* trend in the use of custody, thus placing it with the top four members which incarcerate a higher proportion of their general populations.

Conclusion: The fiscal and social control crisis

The preceding discussion supports the view that what we understand as 'prison crises' are not new to the 1980s. As Chapter 1 has sketched, there have been similar crises since the inception of the prison institution. Similarly, attempts to find alternatives to custody are not new. They are new in form but not in substance. In the main, particularly since the early 1980s, efforts to control the numbers of prisoners and thus crowding have relied on two main options: making more space available, and thus expanding the capacity of the prison to hold more prisoners, and expanding alternatives to custody. But despite these efforts the prison population in England and other countries continues to rise in a relentless manner. In effect, this is not just a crisis about what to do with offenders and how to punish or contain them. It is effectively a crisis about *policy*: it is a *fiscal* and *social (or maybe state) control crisis.* Lack of space creates crowding and social conditions which are inimical to safe security. Expansion temporarily relieves the pressure but adds to the contradiction and the human suffering: it sustains the prison establishment instead of depleting it of its resources and existence. The financial costs are high and the benefits of that expensive investment are short-lived. Hence the need to look elsewhere — to alternatives to custody — for ways to relieve pressure from the prison institution and perhaps reduce the expenditure. There appears to be a genuine desire to control overcrowding and improve conditions in prisons. However, despite the rhetoric of diverting offenders from custody by enacting alternatives, the previous discussion offers little real indication that there is a commitment to *reduce*, in an absolute sense, the prison population. Controlling overcrowding and reducing populations are not synonymous terms and there appears to be little realisation thus far of their difference with regard to current policy. The government, as well as its predecessors, is concerned about an increasing prison population which requires control, security and substantial resources. Space and facilities which make control and security less risky and cumbersome become a priority. After all, historically much change or improvement in prison establishments, as well as the quest for alternatives, emerged out of fear and concern that overcrowding creates social conditions which are inimical to order: they create pressure on the system and lead to security and other risks including internal and external challenges to government (cf. Home Office, 1984a: 22; Vass, 1984: 6–41). In effect, this leads to a fiscal crisis. Therefore, alternatives are expanded as a means of relieving the prison from further crowding pressure and the need to spend more on refurbishment and construction. As they are deemed cheaper, they are desirable in terms of checking further expenditure on prisons — in the sense that if they are absent, more places may be required by the authorities through further construction, refurbishment and expansion. That they may be cheaper (see the next chapter for a detailed discussion), can be observed by the difference in money spent on prisons and alternatives. For instance, referring to the example of the Chancellor making available £720 extra million to the Home Office for the financial years 1989–92, most of the money will be consumed by the construction and operation of two new prisons. In contrast, the opening of nine new bail hostels will consume a mere £3.8 million (cf. Home Office, 1988a: 3). In that sense, alternatives to custody are in fact peripheral. There is little concrete evidence that there is any real shift away from a dependence on custodial sentences in maintaining a high profile against crime and offenders. However, alternatives may be important in cushioning the effects of high spending on construction and maintenance of the prison establishment. There is no substantive evidence for this (indeed, as I shall argue later, costs may escalate by running both systems — prison and alternatives — in parallel) but Hylton (1981b: 24) provides a fairly convincing example of such a state of affairs in the Canadian context. Using a number of comparative indices of costs and distribution of costs, he finds that the role of alternatives to custody in reducing the costs of custodial establishments is clearly evident in Saskatchewan. The expansion of alternatives to custody allows for a smaller (than would have been required) increase in prison spending.

Furthermore, the expansion of the prison establishment to apparently relieve overcrowding contains an inherent, though not uncontroversial, risk. Expansion has not yet been shown to reduce pressure. It has been observed that constructing more prisons and expanding space and, therefore, capacity to contain more inmates, may simply act as an open door policy of increasing the prison population. That is, the policy of expansion may offer a temporary relief both to the state (reducing fear of disturbances) and to inmates (making their stay a bit more bearable and humane) but in the long term it tends to widen the net of the prison by enabling it to contain far more people than before. Usually demand for places outstrips supply and new places are rapidly overtaken by the number of new inmates sent there. In a sense, expansion without a clear policy about how to reduce the prison population may create new and far more disturbing crowded conditions than in the past (cf. Nagel, 1973). Some evidence for this may be seen with reference to the attempt by the government to contain the steep increase in the prison population in July 1987 when it reached a record peak of 51 200 (in prison and police cells). The capacity of the prison — despite the deployment of temporary measures through what the Home Office calls the 'tactical use of accommodation' — was stretched to its utmost limits in that period. Lack of space forced the government to introduce new rules in August 1987 so that prisoners serving 12 months or less became eligible for remission of half of their sentence. This reduced the prison population by 3000 almost immediately. However, the respite was short-lived for by March 1988 the extra space (plus a further 1900 spaces made available by the opening of four new prisons) was once again taken up by a new wave of prisoners, bringing the prison population up to 50 700. The Home Office (1988a) estimated that by the end of 1989 the prison population would have risen to 56 500. This example may point to two issues. First, as suggested, making more space available may in fact negate the intention of relieving crowding in the long term, and may add to the problem as the system has now to cope with far more prisoners. It is as if the more the supply, the higher the demand. Secondly, that the fast reaction from the government to contain the crisis by using executive powers shows how building more prisons and making more space available is not the answer; and that determined *policy* and the will to *reduce* the *social problem* of prisons, even if that will is subject to political expediency, is perhaps the key to finding appropriate solutions to this recurrent problem. That further expansion may not be the answer — though it may be seen in the first instance as a desirable but temporary antidote — to the problem is well captured in a rare joint statement by the Director General and Deputy Director General of the Prison Service (Home Office, 1988e: 1, my emphasis):

> The pressure of the population . . . reached an intensity not experienced before. There was a nightmare-like sense, felt more sharply than ever before at the top of the Service, and, we know, shared by regions and establishments, of always running and never catching up. Two major policy initiatives in July 1987 and March 1988, together with the outcome for the building programme of the 1987 public expenditure round, gave some short relief and opened the prospect of more, *though the forward projections of*

population are not encouraging. A reassessment of position is certainly required in the 1988 expenditure review.

A reassessment was undertaken, with the result that in addition to an expansion of alternatives to custody, two extra prisons, to be added to the previous 26, will be built to cope with the escalating problem of space and crowding. If the government's own projections are to be believed (conservative as those projections may be), even the new prisons will be filled to bursting point by 1995. Even if construction of new prisons and the expansion of the system had unanimous support from all quarters, it is quite clear that as a society we cannot expect to find our way out of crowded prisons through such an approach. The poverty of such policy — in terms of costs and failing to deliver any real social returns — means that alternative solutions become necessary. The following chapter critically examines one such option: the rationale for an expansion of alternatives to custody.

Note

1   Youth custody and detention centres were abolished under the Criminal Justice Act 1988. They have been replaced by one single custodial penalty, detention in a young offender institution — new label, same policy. The only difference is that by breaking down the barriers between youth custody institutions and detention centres, it will offer more space to the prison establishment to accommodate young offenders (see Home Office, 1988e).

3 Alternatives v custody: The debates rage on

On 30 March 1988 the then Home Secretary, Douglas Hurd, made a statement in Parliament about the prison population and the sentencing system. In his speech he emphasised the government's intentions to tackle the problem of prisons through determined action. He said (Home Office, 1988a: 1–3):

> It is not my role to decide who and how many convicted offenders should be sentenced to imprisonment: that is for the courts. It is my role to see that the courts have a satisfactory range of sentencing options open to them, and that when they do commit someone to custody there is suitable accommodation available for him or her. This dual responsibility is reflected in the measures I announce today.
>
> First, work is already in hand to make community service orders more demanding and more strictly administered through, for example, the introduction of national standards. Second, I have already announced a substantial expansion of the programme for providing bail hostels, involving an additional nine hostels at a cost of some £3.8 million. Third, I propose to issue next month a circular designed to help courts in taking decisions on bail. Finally, and in the slightly longer term, I am considering how to build up forms of punishment in the community which are seen by all to present a firm and fair way of dealing with those offenders who do not merit a custodial sentence.

Alternatives to custody, or 'punishment in the community', are again in the forefront of developments towards the reduction of the prison population. But the Home Secretary added that 'the most serious crimes are rightly punished by imprisonment' and announced extra money to be made available to expand the capacity of the prison system to accommodate more offenders. The idea of expanding both alternatives and prisons at one and the same time is not seen as contradictory. Imprisonment is seen as the correct and necessary sanction against serious crimes, and courts must have that option when they need it. The government considers that for other, less serious crimes, alternatives should be available to courts to divert offenders from custodial establishments. This is seen as a long-term aim. It believes that pressure on prisons could be relieved by expanding penal measures which tackle the size of the sentenced population: creating a greater scope for the greater use of community penalties (Home Office, 1988b). As most of those who are sentenced to custody for indictable offences in England and Wales (95 percent of all crimes) are there for property offences and about half of the adult sentenced prison population have been convicted of theft and burglary, the government sees it as fitting that many of those individuals could be given punishment in the community. Punishment in the community is seen as a means of keeping prison places available for more serious crimes and alleviating overcrowding.

However, punishment in the community is not just what it implies: that it refers to the administration of pain. Rather, it is suggested that such punishment, as it is administered in the community, is also 'humane punishment' because it helps offenders to remain in their natural habitat, community and families. It helps them to retain their jobs and teaches them to be self-reliant and responsible. Through their supervised activities (under the close supervision afforded by agencies such as the probation service), offenders can contribute to their own well-being as well as that of the community.

The rhetoric

In order to put those aims to work, and expand the system of community alternatives further, the Home Secretary's statement was followed by a Green Paper on the development of new alternatives entitled *Punishment, Custody and the Community* (Home Office, 1988c). As it is interesting to see how the government sets out the method and rationale of its policies towards further expansion of penal sanctions, it is helpful to quote the Green Paper at some length (Home Office, 1988c: 1–2, my emphases):

> Last year, 69 000 offenders were sentenced to custody for indictable offences in England and Wales. For many of them, this was the right punishment, because their offences were very serious. The courts have responded to public anxiety about violence by lengthening the sentences for violent crimes and the Court of Appeal will soon be able to increase over-lenient sentences. But for other, less serious, offenders, a spell in custody is not the most effective punishment. Imprisonment *restricts offenders' liberty, but it also reduces their responsibility*; they are not required to face up to what they have done and to the effect on their victim or to make any recompense to the victim or the public. If offenders are not imprisoned, they are more likely to be able to pay compensation to their victims and to make some *reparation* to the community through useful unpaid work. Their liberty can be restricted without putting them behind prison walls. Moreover, if they are removed in prison from the responsibilities, problems and temptations of everyday life, they are less likely to acquire the *self-discipline and self-reliance* which will

prevent reoffending in future. Punishment in the community would encourage offenders to *grow out of crime and to develop into responsible and law abiding citizens*. . . People have a choice whether or not to commit a criminal offence. If offenders can be helped to make the right *choices* then the risk of further offending is reduced. This means increasing the offender's *sense of responsibility* and understanding of the need to avoid crime in future. It requires *self-discipline and motivation*. It is better that people should exercise *self control* than have controls imposed upon them. To do this they need to understand the consequences of their actions . . . Imprisonment reduces offending only by restricting the opportunities for a limited period. *Imprisonment is likely to add to the difficulty which offenders find in living a normal and law abiding life*. Overcrowded local prisons are emphatically not schools of citizenship. Prisoners do not have to provide for everyday needs, such as food and clothing, to find or keep jobs, or to look after their homes and their families. If offenders remain in the community, they should be able to *maintain their relationships with their family; their opportunities for work, training and education* will be better; and they should be able to make some reparation for the harm they have done. *Punishment in the community should be more economical in public resources*. On average, holding someone in prison for a month costs twice as much as the average community service order. *Imprisonment is not the most effective punishment for most crime*. Custody should be reserved as punishment for very serious offences, especially when the offender is violent and a continuing risk to the public. But not every sentencer or member of the public has full confidence in the present orders which leave offenders in the community. [Hence] . . . the Government's proposals, which aim to increase the courts' and the public's confidence in keeping offenders in the community.

As can be seen, the reasons for having to expand the choice of penal options in the community are simple: prisons are crowded; most offenders can be safely controlled by other means in the community; prisons only restrict liberty for a temporary period; prisons are not the most effective way of rehabilitating offenders; community penal measures, or punishment in the community, are better because they are cheaper; they allow offenders to make reparation to the community and recompense to the victim; the community helps them acquire self-discipline and self-reliance which they lose by being in prison; punishment in the community helps them grow out of crime and develop into responsible citizens; in prisons they lack choice, in the community they are made to make choices by giving them more options and opportunities; prisons are not schools for citizenship whereas the community is; punishment in the community helps them maintain relationships with their families, sustain a job, and seek their own training and education. In all, prisons are bad, and should only be reserved for the most serious offenders — the really wicked. Community is good and desirable and should be used, as a sanction, for most crimes.

Rhetoric or a meaningful approach to crime and offenders? Who is the government trying to convince about the adverse effects of imprisonment? Surely not probation officers or those responsible for supervising offenders in the community. They have been arguing that prisons do not work for far too long. Of course, there are differences in the way terms are used. Probation officers resent the term 'punishment in the community': they advocate instead 'supervision in the community' (NAPO, 1988a). Their advice to the government is that it should abandon its policy of 'punishment' and retain the concept and practice of 'supervision in the community'! Different terms, but similar intentions.

It is more probable that the rhetoric is part of the same long-running political expediency of having to show that something serious and tough is being done about prisons and crime (Vass, 1984). As in the past, the government is wielding both a carrot and a stick: it is engaging itself in a bargaining process which is characteristic of attempts to promote or enact new penal measures (cf. Young, 1979). On the one hand, it expands the capacity of the prison establishment by spending huge sums of money on such expansion and refurbishment, which is justified on the grounds that the government has a duty to enable courts to deal with serious crimes which call for the ultimate punishment. On the other hand, prison costs are hugely expensive and they fail to do their job of reforming offenders. Indeed, they even lead to detrimental psychological and social effects on prisoners. Something else ought to be offered in their place: alternatives which are capable of controlling offenders in the community as effectively as containing them in prison, and more importantly, can also save money for the taxpayer. In all, the government makes prisons look unproductive but nonetheless socially necessary, thus they must be retained. At the same time as prisons are inhumane methods of dealing with offenders, alternatives to custody become necessary to draw a balance between coercion and rehabilitation. By implication, it is argued that both methods of dealing with offenders have a relevant role to play in the penal system, and thus their existence is fully justified.

In my view, the rhetoric as well as the practical intentions of the government are directed at the judiciary as well as the law and order lobby. It is an indirect appeal to the courts to re-think their activities, but not an attempt to embark on a judicial inquiry on how to restrict their powers to imprison offenders. They are indirectly asked to apply a more controlled approach to their clients by channelling them into alternative sanctions in the community rather than sending many of them, quite unnecessarily, to custodial establishments. There appears to be a problem though in equalising the severity of the custodial sanction with that of alternatives which have a history and an image of being 'soft options'. Indeed, 'alternatives to custody' implies something softer, secondary to the punishment of imprisonment. Therefore, in order to encourage the further use of such penal measures by eliminating or reducing their 'soft option' image, the government is emphasising their *independent* status, not as 'alternatives' but rather as a set of severe sanctions whose purpose is to administer harsh punishment. In addition, unlike prisons, the alternatives are seen as *positively effective* punishment. Hence the careful choice of words. We no longer speak of alternatives. We refer to *punishment in the community*. However, as punishment is administered within the confines of a neighbourhood, a community at large, then some of the most negative effects of incarceration are excluded and restricted to the few who are sent to prison. For those who are punished in the community, the punishment is meaningful. It has a lesson to teach, as well as to emphasise independence; motivation for personal change and development: citizenship. Also, note how labels can change, on both sides of the penal scale, from being loaded with coercion to being more neutral and acceptable in order to fit the change in perspective and the caring nature of community. Gone are those individuals whom governments used to call 'criminals'. They have been replaced by individuals who still commit crimes but who are not 'criminals': they are offenders. 'Criminals', as a label, implies something nasty, which exhibits alien features, and which contradicts the good nature and normality of 'community life'. 'Offenders' is a more acceptable description of individuals who contradict community laws, mores and values. It fits the occasion and the good nature of community. For the community is capable of forgetting and forgiving and assists in the healing process. Offenders break the rules of law, but they are not alien beings. They can still be 'good' and useful people who have something to contribute to their communities if only they could be shown how. Thus, they should be kept away from prison establishments and remain in the community. Punishment in the community applies sanctions coupled with a humane approach to those individuals' actions: punishment imbues them with a sense of guilt as well as purpose: they have wronged their community, and they have to be punished. The community (within which those penalties are applied and executed) teaches them how to readjust to normal life and expectations. Prisons punish, but *alienate*. Community punishes but *reintegrates*: it helps to create a moral conscience and assists offenders in rebuilding their social networks; boosting their morale; engaging in good deeds for others; and treating themselves and others with the respect they deserve.

Building on those intentions, the government published another paper in August 1988, *Tackling Offending: An Action Plan* (Home Office, 1988d). It describes punishment in the community as a way forward in encouraging more use of non-custodial penal sanctions, particularly by making them more demanding and punitive. The 'action plan' is directed towards the 17–20 age group. It invites the 56 probation areas nationwide to establish an action plan in consultation with the courts, police and other agencies. Selected areas will be required to set up 'intensive probation' programmes aimed exclusively at offenders who would otherwise receive custodial sentences. The selected areas are likely to be those where the rate of custodial sentencing for 17–20-year-olds exceeds the national average of 12 percent (National Executive Committee, 1988). 'Intensive probation' programmes will receive priority in capital expenditure allocation.

Reading the government's pronouncements on the benefits of alternatives to custody, one cannot help thinking back to the voices of many sociological studies, liberal reformists and others which, time and again, have trumpeted and amplified the claim that custodial institutions are nothing more than 'universities of crime', which have little effect on crime rates; and which stigmatise as well as exclude individuals from normal relationships. That is, the thrust towards alternatives to custody, under its guise of 'punishment in the community' and its rationale, is not new. It is the same old story of governments trying to promote penal policy by falling back on to highly rehearsed and overused ideas. The process or thrust of policies of diversion — by inventing alternatives to custody — towards community penal measures in the 1960s and onwards was based to a large extent on the conception that custodial institutions do not only fail to deter, but also tend to destroy inmates by dehumanising and degrading them. In addition, that they are highly expensive. Indeed, in the 1970s, as now, one of the most cited reasons for the need to look to the community as a more progressive way in dealing with offenders was that custodial penalties are, by and large, 'decaying institutions' (Inner London Probation and After-care Service, 1975). As the Advisory Council on the Penal System (1977: 4–5) wrote at the time:

> . . . society, by labelling the prisoner a convict and thereby socially and personally handicapping him on his return to the community, alienates itself from offenders. . . . The maintenance of the prison system is as much a direct cost to society as crime itself . . . [F]ew of those who know the prison system today retain much of the simple faith in its effectiveness as an agent of reform.

The above — present, and past — conception of the prison, as a negative sanction and experience, represents a broader argument about the failure of the prison and the need to look at community alternatives for an answer or solution to the problem of crime. Much of the original literature on the merits of community penal measures (and other services, particularly in the mental health field) and defects of the custodial institution originates in the USA. Thus, for example, Martinson (1972), in a series of articles, reiterates the ideas about the desirability of punishment in the community: it reduces isolation, labelling and the disastrous personal — mental and physical — effects of incarceration. He observes that attempts for over 150 years to improve the prison environment (prison design, new building programmes) and to intensify the rehabilitation of inmates has not succeeded in reducing the reconviction rate. According to Martinson, recidivism is a function of the institutionalisation process which interrupts normal occupational and lifestyle processes. Removal from society for a period of time — short or long term — produces irreparable personal and social damage. In a similar vein, Rothman (1971) suggests that rather than trying to improve and rehabilitate the prison establishment (and asylums), we ought to get on with the task of emptying them and closing them down (see also Klapmuts, 1975; Schulberg, 1973). Alper (1973: vii–viii) summarises, in colourful language, the issues raised by such claims that dealing with offenders in the community is a superior and more desirable method than locking people up in institutions:

> nothing succeeds like an idea whose time has come. The institution as a means of coping with the problems of specific sectors of our population seems at this point to have run its course. Whether one is aged, below par intellectually or emotionally, delinquent, alcoholic, or drug-addicted, the source — and the remedy — of the problem lies in the communities where such people come from. By bringing them back into the community, by enlisting the good will and the desire to serve, the ability to understand which is to be found in every neighborhood, we shall meet the challenge which such groups of persons present, and at the same time ease the financial burden of their confinement in fixed institutions.

The reality: The effects of imprisonment

Prisons, and custodial establishments in general, are regarded as the ultimate punishment which restricts liberty and leisure in the type of society we live in. But the word *imprisonment*, as Bottomley and Pease (1986: 95) remind us, is equivocal. Thus whereas in England imprisonment is the ultimate sanction, it is, as Bottomley and Pease (1986) suggest, difficult to measure both in quantity and quality because behind the word imprisonment there lies not just purely defined and designated prisons (for keeping offenders incarcerated) but many other types of imprisonment which escape the attention of the public as well as criminologists (putting people under 'curfew' orders in the community is prison of a different kind, people in police cells, juveniles under care orders, 'voluntary' patients in psychiatric hospitals). According to Bottomley and Pease (1986: 95–6), 'prison is near one end of a continuum from total restriction to total liberty'. As they suggest further, 'It depends on what one counts as imprisonment and it depends on what one means by [its] use'.

In keeping to the more restricted definition of custody — prisons as they relate to offenders — *custody* is in effect, as the name implies, an antithesis of what human social existence is understood to be and violates basic fundamental values: liberty, dignity and fraternity. Liberty is curtailed; dignity and self-respect are seriously limited by the oppression of those individuals through an artificial and squalid environment; and fraternity is a meaningless concept, for inside the prisons fraternity changes into associations which prohibit natural social relationships and which are assumed to erode prisoners' capacity to establish, on their release, normal relationships. In short, custody is supposed to be what one could call the *anti-community*: it is a place where the rotten apples are thrown to protect others from contamination. However, as with all rotten apples, their concentration together leads to further rot, squalor and rapid decomposition. Men and women are expected to survive an environment which goes against every aspect of human dignity and sanctity and come out clean. But they do not. Prisons do not appear to reduce crime and deter offenders from committing new ones; and, it is argued, have serious adverse effects on prisoners and their families (cf. Cohen and Taylor, 1972; Clemmer, 1958; Goffman, 1961; Morris and Morris, 1963). On top of all that, they also cost an awful lot of money. As the *Sentence of the Court* (Home Office, 1986: 7–8, emphasis in original) explains:

> It is with regard to *custody*, the most severe penalty open to the courts, that [choice of sanctions and effectiveness] are particularly relevant. It would be wrong to impose a custodial sentence in a case where that severe a penalty was not warranted by the crime in question, merely in the hope of achieving a deterrent or reformative effect which experience suggests is unlikely to materialise. It is indeed important to bear in mind custody is not only the most severe penalty available . . . and the one which consumes most resources, but it is also the one likely to have the most serious side-effects. These include not only harm to the offender's personal and financial prospects on release but also the particular likelihood of inflicting hardship on the offender's family as well rather than merely exacting proper retribution from the actual criminal.

As retribution then goes beyond merely the offender and begins to affect others and by implication the very people who are supposed to be protected from the ravages of crime (the family or the community at large), the general view is that custody is bad, though necessary for the most serious and dangerous offenders. Custody 'should only be imposed when it is truly necessary in the circumstances of the case, and that if it is necessary, the sentence should be as short as is consistent with the need of punishment' (Home Office, 1986: 8).

It is not surprising that in view of those problems of imprisonment, advocates of community-based penal measures seem to suggest that community penal sanctions are obviously desirable. However, much of the problem in identifying both the measures and the practices lies in separating the content of conceptions from the value-laden imagery of warmth and camaraderie attached to 'community'. The expansion of penal sanctions and community service has come to denote a rather wide assortment of tasks, sentences and dispositions. Thus almost any measure which is seen as falling outside the walls of custodial institutions has been placed in the 'community' category. The impression is given that the very fact of labelling or designating a measure as 'community-based' is supposed to connote that it is 'innovative', 'enlightened', and 'progressive' (Warren, 1972: iii). 'Community' is used, to borrow Benington's (1974: 260) phrase, as a 'kind of "aerosol" word to be sprayed on to deteriorating institutions to deodorise and humanise them'. Apart from the irony that what we may now call undesirable and decaying institutions — prisons — were once in the vanguard of our rehabilitative and reformative ideals (Cohen, 1979a; Foucault, 1977; Scull, 1977) whose adoption 'aroused an almost precisely parellel set of millennial expectations among their advocates' (Scull, 1977: 42), alternatives to custody suffer from a lack of clarity with regard to their role and tasks in the criminal justice system. They appear to be all things to all people, trying to satisfy all kinds of penal philosophies. They punish, rehabilitate, reform, save money for the taxpayer, are humane, and give something back to the community by requiring offenders to make reparation to the community.

Whether they do or do not satisfy any of those requirements or confused and contradictory penal philosophies is a different matter. Prisons are believed by many people to be socially, psychologically and economically undesirable. However, such a belief does not exist without challenge. There are studies which purport to show that in fact we know very little about the effects of 'prisonisation' or institutionalisation, and that the belief that institutions are 'bad' and have debilitating effects on inmates is more of a moral than an empirical statement. As Terence Morris (1965: 77–8) observes:

> some of the cherished notions that penologists have had for years about the nature of prison life and its effects upon the individual offender need modification. It has for long been believed that the longer a man remains inside, i.e. the greater the extent of his prisonization, the poorer his chances of successful rehabilitation. [Some findings do] not support this view . . . it remains that the proposition that prisons can only make criminals more criminal is one which should be regarded with considerable reserve.

This sort of claim may appear unconvincing as it violates acceptable values and expectations about the undesirability of imprisonment and its social and psychological ill-effects on inmates and their families. Also, by accepting it there is a danger of throwing away all the positive efforts which have been made to limit the rate of incarceration and find more humane alternatives. In short, as Howard Parker has suggested in a rather vitriolic response to a collection of papers on the subject (Bottoms and Light, 1987), such a claim is absurd in the face of knowledge about the ill-effects of imprisonment; gives unwelcomed credence and support to a harsh and punitive system; and assists that system in continuing to treat fellow human beings in an inhumane and degrading way. Unfortunately the issue is not as clear as Parker argues. At the abstract and moral level nobody can deny the fact that imprisonment can have negative effects on inmates and adverse social consequences for them as well as their families. But on empirical grounds, the argument about the effects of imprisonment is far from settled.

Autobiographical evidence (e.g. Cobb, 1985; Parker, 1973) and independent research (cf. D'Atri, 1975; Ellis et al., 1974; McCain et al., 1980; Megargee, 1977) suggest that there may be specific (such as deterioration in mental or physical health) or general and irreversible deterioration in prisoners' behaviour (such as depression or excessive violence) during the time served and after release. Although findings are not clear as to what exactly causes this deterioration, it appears that the loss of privacy and stress from crowding are contributory factors. However, in direct contrast to those claims, Sapsford (1978) argues that men who spend a long time in institutions may not after all lose interest in the outside world; and that they do not appear to experience personality changes by becoming more apathetic about themselves or their social world. He argues that his study of life sentences offers some evidence for certain specific changes, which in some cases 'might amount to "deterioration" associated with the length of time a man spends in prison': an increase in introversion, and a tendency for men who were not already dependent on routine and on staff support when they first came into prison to be seen by staff as becoming so as the sentence progresses (Sapsford, 1978: 143). He argues that there is no evidence to suggest that such changes affect all areas of a man's life. Sapsford (1978: 143) says:

> there is little clustering among the many measures considered in this paper, no definite increase in apathy, and no measurable decrease in motivation or in interest in the outside world . . . it would not seem unreasonable to conclude that the extreme conditions of apathy and reversion to childish attitudes which are reported from concentration camps and long-stay psychiatric hospitals may be rare in prisons, even among men subject to the uncertainties of life-sentence.

Similarly, Banister et al. (1973: 322) report that they could not find, following 'a battery of cognitive tests', any decline in general intellectual capacity among prisoners except some reduction in perceptual-motor speed which in itself was not 'a direct function of length of imprisonment'. Richards (1978: 167–8), in an exploration of psychological stresses experienced by long-term prisoners and the methods of coping with them, concludes:

> Neither the problem rating nor the interview data suggest that prison is experienced by most of these men as a fundamental threat to their mental health . . . These findings do not contradict the more dramatic analyses of, for example, Cohen and Taylor (1972) but taken together they show the need for caution in generalising from one kind of penal institution to another . . . They remind us of the need to consider an institution, however 'total', in the context of the society in which it functions.

Reckless and Sindwani (1974: 369) also caution against accepting without question the assumed effects of imprisonment. They suggest that factors other than custody have to be considered in measuring the effects of institutionalisation:

> In spite of great improvements in the programmes of correctional institutions for adults and juveniles, there are still no feasible ways of measuring the impact of institutional stay on the inmate. Outcome on after-care and outcome after expiration of sentence, say a year or more after release, appears to be almost completely unrelated to the impact of the institutional programme. The reasons for this are that post-institutional outcome depends very much upon the type of environment to which the releasee returns, the personality of the releasee, the releasee's involvement with associates, and the readiness of the after-care officer or the police to take the releasee into custody. When the latter happens, failure is recorded.

Cornish and Clarke (1975) in their study of the effectiveness of residential intervention in reducing offenders' subsequent criminality, find that reconviction rates among a total of 280 people in the sample are high. About 70 percent of those individuals committed further offences within a two-year period but the authors say that the true figure is nearer to 80 percent. This is because, of the overall successes ($n=87$), 30 committed offences after the end of their two-year follow-up period (Cornish and Clarke, 1975: 17). They compare their findings with previous studies on approved schools and studies on the effectiveness of custodial and non-custodial institutions and conclude that no particular method of intervention or penalty seems to be successful enough. However, they also draw attention to the fact that not much is known about the effects of custodial institutions in general. They write that 'The extent to which institutions can or do perform the functions of care, custody and deterrence satisfactorily (or indeed cost-effectively) should now be the subject of empirical investigation' (Cornish and Clarke, 1975: 50–51).

In a similar vein, Walker (1983a: 69–70), in a review of studies on the effects of incarceration — from physical to mental health, and the effects on both prisoners and their families — concludes thus:

> Imprisonment is almost always boring, irksome and humiliating; in some prisons it is also squalid, and some prisoners suffer from grievances or anxieties. Condemnation of prison conditions is so universal that even to ask how serious is the harm they cause sounds heretical. Yet it does seem possible to exaggerate the harms. Exaggeration can take the form of attributing to all prisons the evils of the worst kinds of total institution; of attributing to short sentences effects which have been demonstrated only in some long sentence men; or simply of accepting (to say nothing of encouraging) prisoners' beliefs about their own deterioration. The most remarkable omission, however, in the literature of unwanted effects, is any attempt to find out to what extent the harm in question is permanent or lasting . . . The one exception is the finding that reconviction rates increase with length or frequency of custody; yet this too requires much more investigation before we can interpret it.

In sum, far from having a clear picture of the assumed effects of imprisonment which can help the process of diversion and the search for alternatives, there exists a small body of literature which is unclear and sharply contradictory. I think that much of the argument about the effects of imprisonment lacks credence because it appears that each study or finding adopts its own perspective, focus and form of analysis which may, inevitably, lead to different results and contradictory findings. For example, it is difficult to know how to reconcile sociological and psychological literature on the subject. The first looks at broader *social* issues; the second, at more specific *psychological and cognitive* issues. Furthermore, it is difficult to draw firm conclusions about the reliability of such studies as many effects may go unnoticed since they may not be amenable to immediate measurement or observation. Nonetheless, in respect of what knowledge we have about the effects of imprisonment, and allowing for the incompatibility of such studies with each other's perspectives, focus, scope, methods and analysis, it seems that the claim that prisons dehumanise their subjects and lead to a general and irreversible personal and social damage, needs to be considered with some caution.

The rehabilitative powers of custody and alternatives

Various attempts to review research studies on the rehabilitative effect of penal measures in general conclude on a rather pessimistic note (e.g. Brody, 1976; Lipton et al., 1975). The Home Office in its review of the criminal justice system in 1976 (Home Office, 1977) states that alternatives to custody should be considered with caution and that it is questionable whether they can seriously have any real effects on crime rates and in reducing recidivism. It states (Home Office, 1977: 9):

> Although it may not always have been central to policies for reducing crime, the assumption that the type of penal disposal given to a convicted offender would have some effect upon his likely recidivism has figured prominently in justification of various alternatives to imprisonment and the treatment concept still underlies to some extent the current approach . . . This assumption is now under serious attack on the basis of the evidence.

As if to discourage any further optimism about the effectiveness of sentencing practices and sanctions, the Home Office in its *Sentence of the Court* (Home Office, 1986), reports that the incapacitation theory, that is the ability of custody to deter, is of limited value. It argues that findings point to the realisation that increased terms of imprisonment (often advocated and enacted by politicians and adopted by courts) have no real effect on crime rates as regards deterrence or recidivism. On a more general note, the Home Office (1986: 6) states too that the idea that penal measures, including prisons, and particularly alternatives to custody, have a positive effect on crime rates is far from the truth:

> The almost invariable conclusion of the large amount of research which has been undertaken (in various Western countries) is that it is hard to show any effect that one type of sentence is more likely than any other to reduce the likelihood of reoffending, which is high for all. Equally, longer periods of custody do not produce better results than shorter ones, nor, generally, particular institutional regimes better results than others. Studies comparing the reconviction rates of offenders given community service orders with those given custodial sentences have also shown little difference.

An illustration of this failure of alternatives to show any serious positive effects on the reconviction rate, is the case of the community service order.

The Home Office's attempt to assess the success or failure of community service in terms of early reconviction (Pease et al., 1977) was, despite methodological problems, not particularly supportive of the new penal measure. Allowing for the small samples (617 offenders in the experimental group and 111 offenders in the control group), and the not fully comparable samples (the control group was found to be significantly older than the community service treatment group), the study did not show any 'apparent reduction of reconviction in the group given community service relative to those given other disposals' (Pease et al., 1977: 19). Combining data from all six areas from which samples were drawn, 44.2 percent of all those sentenced to community service during the first year of the scheme were reconvicted within a year of the sentence, as against 33.3 percent of the control group of offenders who had been recommended by the probation service for community service but received alternative sentences. It would appear that though further assessment in this area is now overdue, this particular study may cast some doubt on the belief that community alternatives can do much to bring about any significant changes in the reconviction rate. In point of fact, the study concludes on a rather pessimistic note, that 'The data did not show that community service had a stabilising effect on the criminal careers of the offenders studied' (Pease et al., 1977: 23). A similar conclusion is reached by research on community service orders in the USA. For instance, McDonald (1986) found that community service did not show much effect on offenders in terms of stopping them from reoffending. Although he argues that in all it is better to divert offenders from imprisonment on economic and humanistic grounds, he is nonetheless emphatic about the failure of community service to control crime (McDonald, 1986: 186): 'the community service sentence is not a cure for crime, at least in the population of recidivist offenders (mostly thieves) that the New York courts sentenced to the Vera Institute's project. Approximately 40 to 50 percent of those in our sample were rearrested within six months of having being sentenced.'

This pessimism about the capacity of particular alternatives to have any positive impact on the crime rate reflects a general concern shared by other writers about the ineffectiveness of community-based programmes in overcoming the weaknesses and harmful effects of custodial institutions (e.g. Davies, 1974: 164).

However, this pessimism on the one hand (that alternatives to custody are not immune to criticism and failure) and optimism on the other (in the context of the current push towards more rewarding and effective alternatives to custody in the form of 'punishment in the community') throws up serious contradictions and confusion about the role and relevance of such measures in combating crime and controlling the activities of offenders. The idea that 'nothing works', with the wishful thinking that *something* must surely work (otherwise the obvious question that comes to mind is 'why bother?'), calls for research which attempts to identify particular sanctions and parts of the *process* (cf. Smith, 1987; Vass, 1988b) of administering and enforcing those sanctions to see whether indeed anything at all works which is not immediately open to analysis on the basis of pure arithmetical comparisons, such as those offered by looking at the recidivism rate. Thus, for instance, a study in England by Phillpotts and Lancucki (1979) considered the reconvictions of a sample of 5000 offenders. Fifty percent of the male and 22 percent of the female offenders were reconvicted within a six-year period. Although the results were not encouraging for any one particular sentence of the court, the authors were able to conclude that, in the main, offenders given custodial sentences appear to have higher reconviction rates than those given suspended sentences or probation or supervision orders; but that the latter do worse in comparison to a fine or an absolute or conditional discharge. However, it is difficult to draw any realistic conclusions because recidivism as a measure for counting success or failure has serious limitations and usually matters relevant to the question are left untouched. For instance, recidivism is not just a function of committing new offences. There is a difference between reoffending and recidivism. The first may take place without the offender being found out or apprehended. The second is more of a 'bureaucratic' decision by supervising or prosecuting officers to treat the commission of a new offence as a failure. The way in which they act or react to identified infractions of the rules is a material source of influence on whether an offender will be processed through the courts as a recidivist or whether he or she will be shielded by those supervisors or enforcers from a re-exposure to the criminal justice system. For instance, probation may do better not necessarily because those offenders commit fewer offences after conviction and sentence but because they may, as they are now known to welfare agencies, receive preferential treatment; infractions of the law may not be reported and attempts may be made by supervisors to deal with the new situation through internal, administrative, or informal sanctions as opposed to external, legal and formal penalties (cf. Day, 1981; Fielding, 1984, 1986; Lawson, 1978). Besides, even when the relevance of outcomes is taken for granted without questioning how they are achieved and under what circumstances, the evidence is contradictory and subject to different interpretations. Thus Sheppard (1980) finds that 67 to 71 percent of those completing two-year probation orders are reconvicted within five years. There is some evidence, though, that individual penal sanctions appear to work differently with different types of offenders and therefore, whereas they can be effective with some offenders, may not be so with others. For instance, Walker (1985), in considering various findings, suggests that for some offenders at various stages in their criminal career, different sentences may have different effects. Thus, probation orders appear to be more effective in controlling recidivism if they are used for offenders with previous convictions — particularly between two and four — though once again why that should be so is not clear from the evidence (Walker, 1983b). As Bottomley and Pease (1986: 164) state, in our ignorance we suffer a sort of 'penal agnosticism'. They suggest that we tend to look at all prisons, probation officers, alternatives to custody and so forth as having the same effect on people, when in fact they may not. In order to avoid distorted perceptions of the effects of penal measures, they call for more 'differentiation among sanctions in the same nominal category'.

Hidden flaws and the 'halo' effect

A clearer understanding of the problems and complexities of the arguments for or against alternatives and the desirability of community-based penal measures can be gained with reference to experience and findings emanating from the early attempts to divert offenders to the community in the USA. Although these findings are rather outdated and have been much rehearsed in the literature, they offer good illustrative material. This is so because advocates as well as critics of alternatives to custody have by and large drawn their respective arguments from those experiences, and particularly from two pioneering experiments: the Provo Experiment and the California Treatment Project (CTP).

The Provo Experiment was a non-residential programme featuring work in the community and the use of guided group interaction techniques (Empey and Erickson, 1972). Members of the experimental programme were compared with two control groups of court wards in the Provo area: boys on regular probation and boys sent to the state training school. Two major findings stood out. First, when pre- and post-programme delinquency rates were compared, there were significant reductions in every programme, including incarceration. Secondly, the reductions were greater for the boys who remained in the community than for those who were incarcerated. As a result, the inference was drawn that 'efforts to improve correctional programs might be far more fruitful if they concentrated upon the improvement of community rather than institutional designs' (Empey and Erickson, 1972: 261).

Similarly, the CTP has been characterised as 'one of the most comprehensive attempts to develop community-based treatment alternatives for juvenile offenders' (Moos, 1975: 240). The CTP's major purpose was to investigate the feasibility of substituting community programmes for traditional custodial programmes with a sample of delinquents committed to the California Youth Authority. It began in 1961 and ended in 1974. Young offenders who were committed to the Youth Authority were allocated at random to the CTP or to a custodial setting. The aim was to compare the two groups in terms of revocation of parole and reconviction rates. Those who were allocated to the CTP were subjected to intensive supervision which included 'matching' techniques, placements in group homes, tuition and assistance with outside agencies such as schools, employers and welfare agencies. The overall results of the project appeared to indicate that the CTP was at least 'as effective if not more effective, than traditional programs' (Moos, 1975: 241). Over a period of four years the experimental group showed a reconviction rate which was slightly lower than that of the control group. This prompted various writers to claim that treatment in the community did appear to reduce recidivism (Palmer, 1971, 1973).

Critics were quick to react and review findings from a different perspective. Thus, as Moos argues, the CTP and other programmes have been wrongly designated as 'treatment projects' and that 'More than 30% of community-based programs have social environments that are not specifically treatment-oriented' (Moos, 1975: 250). Grygier et al. (1970) argue that although community-based programmes in general may offer certain financial rewards or savings for the public purse, vocational guidance to offenders, encouragement and moral support, they also allow for a concentration of offenders — in association with each other — which may reinforce (as custodial institutions are thought to do), rather than reduce, criminal values and patterns of behaviour (see also Millham, 1975). Sarason (1974) notes that community-based penal measures may not be as different from regular custodial institutions as the current literature seems to suggest. The difference has mainly to do with degrees of freedom and mobility. Otherwise, the two regimes share similar means and objectives. For example, community programmes usually rely on a traditional conception of professional responsibility rather than an alternative conception of *community* responsibility. He points out that the Provo Experiment and the CTP, as well as most other community penal programmes, are, for instance, organised along hierarchical administrative lines very similar to those characteristic of custodial regimes.

This is a valid point, as research into the hierarchical structures of community service organisation (cf. Vass, 1984; Vass and Menzies, 1989) demonstrates. There are distinct structures of organisation which resemble the 'pyramid' type of organisation in custodial establishments. This is even more evident in other types of community penal measures, as for instance the attendance centre order in England. The attendance centre order is an alternative to custody (cf. Home Office, 1986: 9) which is given to 'Anyone aged under twenty-one who is found guilty of an offence for which an adult may be imprisoned' (Home Office, 1986: 48). The aim of the order is to 'impose, in loss of leisure over a considerable period, a punishment that is generally understood by young people and to encourage them, in a disciplined environment, to make more constructive use of their leisure time' (Home Office, 1986: 48). In 1986 there were 127 centres in England and Wales; 89 of them catering for boys aged 10–16; seven for girls aged

10–16; 13 for boys and girls aged 10–16; and 18 for young men aged 17–20. The centres are usually situated in school buildings equipped with a gymnasium and showers; youth clubs; police premises 'out of sight of the public and community centres'. Centres are often organised and administered by police or ex-police officers. Sessions are held on Saturdays and last for up to two hours for juniors and up to three hours for seniors. Much of the offenders' time is devoted to physical training and discipline. Most of these centres are run on almost identical administrative patterns to those adopted in prisons whereby staff members do not only belong to strict hierarchical structures of command but they also wear special uniforms to emphasise the ceremonial aspects of power and subordination. Staff expect youngsters to address them in specific and formal terms. The status, allocation of tasks and roles, uniform, posture, and manner of communication act as rituals which help to stress the existence of formal rules which necessitate submissiveness and compliance by the offender.

Sarason (1974: 188) adds that 'there is little reason to expect that the adverse consequences [of custodial establishments] will be discernibly less in the community'. In fact, he sees the existence of alternatives to custody as virtually guaranteeing the continued existence and expansion of custodial institutions. For without the latter, there would be no sense in sustaining measures as alternatives to custody (see also Mannheim, 1939; Hudson, 1984; Vass, 1982a). Lerman (1975) makes a similar point and suggests that the claims of the CTP, particularly in relation to the Probation Subsidy Scheme, concerning the success of community programmes, are not correct. Lerman (1975: 15) argues that the introduction of the Probation Subsidy Scheme may have increased, not decreased, institutionalisation:

> at a county level many more youth were experiencing detention in county facilities than during the presubsidy years (controlling for population changes and the rise in drug arrests) . . . for while fewer youth were being deprived of their liberty at the state level, many more were being detained at the county level; and while fewer youth were experiencing lengthier lock-up periods at a state level, more were experiencing shorter lock-up periods at a county level . . . [T]here is a lack of evidence that California has, in fact, reduced the net amount of statewide institutionalization when state and county figures are combined. It appears, contrary to conventional beliefs, that probation subsidy need not be associated with economic savings or a reduction in total institutionalization.

A more serious criticism of the so-called success of community-based penal measures such as the CTP refers to the spurious relationship between community-based supervision and reconviction rates. In the CTP, the 'halo' effect in terms of results (that is, the influence of the supervising agent in determining success or failure) was noted by critics. Studies of community-based penal measures which attempt to demonstrate that offenders who are supervised in the community have fewer reconvictions than those who serve custodial sentences may not, in fact, demonstrate the superiority of those measures in terms of effectiveness in controlling recidivism but, rather, they may show the effects and the importance of differential reactions to offenders (and their offences) by the enforcement agencies. Thus, Lerman (1968) and Gibbons (1970) argue that the basis of the claim that community penal measures are better than custodial sanctions rests on the evidence that recommittal for parole violation is much lower for the experimentals than for the controls. But when known offences (rather than reconvictions) are examined, it turns out that the experimentals have as many offences as the controls, if not more. The two groups — experimentals and controls — have comparable technical violations and comparable chances of being sanctioned by the police and parole agents via court proceedings. However, the former group seem to do better in terms of reconviction rates because 'the noticed offences [are] treated differentially by the experimental and control organizations' (Lerman, 1968: 57, 1975; see also Scull, 1977: 100). In short, reconviction (and thus failure or success) may be, in the final analysis, a function of the process of law enforcement rather than the actions of offenders or the positive effects of supervision in the community. Similar findings are reported by Taggart (1972), who suggests that the successes of community penal measures may be due to favourable reactions towards offenders by their supervising officers relative to the reactions to other offenders violating the terms of probation or parole. In such programmes, what one may measure is not degrees of rehabilitation or reformation of character but in fact the *processes* which lead to the *construction* of outcomes. In other words, one may be measuring the type of interaction that takes place between law enforcement agents (who act as supervisors or administrators of those penal measures) and offenders rather than the latter's reoffending behaviour. Taggart (1972: 37), in reference to the CTP, writes: 'The [CTP's] apparently positive impact was to a large extent the result of the favourable treatment given to participants relative to other offenders violating the terms of probation or parole . . . When the offence is of low or moderate severity experimentals are less likely to have their parole revoked; and they thus have a lower recidivism rate'.

The public v private world of alternatives

In short, what concerns us here is the mechanics of law enforcement which will receive fuller treatment later, particularly in Chapter 5. It is important, however, to air this issue now as its relevance to the argument that alternatives to custody are more desirable if not more effective than custodial sentences is quite strong and thus merits attention.

The problem here can be summarised in a few words: policy is one thing, practice is another. Supervising officers have a 'bag of tricks' which can help them cope with pressures and, in so doing, form policy on the spot; deviate from the rules; and control situations according to their own ends. Usually, those ends relate to a discernible goal: a positive and successful portrayal of their practices and the effectiveness of their work. The realisation that outcomes are not merely the result of the actions of offenders but also the actions and reactions of supervising officers is not a new one. It has been observed in many other forms of social organisation where rules and regulations inform social relations, not just in the workings of alternatives to custody (cf. Vass, 1984: ch. 2). For example, research on the enforcement of regulations by foremen and supervisors; the factory inspectorate; bureaucratic organisations; the police; parole agents; store detectives; miners; debt collectors; and even prison guards, among others, shows that 'systems of control expedite, evade, routinise, alter and distort. Formal rules . . . are applied in a climate of reciprocity, fraternity and coexistence' (Vass, 1984: 57). Therefore, even before the above attempts were made to critically evaluate community penal measures, research showed that law enforcement does not take place indiscriminately or in a rigid fashion — according to the letter of the law. Certain allowances are made and some rule-breaking is tolerated in the process of encounters between offenders supervised in the community and supervising officers. For instance, some studies (cf. Nuttall et al., 1977; Home Office, 1978) '*suggest* that parole may reduce the likelihood of reconviction' (Bottomley and Pease, 1986: 164, emphasis in original). What the authors of those studies and secondary sources do not say or acknowledge is that such an interpretation, though feasible and worthy of consideration, has serious flaws: methodological problems in terms of sampling issues and the difficulty in separating known from unknown offences. It also ignores how those outcomes are reached. Various studies show (see for example Takagi, 1969; Takagi and Robinson, 1969) that the failure or success of parolees depends largely on the willingness of supervising officers to take bureaucratic action in referring deviants to the recall authorities. In Takagi's study, reactions to deviance (that is, violations of licence) are not simply a matter of a parolee being a law-breaker because each parolee in the study is a law-breaker either legally or technically (Takagi and Robinson, 1969: 80). Rather, rule-breaking is *accommodated* in many instances via selective enforcement which depends on the supervising officer's perceptions and interpretations of the violations and the office's mores within which he or she functions. These define what offences can, under what conditions, be ignored; which can be treated in an informal and lenient manner; and which necessitate or warrant drastic responses through the activation of formal sanctions. In that sense, success or failure (apparent recividism) can be 'controlled' by officials (Takagi, 1969: 198).

In a similar fashion, in an empirical study of the enforcement of community service orders in England, I observed that the 'success' of the schemes had more to do with the actions and activities of probation officers than with the willingness of offenders to complete their sentence successfully (Vass, 1984). Failure to appreciate or recognise that supervising officers are capable of *creating* outcomes according to choices made, often leads officials to make extravagant and inaccurate claims about the success of such alternatives to custody. For instance, in 1982 one Chief Probation Officer (cf. Griffiths, 1982), called for more 'punishment in the community' and suggested that the role of the probation service ought to be to offer more real alternatives to custody, based on the principle of punishment. In doing so, he illustrated the point by referring to the effectiveness of the community service order as a penal measure working on the principle of punishment and containment in the community. However, what Griffiths failed to say was that there is a difference between what is *publicly portrayed* (official statistics or reports) and what is *privately portrayed* (what actually takes place in practice far away from popular awareness). Official reports may give a very positive picture of such community penal measures. For instance, that approximately 75 percent (on average) of community service orders are successfully completed; that approximately only 11 percent of orders are breached by offenders; that approximately 10 percent of offenders under community service are convicted for other offences in the course of their community service order. In short, overall community service orders are seen as an efficient and effective way of keeping offenders out of prison. Similarly, that about 80 percent of probation orders are successfully completed; that 12 percent are terminated early for good progress; that only 2 percent (in 1986 as compared to 18 percent in 1978, 12 percent in 1982) of offenders fail to comply with requirements; and that 14 percent are convicted for other offences during the course of a probation order (NAPO, 1988a: 17). The statistics and presentation are preceded with the statement (NAPO, 1988a: 1): 'the [probation] service has the energy, the vision, the skill and the experience to make a significant contribution to a reduction in the use of custody and the incidence of crime by providing safe and effective supervision in the community.'

This is the public face of work. The private face is something different. In the private and more discreet domain of supervision, the transactional process (that is, the interactions between supervising officers and offenders) depicts a series of connected stages leading to a lofty goal: the successful completion of sentence. In this process, the offender's career in community service, probation, parole or any other penal measure including imprisonment (where control and supervision are part of the contract) is regulated and shaped by the actions of supervising officers who act as law enforcers. Of course, that is not to imply that offenders are passive participants. That is far from the truth. Their actions colour the responses of their supervising officers. But their deviance or failures in general are by and large characterised by low visibility. For instance, the definition of rule-violation in community service or probation resides in the offender's refusal or unwillingness (other than committing new offences) to perform his or her duties as ordered by the court and interpreted by the probation officer. These rule-violations and interpretations occur in often discreet social settings — geared away from unnecessary publicity — which do not invite the attention of outsiders in either knowing what is really going on, criticising or raising public anxiety about enforcement and the informal procedures adopted in controlling offenders. Failure, success or rule-violations in such a context are defined according to the 'world views' of the participants, and often exist and are policed in a context of 'popular unawareness' (Rock, 1973: 5; Vass, 1984). This being the case, the supervising officer and his or her assistants are vested with considerable discretion in interpreting policy; the degree of seriousness of violations; and the type of appropriate responses to those violations or breaches of regulations in general. Therefore, in the final analysis, the supervising officer is not merely an administrator, someone who applies the rules as they are formed by others (legislation and courts). Rather, such supervising officers — as 'people in the middle' (Roethlisberger, 1945) — act as *policymakers in miniature*. Through their interpretations, decisions, and actions they determine the shape and character of relationships: their means and ends. In the case of community service, when one considers the relations between officers and offenders in practice one observes that officers create the conditions and the environment for the promotion of the successful completion of orders through serious evasions and distortions of the formal rules; by creating special concessions or 'privileges' which allow offenders to accrue hours which have not been worked for the 'benefit of the community' and which cover up violations of the order; by interpreting rules in a relaxed and flexible way to suit officers' means and ends; and making conscious efforts to avoid formal sanctions (court proceedings) against defaulters for the sake of creating stable social relationships (avoiding conflicts) with offenders; and thus assisting offenders by accommodating their failures and violations of the order, and helping them in very practical ways to complete orders successfully. Indeed, if breach of community service orders and the general problems of organisation and administration encountered in the process of administering and enforcing a community service order were not to be accommodated and negotiated by probation officers, probably 80 percent of offenders serving under such orders would, at some point in their career as community service workers, face failure, and prosecution for non-compliance or other lapses (Vass, 1984, 1986a; Vass and Menzies, 1989). In that respect, when one looks at the arguments for the desirability of such penal measures and observes interesting statistics about rates of successful outcomes, such presentations should be considered with caution and the reader should be sceptical about the claims made.

Recognition of the effects of those relationships and the role supervising officers play in colouring outcomes has prompted Bottomley and Pease to write that none of the main alternatives to custody (suspended sentences of imprisonment, probation orders, community service orders and so on) have been used exclusively as alternatives to custody. Although 'The best estimates of their use in place of active custody has approximated 50%', they argue that whether 'this partial success is worthwhile is open to doubt, given the confusion and active trickery which often attend the imposition of serious non-custodial penalties' (Bottomley and Pease, 1986: 107). Bottomley and Pease have somewhat exaggerated the issue here, or they have failed to recognise its 'normality' as a feature common to almost every formal organisation. For as said earlier, it is not really 'trickery' applied but a flexible interpretation of the rules to make those rules both applicable and relevant to the expectations, needs and perspectives of the participants and to satisfy the structural constraints of the context within which they relate to each other.

Alternatives as a Pandora's box

Bottomley and Pease's above criticism or indeed rejection of alternatives to custody does not imply that 'nothing works' (Martinson, 1974). Martinson, who only two years earlier (Martinson, 1972) had criticised custodial institutions for their failure to halt recidivism and for inflicting irreparable damage on individuals and families, now in a much-quoted review of 231 studies on community penal sanctions reported from 1945 to 1967, concludes that no particular method (custodial or non-custodial) has any appreciable effect on recidivism. In conclusion, he declares that 'nothing works' and that correctional programmes of all sorts have been a waste of taxpayers' money. Later he (Martinson, 1979) revised his conclusions by suggesting that his original interpretations of the data were not entirely correct and that he had oversimplified the complex processes at work (for instance that different methods may suit different types of offenders — thus in the case of juveniles he claimed that 'shock probation' appeared to result in better than average reconviction rates). Despite the correction, his original thesis may have had a fairly dampening effect on the quest for alternatives and created an aura of widespread pessimism about the capacity of alternatives to offer a more positive approach to custodial institutions. This pessimism has filtered through the debates to the point where researchers, even before they embark on their projects, tend to conclude and explain 'alternatives' as a Pandora's box (see Chapter 4 for details). They see alternatives as a highly unreliable, unpredictable and dangerous practice which leads to a multitude of nasty and obnoxious sins. Rather than checking or retarding the incarceration process, alternatives, it is argued, help to expand the net of social control and surveillance.

The pessimism that alternatives to custody are merely a waste of time and are not capable of making a positive contribution is not altogether shared by all writers in the field (cf. Walker, 1985). Walker, in a rather caustic remark about the 'nothing works' statement from Martinson and his later revision of his original thesis states laconically: 'I won't give all his [Martinson's] findings, partly because they relate to the USA, but partly because for technical reasons I don't trust them any more than his original careless article' (Walker, 1983b: 99). In a similar fashion, Bottomley and Pease (1986: 164) suggest that:

> Continued doubts about research methods in this area [of effectiveness], and an increased fashion for retribution as a penal purpose, has resulted in widespread scepticism in many quarters about the capacity of any sentence to change the future behaviour of an offender significantly more or less than any other sentence . . . We think such a conclusion is overstated, and that a much more open-minded approach is necessary. The 'nothing works' pessimism of the 1970s was premature.

They echo, in some respects, Walker's (1985) claim that we have to stop generalising about failures: that for some people some penal measures at some point may have a positive effect. Thus, in a sense, we have to allow for more differentiation among offenders; sanctions; length of sentence; and perhaps re-evaluate outcomes with a more open mind than has been practised in the past. These arguments, and it is not clear if the authors do recognise the similarities, reflect the gist of Palmer's (1975) counter-criticisms of the 'nothing works' perspective. Palmer, in response to Martinson's original thesis, suggested that criminologists and penologists, instead of wasting their time in arguing about what does or does not work, should be looking at the 'degree of effectiveness' and asking questions about what methods suit which offenders under what conditions. That is, Palmer's argument was that greater awareness of differentiation among sanctions, types of offenders and conditions under which they apply ought to be the aim of any evaluative study of the effectiveness of penal policy. Methodologically that is again where new problems emerge: what to control; what to observe; how to assess the effects of length of supervision or sentence. These problems and the outcome of such attempts are well illustrated by the Home Office studies on intensive probation. Palmer's ideas were, in some sense, put into practice by the Home Office (Folkard et al., 1976). Four probation areas — Dorset, Inner London, Sheffield and Staffordshire — were involved in an experiment to evaluate the provision of more intensive and matched treatment for relatively 'high-risk' offenders. Attention was paid to situational variables in family, work and leisure. Experimental and control groups were set up in each area by random selection. All cases were followed up for about 15 months, though many of the offenders were, in fact, followed up for a full two years. The findings showed that 'in respect to subsequent reconvictions within one year, experimental treatment as opposed to control treatment made no difference' (Folkard et al., 1976: 14). Indeed, with one exception, the experimentals showed a slightly higher proportion of reoffending. Thus, whereas the study showed the feasibility of Palmer's ideas, the results provided no evidence to support a general application of more intensive treatment or methods of control in the community. The authors conclude that their findings are consistent with Martinson's view that no particular method of treatment is better than any other (Folkard et al., 1976: 2).

The failure of 'intensive probation' to yield any real positive results and its abandonment in the late 1970s has not discouraged the present government in 1988 from attempting to reactivate the original idea under the slogan, *Tackling Offending: An Action Plan*. In the current search for new methods of control in the community and under the banner of 'punishment in the community', the government has produced tentative plans to use existing legislation to encourage more use of alternatives to custody by making them more demanding and punitive in order to appeal to sentencers. Under proposals published in August 1988 (Home Office, 1988d) the government is asking all 56 probation areas in the country to establish an action plan in consultation with courts, police and other agencies (such as social services) of how to create the right conditions for the administration and enforcement of the new sanctions (particularly in the creation of a new 'order' which will combine a number of existing community penal sanctions at one and the same time). Selected areas will also be required to set up 'intensive probation' (IP) programmes aimed exclusively at offenders who would otherwise receive custodial sentences. Although the National Association of Probation Officers states that they 'unreservedly support a determined attempt to reduce the use made of custody and to limit imprisonment to those who have committed the most serious offences' (National Executive Committee, 1988: 2), it rejects 'intensive probation programmes' on the grounds that (National Executive Committee, 1988: 4): '[The] likely effect of IP programmes is an increase in the failure rate leading to breach and imprisonment. Many young adults who can be worked with successfully on probation and CS [community service] would have little chance of coping with the demands and control implicit in IP . . .'.

As if to contradict the message (that community service and probation work), the Association (National Executive Committee, 1988: 4) adds: 'IP programmes will go the same way as other alternatives to custody such as suspended sentences and community service — they will become alternatives to alternatives. What is required is a consistent sentencing policy which makes more use of existing and proven sentences.'

Support for alternatives to custody seems to be guided by a need to be optimistic, and to appear loyal to what, after all, is for most commentators a good cause: a need to offer more humane treatment, and to search for new ways in dealing with offenders which may not be totally effective and foolproof against failures or criticisms but which, nonetheless, are more appropriate and desirable than locking up people in prisons. The practice of resigning to the view that alternatives may not be that much 'better' in terms of effectiveness than prisons and that not too much in terms of practical results should be expected from them, other than more humane treatment — and perhaps savings for the public purse — is shared by even some of the original, most fervent supporters of community-based penal programmes (cf. Shichor and Kelley, 1980). Empey (1978) was able to acknowledge that community-based penal measures do not seem to be very effective in containing the rising crime rates. Nonetheless, he was also able to argue that they are still more humane, less costly and though they do not decrease recidivism, do not increase it either. However, two years later (cf. Empey, 1980) he wrote that the rehabilitative philosophy which has guided the development of alternatives to custody 'is in a shambles', and added (Empey, 1980: 168):

> the findings of science on the effectiveness of correctional programs have been inconclusive, at best, and devastatingly negative, at worst . . . On the one hand, the most scientifically defensible experiments have tended to indicate that one correctional alternative is rarely found to be clearly superior to another in reducing overall recidivism rates. For example, while

a series of experimental community programs have been shown to be at least as effective as incarceration in reducing recidivism, and usually much less costly, they are not clearly superior.

This apparent failure of alternatives to show in terms of measurement any substantial rehabilitative impact on offenders; and the unlimited urge expressed by politicians to search for new alternatives and methods of sanctioning offenders in the community led to predictions on both sides of the Atlantic that penal policy would experience a throwback to a philosophy of 'just deserts' characterised by a more overt emphasis on punitive penal measures and with 'punishment' being the new vogue word of the 1980s and beyond (cf. Erickson and Gibbs, 1980; Horton, 1981; Hylton, 1981b; Jordan, 1983; Mathiesen, 1981; Vass, 1982a, 1982b, 1984: 178–80; Walker, 1983c; Williams, 1981). In many respects, such a prophecy, at least in terms of expansion of the means of punishment and control, has come true — depending, of course, on one's perspective. Since the late 1970s, criminal justice policy has not only expanded on an unprecedented scale but has also shifted towards the more traditional conceptions of punishment and deterrence (cf. Home Office, 1984b, 1988c). Platt and Takagi wrote that since the 1970s there has been an increase in the imprisoned and legally supervised population; an increase in the type and severity of punishment; a proliferation of 'law and order' legislation; and a rapid deterioration in conditions within and outside prisons. They point out that 'With this increase in the imprisoned population and cutbacks in social services, there has been a corresponding increase in the severity of penal discipline' (Platt and Takagi, 1981: 1–2).

One may argue that this search for new ways of punishing offenders or reforming and upgrading the means of the 'theatre of punishment' is part of a more generalised punitive political process which is gradually introducing cultural and structural changes in western states. In England, these changes (that is, the introduction of new ideas about the role of the state, the meaning of citizenship, and the rights of the individual) which have been socially engineered by the Conservative government since 1979 have led to an expansion of controls and restrictions in almost every possible sphere of social relationships. The onset or the creation of a 'punitive city' has been guided and legitimated by law. Since 1979 an unprecedented amount of legislation has been introduced to limit or restrict particular individuals or groups from open or free participation, association, mobility, criticisms, or debate about 'politics' or the way government operates. The long list of legal measures which are leading to more refined and coercive methods of regulation and surveillance which have been enacted (or are about to be enacted) since 1979 include: the Imprisonment (Temporary

Provisions) Act 1981; the Nationality Act 1981; the Contempt of Court Act 1981 (which restricts press reporting trials); the Employment Act 1982; stiff immigration procedures (for instance, the 'Primary Purpose Rule' 1983 which excludes many Asian men married to British women from entering Britain); the Criminal Justice Act 1982; the Prevention of Terrorism Act 1984; the Police and Criminal Evidence Act 1984; the Local Government Act 1985; the Interception of Communications Act 1985; the Criminal Justice Act 1988; the Public Order Act; Section 28 of the Local Government Act 1988; the union ban at GCHQ; the Education Reform Act 1988; the Immigration Act 1988; the Community Charge (or 'poll tax' which acts as a regressive tax system that will lead to an upsurge in criminal statistics as many people who cannot afford the charges default on payments, and offers a legitimate means to the state in monitoring most adults' movements around the country); the Official Secrets Bill; the introduction of identity cards; the Security Services Bill; limits to the right of silence by defendants; and the Housing Bill (which will outlaw any 'political' activity by local government employees earning £13 000 or over and the establishment of a designated official who will police individual employees about their political activities). These illustrations help to show that the coerciveness of the criminal justice system is not an isolated or peripheral matter. It is, it seems, part and parcel of a general trend towards more regulation and restrictions and the growing importance and role of centralised control.

Although there is little doubt that there has been an overall expansion and shift in policy towards more refined and coercive methods of control and surveillance, there are many qualifications which need to be made about the view that such an expansion is gradually leading this and other western states towards becoming 'carceral' societies. There is a difference between policy intentions and actual practice. Standards and structures are not merely the function of laws and governments' wishes or intentions. They are also the function of those people who have the task of either administering or enforcing them. At that level, rules and regulations or expectations are often evaded, distorted and interpreted by the 'on-the-spot' authorities according to prevailing organisational and personal needs. These evasions occur out of expediency: to make those laws and expectations both manageable and workable as well as relevant to the world views of those who apply them. In short, what is often intended in terms of policy may not always be what is created and practised in the daily routine of social relationships.

Alternatives on the cheap

It is apparent from what has been covered so far that a major justification for alternatives to custody is that financial savings are accrued by such methods of dealing with offenders. If they do not rehabilitate or fail to act as true alternatives, they can at least save money for the public purse. In that respect, governments, as well as advocates of such penal measures, in the past and present, have put forward the proposition that alternatives are cheaper than custody and thus more desirable. Certainly the statistical evidence supports this proposition.

The available statistics which compare the costs of custodial versus non-custodial sentences are quite impressive: they do support the argument that alternatives *are* substantially cheaper than custodial establishments. Table 3.1 shows the costs of custodial sentences and selected alternatives to custody.

As can be observed, from the known figures and estimates supplied by official sources, the differences in costs between custody and alternatives are quite real. It costs, on average, £14 300 to keep a person

Table 3.1 *Average cost of sentences: custodial v alternatives to custody*

Sentence	Average cost per offender per week	
	1982/3[1]	1987/8[2]
	£	£
Custody (overall average)	218	275
For male offenders		
— Dispersal (i.e. high security)	433	569
— Other closed training prisons	205	253
— Local prisons and remand centres	200	249
— Open prisons	158	189
— Young offender institutions	212	330
For female offenders		
— All establishments	308	379
Community service order	10	13[3]
Probation order	11	15[3]
Supervision order	9	12[4]
Attendance centre order	67	89[4]

Sources:

[1] Figures derived from Home Office (1986: 101, Appendix 3).

[2] Figures derived from Home Office (1988e) by combining a number of tables; therefore the figures may be approximations to real costs.

[3] Figures refer to year 1986–7 and derive from NAPO (1988a: 1) based on official publications.

[4] Figures are estimates from 1986–7 which have been arrived at by using the base figures for 1982–3 and adding on a nominal increase in costs (approximately 33 percent including inflation at 5 percent a year) as is apparent from the known costs of community service and probation orders.

in prison for a year at 1987–8 prices. In comparison, it costs about £700 to supervise an offender under the requirements of a community service order at 1986–7 prices! King (1983: 124), in a comment about 'the price of prison', using figures available for 1980–81, states:

> According to the Report of the Prison Department for 1981 [the] average cost [per offender] was £177 per week . . . [which represents] . . . a commitment of £9225 [a year]. . . Suppose that such a sum was 'available' to deal with [an offender] and suppose the same offender could be dealt with by a two year probation order at a total cost of £800 . . . without a significant difference in outcome as far as the offender's likelihood of re-offending is concerned. Would it not make better sense to sentence the offender to probation and to use the 'savings', say, to send the victim and his family on a round the world cruise on the QE2? . . . The cost of a young man serving a short sharp shock in detention centre for 3 months in 1980–81 was £1892 — enough to send a boy to Eton for a term. And at the other end of the spectrum an armed robber sentenced to 30 years, who did not get parole and spent most of his sentence in maximum security might cost £350 000 over 20 years at 1980–81 prices: allowing a modest 5% inflation per annum it would mean a cumulative commitment of over one million pounds over the period of his sentence. Given what we know of the effectiveness of imprisonment (50% of adult males reconvicted within two years, 63% of those passing through detention centres) one wonders how many people can seriously regard these as good investments.

Similar comparisons are evident from other sources outside England. For instance it is argued that in 1978 prices, the cost of probation supervision in Saskatchewan (Canada) was approximately $400 per person per annum as opposed to the cost of prison at $9100 per person per year — nearly 23 times as much (Hylton, 1981b: 24). However, this apparent cheapness of alternatives to custody is also one reason, Hylton argues, that the state can sustain both the prison establishment (by being left, from the savings made, with more money to spend on refurbishments and expansion) and exert further control over more of its citizens. Hylton (1981b: 24) writes:

> From these figures it can be estimated that the costs of providing institutional services to the 2300 probationers under supervision at any one time in 1977 would have been over $20 million. Since this amount is nearly three times the total corrections budget for 1977, it is clear that vast increases in expenditures would have been required had probation services not been available. In all probability, demands to reduce excessive expenditures would have resulted in some offenders being released outright and without supervision. From this perspective, community programs may be seen not as an alternative to incarceration but as an alternative to outright release.

In the USA, an analysis of prison costs by Gail Funke, an economist and public policy analyst, claims that official data for the cost of prisons ($35 million per prison over a 30-year period) are grossly unrepresentative of the true economic costs of maintaining and running a prison regime. In revising official figures, she makes a cogent argument that in the United States, the construction of a 500-bed prison requires about $350 million (in 1981 prices) over 30 years; $135 million for construction and $210 million for operation. On average, a prison costs, in real terms, $11.5 million per annum. Funke points out a useful concept deployed by economists in calculating the real cost of a service: the *opportunity cost* of a prison is the *alternative* goods and services that $350 million — not $35 million — can command: 'These might be other corrections projects, education, vocation, or other social service programs — or simply no new taxes' (Funke, 1985: 93–4). Thus for example, given that, in 1981 prices, the cost of probation was estimated to be $600 per person per year (Funke, 1985: 96), the huge sums of money spent on prisons could usefully be deployed to expand facilities in the community at no financial cost and perhaps to social benefit (given assumptions about humane treatment and no difference in the effectiveness between different penal measures). Funke (1985: 96) writes:

> A substantial number of alternative punishment experiences can be bought with $11.5 million, depending on the option selected and the average length of stay. Nearly 10 000 probation punishment experiences — with an average length of stay of two years — can be bought annually [for 30 years]; over 1000 residential punishment experiences of a year's duration or less would be possible . . . If the average length of stay is two years, then over the 30-year financing lifetime of the prison, an agency could purchase either 7500 prison punishments or 300 000 probation punishments or nearly 16 000 community residential punishments . . .

Translating those calculations into costs per offender in prison, as King has shown above, there is a vast amount of money spent per person for each year which increases substantially as prison sentences get longer. For example, using the above average prison cost of $11.5 million annually, a 500-bed prison will mean that each offender may cost $23 000 annually to the taxpayer. If one is sentenced for five years, the cumulative cost becomes $115 000, and where someone stays in prison for 10 years, that yields a cost to the taxpayer of nearly one-quarter of a million dollars (Funke, 1985: 97). Funke also (1985: 97) argues that if penal policy is measured according to a cost–benefit analysis, then the benefits (in the prison's case meaning 'incapacitation', 'deterrence' and 'reduced recidivism') should outweigh the economic costs. As prisons fail to meet those benefits and those lofty goals do not seem to materialise, there is little to justify the high costs of maintaining prisons. Hence, the sustainment of prisons, according to Funke (1985: 98), is an irrational and uneconomic policy. Prisons are vastly expensive because they comprise 'capital costs, phased construction costs, financing costs, and operating costs' (Funke, 1985: 90) which are not normally experienced or required by alternatives to custody. Prisons are expensive because they have to be maintained. In England, in 1987–8 approximately £24 million was spent on repairs and maintenance. Further, when new prisons are constructed it is often a few years before they are operational, thus creating unforeseen planning and financial liabilities (inflationary spirals leading to higher labour costs and materials, for example). When they become operational, the daily costs of staff, administration, organisation (accommodation, fixtures and fittings, relationships, medical, educational and training services and so forth), security and control all add up to a considerable and always increasing expenditure.

By 1991 nearly £900 million will be spent on prisons in England and there appears to be no end to the escalating costs. By and large, the vast majority of the huge sums spent on prisons (nearly 80 percent) goes on operating costs, much of which goes in return to manpower, security and control services. Manpower has seen a huge expansion in recent years (cf. Home Office, 1988e). Morgan (1982) points out that in the period between 1947 and 1981 the number of prison officers increased by 607 percent, which outstripped the rate of growth in the prison inmate population. Security consumes nearly 40 percent of operational costs (King, 1983: 125). As can be seen from Table 3.1 costs vary according to type of institution as well as, though not observable here, the geographical situation of institutions (cf. Home Office, 1988e). Added to the daily aspects of security and control, the service has to contend with various incidents. In 1987–8 there were 42 demonstrations — the most serious incident took place in Bedford Prison in March 1988 when remand prisoners protested at the removal of food privileges and severely damaged cells; 25 incidents of roof climbing; 22 hostage incidents involving injuries in four of them; 177 escapes; and an unprecedented rise in suicides in comparison to previous years (Home Office, 1988e). All these daily concerns create extra pressure for vigilance, improvements and upgrading of security facilities and systems, thus adding to costs (cf. Home Office, 1988e: 13).

Suggestions then that alternatives to custody are preferable because they are cheaper appear to be well founded. However, there are uncomfortable flaws in such a rigid interpretation. Arguments that alternatives are preferable to custodial institutions because they are more cost-effective must, if they are to bear any real credibility, be acccompanied by either a clear *diversion* of resources from custodial institutions or by a formidable increase of expenditure in the field to accommodate the desirable measures. As has already become apparent, when the actual and projected expenditure by both central and local government is considered, the picture is far from satisfactory. Expenditure in the last 20 years (particularly since the early 1980s) on custodial institutions far outstrips the resources made available for the administration and expansion of alternatives to custody. For example, whereas the probation service — which is responsible for most offenders supervised in the community — will continue to absorb an increasing share of public expenditure, its share may not grow as rapidly as one should expect given current expectations about increasing the use and choice of alternatives to custody; and will probably remain, as it has always been, relatively small — about 5 percent of criminal justice expenditure — in relation to police, courts and prisons in particular (Home Office, 1977: 29, 1979: 73–7, 1984a). Despite government pronouncements about the desirability and expansion of alternatives to custody and an expressed intention to divert resources to the community, between 1956 and 1979 (NACRO, 1982: 8), and currently between 1979 to the present, prison spending has expanded considerably faster than most other agencies within the criminal justice system and 20 times faster than public expenditure as a whole. These comparisons may point to the conclusion that, as Hylton (1981b) argues, alternatives play a secondary, if not supportive, role in relation to the preservation and maintenance of the prison establishment. By being cheaper they effectively reduce the net cost to the prison.

However, moving from the expensive nature of custodial institutions to the relative cheapness of alternatives there are serious questions to be asked about how one really calculates the cost of those alternatives. I use the phrase *relative* cheapness because as in the case of prisons — where there are hidden costs as shown above as well as others (cf. King, 1983: 125) — exact figures or methods of calculation of costs are hard to determine and will not bear too close an analysis. For instance, how does one calculate the cost of a probation order, or a community service order? Merely dividing the number of orders by the amount of resources made available or spent on supervision is a very crude method of reaching proper estimates.

In order to illustrate this method, let us take an example from the late 1970s which was used to promote the idea that the community service order saved money for the taxpayer. In 1979, £5 million was spent on community service. The number of community service orders made in that year was 14 155. Crudely, this gives, on average, a cost of £353 per order. One can even take this method of measuring costs to its extreme by suggesting that the *net* cost is in fact less because when the hours which, allegedly, have been worked for the benefit of the community on a voluntary basis are considered, the actual cost of community service may not be £5 million in total but, as one source has even suggested, without explaining the nature of that calculation, just £1375 (*Justice of the Peace*, 1981: 110)! Even if that were true in terms of calculation, the reality of practice as opposed to policy nullifies such extravagant claims. For a third of all hours imposed by courts are not used for work under the conditions of a community service order but are aspects of administrative and organisational fringe benefits offered to offenders by probation officers to maintain order in social relationships and to negotiate personal, interpersonal and organisational conflicts (cf. Vass, 1984).

Usually the estimates, as far as one can understand the analysis given the ambiguity of those calculations, stem from an oversimplified process of giving per capita annual cost of supervision based on salaries, grants and miscellaneous expenses. Rough as these calculations may be, they are nevertheless effective in sustaining the virtue of alternatives to custody and help to attract support and attention from governments and other institutions concerned with economic stringency or expediency. However, the cost-effectiveness of such penal measures, though relatively cheaper than custodial penalties, can create unnecessary illusions about *absolute* economic benefits and savings (cf. Hylton, 1982; Lerman, 1975; Stanley, 1976: 182–3). Although the differences between the costs of prison and those of alternatives are quite impressive, the comparisons based on per capita cost do not take into consideration secondary or hidden costs. For example, omitted are the added costs of community penal measures when breach proceedings are initiated for violation of requirements by defaulters. In 1987, 30 400 people were sentenced for breach of alternatives to custody: suspended sentences (25 percent of sentences); probation (19 percent of orders); community service (18 percent); conditional discharge (11 percent). With regard to suspended sentences, 75 percent of those prosecuted had their sentences activated and an immediate sentence of custody was imposed. In 1987, 35 900 offenders were placed on community service orders which represented 8 percent of all indictable offences. Of these, 6600 (18 percent) were prosecuted for failure to comply with requirements; 2300 of those prosecuted (35 percent) were given immediate custodial sentences for breaching their order. In addition to those offenders who breach requirements there are also others (well over 10 percent of orders made) who have their orders revoked for committing further offences. Similarly, in the same year, 42 200 probation orders were given to offenders which represented 9 percent of all indictable offences. Of these, 8000 (19 percent) reappeared in court for breach of requirements with the result that 4300 (54 percent) received an immediate custodial sentence (Home Office, 1988f). Thus such measures not only do not count the *double* costs incurred in first supervising those offenders in the community and then locking them up (that is, there is here a *double jeopardy* at work in the sense that neither custodial nor community alternatives fare well) but also breach proceedings and the organisation of laying information to courts require a considerable and often unmeasurable amount of time and resources by probation officers or other supervising officers (cf. Vass, 1984); and altogether the 30 000 court hearings (without even considering adjournments and other delays or contested cases) must call for an immeasurable liability to the taxpayer in legal and administrative costs.

The broader implications of this illustration are relevant to both alternatives to custody and prisons, for similar costs are incurred with regard to prisoners released early following remission of sentence, parole or who complete sentence and are reconvicted and sentenced to new terms of imprisonment. The point made here is that costs per capita are suspect and camouflage a host of other conditions and situations which, if included in the calculations, inflate the figures and may make alternatives (and prison) more expensive than generally assumed. Indeed, one cannot even pretend for a moment that actual savings are made by offering alternatives because the double jeopardy mentioned earlier works on a broader scale than merely in terms of hidden costs. No real or appreciable savings can be claimed by politicians or practitioners *unless the prison population is so reduced that a whole establishment or a wing is closed and staff laid off.* By having the prison establishment *growing* at an accelerating rate in parallel to the growth of alternatives to custody, *costs, in a very real sense, escalate and the taxpayer is left to pay both the bills of the prison and its peripherals of community alternatives.* But even there, though an unlikely proposition, it is inappropriate to assume that savings will accrue by closing down penal institutions, for the corresponding expansion in community alternatives and the cost of operating those penal measures will call for vast sums of money which — through economies of scale — will escalate with time. This problem of diverting resources to community penal measures brings me to the penultimate point I want to make that alternatives, things remaining as they are, are unlikely to command in the present or near future the financial muscle of custodial establishments.

In addition to the reservations voiced that cost-benefits are hard to determine, there is also the less appreciated *economic and political* need to *constantly reinforce the virtues of the cost-effectiveness of such measures by keeping them cheap.* Claims which are often unjustified can be taken for granted and used by resource-allocation bodies (voluntary or statutory) as a basis for cutting back expenditure on community alternatives to prove that they are cheaper and to make savings. In effect, such a policy starves administrators and practitioners of the necessary funds and staff resources in dealing successfully with the demands and pressures of supervising offenders in the community. Indeed, as has always been the case, there is a lot of rhetoric about the desirability and cheapness of 'community', but little practical illustration that governments are willing to demonstrate that belief through proper financial and other investment in community programmes. For instance, the classic example is that of closing down mental institutions, and thereby forcing the mentally ill to live not only rough in an 'uncaring' community but also to find refuge — occasionally through their own choice as a matter of last resort in securing a roof over their heads — in prison establishments. The Griffiths Report (1988) which looked at 'community care', did not come up with anything new but reiterated the basic weaknesses which haunt attempts to develop viable 'community care' networks. In particular, the issue of limited money and scarce resources in general made available to 'community care' programmes is aired in strong language. The Griffiths Report (1988: iii: para. 7; iv: para 9: ix: para 38) says:

> Many of the submissions have drawn attention to inadequacies of funding . . . [M]any social services departments and voluntary groups grappling with the problems at local level certainly felt that the Israelites faced with the requirement to make bricks without straw had a comparatively routine and possible task . . . At the centre, community care has been talked of for thirty years and in few areas can the gap between political rhetoric and policy on the one hand, or between policy and reality in the field on the other hand have been so great. To talk of policy in matters of care except in the context of available resources and timescales for action owes more to theology than to the purposeful delivery of a caring service. This is not argument in itself for more resources: the imperative is that policy and resources should come into reasonable relationship . . .
>
> The general banner under which many submissions were made carried the legend 'Care in the community is not a cheap option' . . . What cannot be acceptable is to allow ambitious policies to be embarked on without the appropriate funds.

The panacea of community can thus be exploited by governments to abdicate their moral and financial responsibilities towards really viable alternatives to custodial institutions. It works on the principle of a self-fulfilling prophecy: community programmes are cheaper than custodial institutions. If they are cheaper, it means that a lot is being and can be done through the community's goodwill and care. So, why spend more than we have to, when that would be a waste, and when the money can be used more profitably elsewhere? By reducing taxes for the well-off, it is argued that such action generates more wealth and consequently more community care; or maybe building a few more prisons. As the budget for community alternatives is cut, it keeps those alternatives cheap. In turn, that then filters through and appears in statistical form which in turn reinforces the original belief that community programmes are after all cheaper than custodial establishments. This self-fulfilling prophecy works on the principle, well-captured by an ex-Secretary of State for Industry — Patrick Jenkin — who, in a moment of real inspiration, supported the expansion of community alternatives at little cost in order to allow substantial cuts in public expenditure by proclaiming that community alternatives are 'not caring on the cheap — it is a way of getting a great deal more for our money' (Jenkin, 1981: 18). In February 1977, one of the best-known figures of the Conservative Party, Lord William Whitelaw, in a speech at the National Young Conservative Conference at Eastbourne, expounded the virtues of self-help and the spirit of community. He said:

> I visited recently a number of voluntary organisations set up in London by ethnic minority groups themselves. I was most impressed to find voluntary workers, white and coloured, striving manfully with very few resources, a small terraced house, a car engine or two, for example. Their greatest resource was of course, their dedication to the task of running hostels, workshops and classrooms. They were determined to work twenty hours a day if need be to keep youngsters from drifting into despair and indifference.

As can be observed, the community spirit, *deus ex machina*, does occasionally expose itself in a flash of light; leads to inspired commitment; penetrates people's conscience; makes them act in resourceful and caring ways; guides even hardened souls to commit worthwhile deeds by keeping fellow citizens out of trouble. Its moral force is also measured in quantities of cash: it saves the Treasury a lot of money. At the same time as enlisting all these virtues of community, nothing is ever said about why such young people are faced with 'despair'; 'indifference'; or why they should be expected to survive a hostile environment by taking shelter, if they are indeed lucky enough to have that choice (cf. *Guardian*, 1988b), in a 'small terraced house'; with an 'engine or two'; and to have to justify that effort by working 'twenty hours a day'. Although examples such as these are crude and oversimple, they do illustrate how community alternatives can offer politicians and other ideologues a convenient sponge which can be deployed to absorb devious policies — such as starving the community of real resources and diverting them to custodial establishments — and which allows advocates of such measures to wipe clean any small trace of guilt or dirt off their conscience.

Inter-agency relationships

There remains a last major traditional stumbling-block in the efficient administration and application of services or penal measures in the community. Unlike custodial institutions where there is one well-defined structure of social relationships and accountability (crudely, that of prisoners controlled by prison officers within the confined physical structures of the prison), community alternatives may be organised by, say, one agency such as the probation service, but its clients may also share something with the police, social services and particularly courts. In short, since the late 1970s and especially since 1983 there have been attempts to create cooperative links between various community agencies in dealing with crime or related matters. This community multi-agency approach to crime prevention and control is reflected in both official pronouncements (cf. Home Office, 1984b) as well as in the changing patterns of work done by officials in the field (cf. Blagg et al., 1988; Broad, 1988; Henderson, 1986; Scott et al., 1985). Blagg et al. (1988: 204) write:

> Recent official discourses and policy debates on crime and criminal justice have generated and mobilised a number of key terms: 'community', 'participation', 'inter-agency co-operation' and 'crime prevention' are among those which frequently cluster together in these discussions. Implying a co-ordinated effort by both state agencies and voluntary bodies, a closer involvement between services and the public, an avoidance of wasteful duplication and policy confusion, these discourses convey the sense of an unproblematically 'good thing'. When, as they frequently are, they are yoked together in such formulae as 'inter-agency co-operation in community crime prevention' their positive connotations tend to be reinforced. Who could possibly argue that agencies should not co-operate to such worthy ends?

As the authors have discovered, this idea of various agencies combining forces to tackle in a concerted manner common enemies such as crime and assisting each other in the supervision of offenders in the community has serious practical as well as ideological limitations. As I pointed out elsewhere (Vass, 1982b: 104–5), community measures which require the cooperation of diverse social and policing agencies are riddled with problems. There is, first, the problem of knowing what exactly is expected of each agency or what role each plays in any activity which calls for inter-agency cooperation. Secondly, even where an agency — at the administrative and managerial level — may have a fairly clear view of what it should be doing, the front-line officers (those who are vested with the responsibility of applying that policy) remain in the main very unhappy, unclear and confused about their responsibilities (cf. Broad, 1988; Scott et al., 1985). Thirdly, there is also the fundamental problem of how to negotiate the diverse means and ends of each agency. Their terms of reference, which give them their distinct shape and character and which allow them to maintain a separate existence and profile from other similar agencies, remain carefully guarded against contamination by other agencies' values. This prohibits real inroads into attempts to establish workable coalitions.

Those problems are not new and certainly not just problems of the 1980s. In this country the conflicts within and between social agencies, such as social services, the probation service and voluntary organisations, over allocation of roles, responsibilities, tasks, resources and determining objectives in the quest for alternative solutions (for instance, intermediate treatment projects) to the incarceration of young people are well-recognised facts (cf. DHSS, 1972, 1973). The crux of the matter is not that these agencies cannot work together. Rather, as they exist in a social and economic context which offers only scarce resources and thus encourages stiff competition for funds, it is *not* in *their* interests even to make an effort — in a real sense — to cooperate with others as that may mean loss of income, loss of independence and clashes over perspectives. As Miller (1970) perceptively explains, conflicting philosophies and loyalties among such social and policing agencies, and the actual competition for resources, disagreements and schisms about objectives and means of achieving those objectives in controlling offenders, become a major impediment to community penal measures. Cooperative efforts among groups of professionals are difficult to obtain because of a lack of ideological unity, competing interests and a lack of trust in each other's work. In effect, penal measures in the community may run into problems because it can prove difficult to achieve or even envisage how to achieve the right coalition effort required for the proper supervision and administration of such measures. If such coalitions are not easy to build, the call for enlisting the assumed goodwill and spirit of the community (Alper, 1973) may easily turn, as Lerman (1970: 356) suggests, to 'an exercise of rhetoric and good intentions'. This diversity of opinion and goals among interested parties in the community is well illustrated by Blagg et al. (1988). They point to the diverse expectations and suspicions expressed by the various groups trying to establish inter-agency connections: police, community wardens, social services, housing workers, probation officers and so forth. As an illustration of this problem, the following extract (referring to attempts to establish inter-agency links in order to control crime in an estate) captures the gist of the problem (Blagg et al., 1988: 214):

> As a backcloth to these emerging tensions, there is a complex interplay of different inter-agency and intra-agency emphases on what might constitute an appropriate strategy . . . The local police view of crime prevention tends to be purely situational. They want any available funding from central government directed towards providing stronger doors, with stronger locks, together with window locks for all ground-floor windows. The Chief

Executive's department, on the other hand, leans towards a more 'social' approach which would entail the establishment of 'residents' committees' to seek local views on police priorities, on the grounds that crime prevention must begin with 'restoring public confidence in the police'.

The above quote and its implications is almost a replica of a different and earlier source which made a similar and witty observation. Gans's classic study of juvenile delinquency in Levittown brings out these conflicts in a clear passage (Gans, 1970: 387–8):

the parent on the panel said, 'The needs of adolescents should first be met in the home and young energies should be guided into the proper normal channels.' The teacher suggested that 'parents should never undermine the authority of the teacher . . . and the school will in turn help maintain the authority of the parent over the child'. The minister urged parents to 'encourage youth leadership responsibilities within the church', and the police chief explained 'the importance of teaching adolescents their proper relationship to the law and officers of the law'.

Conclusion

In summary, in this chapter I brought together and examined a number of contentious issues which relate to prisons and alternatives. In general, claims about the desirability of alternatives to custody are found to be lacking in clarity, depth and conviction. Although there is a continuous search for the expansion of community penal measures, little is known or appreciated about the nature and consequences of those enterprises and exactly what they entail in practice. These measures exhibit, to borrow a term from Griffiths (1988), a 'theology' about intervention or ways of dealing with offenders. But they fare differently and, it is claimed, in a less positive way than intended. They are faced with often intractable problems (resources are a case in point) and one is left with the impression that 'looking for alternatives to custody is like searching for the mythical pot of gold at the end of the rainbow; both are real enough in the dream, yet never quite attainable' (Raban, 1984: 20).

The fundamental question which needs to be asked is whether alternatives to custody act as 'genuine' alternatives or whether they assist in sustaining and enhancing the prison's status as a necessary and predictable form of punishment which assumes, within the social structure, an unwarranted, though important, social and political role as the bastion of the disciplinary process. This question about the relationship between alternatives and custody is the subject of the next chapter.

4 Alternatives as a Trojan horse: The case re-examined

The expansion of alternatives to custody since the 1970s has taken place amid hopes that they would diminish the role of prisons and engineer a more humane and cheaper approach to containing offenders in the community. However, the evidence sharply contradicts such hopes. Increasing alternatives does not automatically lead to a reduction in costs, and there are questions about their effectiveness in controlling crime and acting in less 'coercive' ways than prisons. More serious than those problem areas, however, is the realisation that the creation of such alternatives does not automatically lead to a decrease in the use of imprisonment. In fact, it has been argued that through such a policy of offering and expanding alternatives, we are still left with overcrowded prisons while at the same time impregnating the system with further problems and confusion by creating 'overcrowded' community penal measures (Vass, 1986a: 103). Harris (1985: 151–2) writes with reference to the USA:

> New programs for dealing with offenders outside the institutions were developed across the country. By 1979, nearly all states and the federal government had laws authorizing judges to impose restitution orders. Nearly one-third of the states had established community service work orders as a sanction, and they were being used as a condition of probation elsewhere. A 1978 survey of parole supervision agencies showed that about 15 000 prisoners in 38 jurisdictions were released to 800 halfway houses in that year. About 1000 beds in community facilities in 19 states were available for use as an alternative to prison commitments. Several states adopted mechanisms to grant funds to local governments to sanction offenders locally instead of sending them to state institutions. Programs also were developed for intensive probation or parole supervision, intermittent confinement, and release to community supervision after brief confinement. Nevertheless, hopes of achieving a diminishing role for the prison through promotion of alternative programs were short-lived. Evidence quickly accumulated that merely increasing community programs did not lead to automatic or corresponding decreases in the use of prisons and jails. New sanctions seldom were used as substitutes for prison sentences. Rather, they were used as alternatives or supplements to fines or regular probation. While the number and proportion of Americans under

correctional supervision in the community grew significantly throughout the seventies, so did the number and proportion who were imprisoned.

In England, a recent review of research findings by Bottoms (1987) of the use of alternatives to custody in limiting the process of incarceration interprets outcomes in a rather pessimistic way. He suggests that 'recent English experience offers no support at all to the optimistic suggestion sometimes made in the past, namely that the progressive adoption of various measures to limit prison use would, in a gradual way, erode the central importance of the prison in modern penality' (Bottoms, 1987: 177). Although he is sceptical of the thesis that alternatives become mere additions to the system of discipline and punishment (Bottoms, 1983), he does conclude (Bottoms, 1987: 198):

> This paper has had to review a considerable number of recent English initiatives aimed to produce 'alternatives to custody' or to limit the length of custodial sentences. Some of the measures seem in certain respects to have had some modest success, yet almost all of them can also be shown to have run into severe difficulties of one kind or another. Perhaps most significantly of all, at the end of this twenty-year period the prison population in England stands at a record high level . . . Additionally, the number of prisoners per 100 000 population in England is among the highest in Europe . . . Not surprisingly, in such a situation those who wish actively to reduce the prison population in England see little point in pursuing further initiatives of the kind reported in this paper . . . Many radical and left-liberal critics of the system . . . are inclined to accept Mathiesen's (1974) view that such alternatives all too often turn out not to be real alternatives, but ways of buttressing the social institutions to which an alternative is sought (in this case, the prison) . . .

The dispersal of discipline thesis

These criticisms are only a small part of a wider and broader critique of alternatives to custody (cf. Austin and Krisberg, 1981; Cohen, 1979b, 1985; Garland, 1985; Hudson, 1984; Lerman, 1975; Rothman, 1974; Scull, 1984; Vass, 1982a, 1986a; Vass and Menzies, 1989; Warren, 1981, among others). In the main, despite the diversity of perspectives adopted and emphases placed on issues under consideration, the criticisms relate to the same theme: the 'dispersal of discipline thesis' (cf. Rodger, 1988). This theme suggests that 'alternatives' are not really alternatives and that they tend to widen the net of surveillance and control. It suggests that at every possible and conceivable level of discourse, alternatives fail to deliver the promised goods which would put an end to the relevance, and continuous expansion, of the prison. Indeed, rates of institutionalisation are increasing, not decreasing. Alternatives fail both to make the application of sanctions cheaper and reduce the incidence of crime and reoffending. They are not as humane as they are supposed to be because they 'disguise coercion, increasing invisible discretion' (Cohen, 1985: 38). Whereas in prison at least one knows one's place, under alternatives much control takes place in settings which are far removed from popular awareness. Alternatives are not being developed out of a moral concern for the plight of offenders who have to live in squalid conditions in prisons and which are an affront to civilised society. Rather, they are advocated in response to government's need — ideological or practical — to demonstrate stringency in fiscal policy and thus control or cut back on public expenditure. In all, alternatives are of no positive consequence and do nothing, or little, to challenge the hegemony of the prison: it is 'business as usual', with the difference that 'overall, the system enlarges itself and becomes more intrusive, subjecting more and newer groups of deviants to the power of the state and increasing the intensity of control directed at former deviants' (Cohen, 1985: 38).

With regard to this dispersal of discipline thesis, Rodger (1988: 563) writes:

> It is argued that the prison has become decentred as the main penal institution and is now looked upon in most western societies as one institution of social control among many, all seeking to perform different tasks within an elaborate penal/welfare division of labour. The institutions of punishment and welfare are, within this emerging analysis, viewed as being inextricably bound together. There has been a 'blurring of the boundaries' that divide them. The movement from 'exclusivist' forms of control over deviants in the nineteenth century prison has therefore been replaced by a more 'inclusivist' gaze, as Foucault would have it, involving dispersed centres of supervision and social control throughout the community.

This idea then that alternatives are another convenient means of extending the process of control and colonising various populations of offenders is well captured by Cohen who likens alternatives, and what he calls attempts to 'destructure' prison establishments, to a Trojan horse: the alternatives are a monster in disguise. Cohen (1985: 38) says: 'The benevolent-sounding destructuring package has turned out to be a monster in disguise, a Trojan horse. The alternatives had merely left us with "wider, stronger and different nets".'

In a nutshell, alternatives do three things: they *widen* the net of surveillance and control; they make that net *denser*; and they produce and reproduce *new and different* nets which are added to the original ones. Cohen offers evidence from a number of sources in England, the USA and Canada which suggests that the above consequences of alternatives are not merely conjectures but are rooted in observations about developments in the field and lend support to the claim that despite some gains and successes, the outcomes of alternatives remain 'ambivalent, ambiguous or wholly negative'. The obvious conclusion reached by critics and summed up by Cohen (1985: 48–9) is that 'the use of community alternatives actually causes an overall system expansion which might not otherwise have occurred'.

The experience of alternatives: The Trojan horse in action

The dispersal of discipline thesis and the idea that alternatives are a Trojan horse are supported by a number of observations and studies on both sides of the Atlantic. The vast expenditure on prisons and the expansion in the rate of incarceration, despite an equal proliferation in the number and types of alternatives offered, are assumed to be witness to this claim. Simply, the system *is expanding* without any real indication that things are improving.

One of the fundamental assumptions about alternatives to custody is that they are what they are implied to be: prison substitutes. But experience shows that when such new powers to sanction offenders are enacted with a clear intention of diverting offenders from custodial sentences, such penal measures are not used as sanctions which replace custodial sentences, but rather as sanctions which replace other existing *non-custodial penal measures*. In England one of the nearest examples of this effect rose from the introduction of the suspended sentence of imprisonment. This measure was introduced in 1967 with the formal intention that it should be given *in lieu* of imprisonment. Soon after its introduction, the number of people incarcerated fell. But after 1968, the number of prison sentences increased to a point which, according to informed estimates, was higher than would have been the case in the absence of the suspended sentence (Home Office, 1977). At least part of this increase has been attributed to the fact that suspended sentences, subsequently activated because of breach of conditions, are being used for offenders who would otherwise have received other non-custodial penal sanctions which do not carry the precondition of imprisonment (Sparks, 1971; White, 1973). Researchers estimate that only between 40 and 50 percent of offenders given suspended sentences of imprisonment would, but for the existence and availability of the suspended sentence, be given custodial sentences (Oatham and Simon, 1972; Sparks, 1971). Indeed, Sparks was so concerned about the unanticipated consequences of this alternative to custody measure that he warned about the risks of introducing similar penal measures in future which could increase rather than decrease the risk of incarceration.

After ten years of operation of the suspended sentence and sustained criticisms, the Advisory Council on the Penal System (1978: 117) reported that 'if the main object of the suspended sentence was to reduce the prison population, there are considerable doubts as to whether it has achieved this effect'.

In similar terms, three years later, Bottoms (1981), having reviewed the effects of the suspended sentence, suggested that since 1968 the suspended sentence had been used not only as an alternative to imprisonment but also in place of fines and probation orders. Bottoms (1981: 25) concluded: 'In view of this dilemma, the case of the abolition of the suspended sentence, rarely heard nowadays, perhaps deserves some serious attention . . . [T]hose who are anxious to reduce the prison population cannot afford to ignore the role of the suspended sentence in helping indirectly to contribute to the total number of people incarcerated.'

A year later, *Justice of the Peace* (1982: 2), in its editorial pages, accused the government of not doing enough to control the prison population, and said: 'Unfortunately the Government has done nothing about the suspended sentence . . . Despite its popularity with the courts, the suspended sentence has given rise to serious juridical problems which have never been satisfactorily answered and has probably resulted in a nett increase in the prison population.'

These claims must be put in context. If estimates suggest that about half of those given the suspended sentence are truly diverted from custody, then that implies that there is a balancing act at work. That is, that such a measure does not divert but it does not contribute to prison crowding either: the 50 percent who would be in prison are now in the community. This is counteracted by the remaining 50 percent who receive suspended sentences as a diversion from other alternatives to custody. However, that is where the problem lies. Courts tend to activate such sentences in the majority of cases where offenders do not keep out of trouble. In 70 percent of cases they impose the full term of imprisonment for the original offence and, in addition, they impose another term of imprisonment for the new offence, that is, instead of running concurrently, the sentences of imprisonment are made in most instances to run consecutively (Bottoms, 1987: 183). That means that there is not just a failure to divert because many of those offenders would not have been imprisoned in the first instance had it not been for the availability of the suspended sentence — in the absence of that sentence they would probably have remained lower down the tariff scale. There is also the disturbing implication that there is a tendency for courts to pass longer sentences which partly explain prison crowding (see also Fitzmaurice and Pease, 1982). And as those offenders who are given a suspended sentence of imprisonment are by definition and implication placed higher up the tariff and next door to imprisonment, this 'certainly leads to a greater tendency to re-imprison, both for the first and the second offence' (Bottoms, 1987:

190). In short, this so-called alternative to custody may not just put offenders at a greater risk of imprisonment. In many respects offenders experience what I have already called the risk of double jeopardy. Many of them are punished unduly: they would have received, in the absence of the suspended sentence, something else but not imprisonment. They are also given *more* and *varied* punishment. They are given a suspended sentence; they are then subjected to a full term of imprisonment for the original offence (even though it might not have been, in the first instance, and in the absence of the suspended sentence, an 'imprisonable' one); that term of imprisonment is imposed irrespective of how long the offenders had served 'time' under the suspended sentence; and, finally, because of the suspended sentence and the implication that reoffending calls on a court to activate the sentence, the offender also runs a higher risk of being sentenced to another term of imprisonment for the new offence (even though the offence may not be serious enough to merit a custodial sentence). This is because reoffending is a violation of trust. Punishment in the form of a custodial sentence becomes necessary to demonstrate the inviolability of that trust and not necessarily the culpability or seriousness of the offence.

In view of those findings and adverse effects of this alternative to custody, Bottoms (1987) returns to the same theme and concludes with despondency:

> In short, most observers have concluded that suspended sentences are by no means always being applied in the way that the law states they should be; and that the introduction of this sentence into English law has contributed little or nothing to reducing the prison population . . . To add to the catalogue of failure, what little evidence there is suggests that the suspended sentence might have a marginally worse reconviction record than other sentences on comparable offenders.

The role of the community service order as an alternative to custody is not much brighter. Of course, a clarification should be made. In England the only clear substitute for imprisonment in legal and unequivocal terms is the suspended sentence. It is defined as an alternative to imprisonment. As I have pointed out elsewhere (Vass, 1984: 59), the legislation defines community service as an order relevant to offences which are 'punishable with imprisonment' and indicates that it could be used in place of the originally intended sentence (that is, as an alternative). But the original sentence which is replaced by the community service order is never in fact made clear (though, following consistent criticisms and suggestions for improvements, (cf. Vass, 1986a) certain changes or improvements are becoming evident in the way in which the order is used — see the last chapter in this book for a critique). The same ambiguity and vagueness about the status of community service versus custody is exhibited in the legislative guidelines concerning the procedure for the imposition of a new penalty following failure to comply with requirements of the order. The legislation says that a court can 'revoke the order and deal with the offender, for the offence in respect of which the order was made, in any manner in which he could have been dealt with for the offence by the court which made the order if the order had not been made' (Powers of Criminal Courts Act 1973, section 16(3) (a)). Whether the community service order actually replaces a custodial sentence or another alternative to custody or generally speaking a non-custodial penal measure is open to interpretation. There is not any clear information in the law which clarifies or establishes the order as an unequivocal alternative to custodial sentences. For the idea that the order should be imposed on offences which are deemed to be 'punishable with imprisonment' means all things to all people: it is not synonymous with its use as an 'alternative to imprisonment'. The majority of offences can be regarded as being punishable with imprisonment (if courts choose to take that action) but that does not necessarily mean that such offences would be sanctioned by resort to custodial penalties. In that sense, the legal and formal status of the order as an alternative to custody is extremely dubious which leads sentencers and those recommending the making of an order to treat it according to their own interpretations. In effect, the order is used as a sentence in its own right; as an alternative to other non-custodial penal measures, including probation and fines; as an alternative to custody; and often as a convenient *deus ex machina* which fills, for some sentencers and probation officers, the gaps which are assumed to exist in the tariff system: if nothing else fits the occasion, community service appears to be the ideal and convenient solution (Vass, 1986a: 106).

The claim then that the community service order may be used as an effective alternative to custody (Home Office, 1986: 7) is ill-supported by both official and independent sources (cf. Andrews, 1982; Pease 1980, 1986; Pease et al., 1975, 1977; Vass, 1981, 1984, 1986a; Vass and Menzies, 1989; Willis, 1977; Young, 1979). Although in general courts still maintain, and are encouraged to do so by official rhetoric (cf. Home Office, 1988b, 1988c), that the order is an alternative to custody, the Court of Appeal states the matter in different terms. Following the case of *R. v. Lawrence (1982). 4 Cr. App. R. (S) 69* it has been stated that the community service order is both an alternative to custody and a sentence in its own right. Indeed, at the risk of contradicting itself, the Home Office recognises this ruling and the fact that the order is not used exclusively as an alternative to custody. The Home Office (1982: 45) writes: 'The legislation specifies that a community service order can be made in respect of a person "convicted of an offence punishable with imprisonment" . . . Different interpretations may be put on this phrase and courts may vary in the extent to which community service orders are used as an alternative to imprisonment.'

Later, the Home Office, in recognising the exact nature of community service as a sanction which can be used for different offenders and under the guise of different intentions is prepared to state first that the order is an effective alternative (Home Office, 1986: 7) and subsequently to correct that statement by instructing sentencers that the order is also a sentence in its own right. It advises courts thus (Home Office, 1986: 41): 'When Parliament accepted the proposal for the introduction of a community service order, it was seen as a penal sanction that made serious demands on the offender and could thus be regarded as a realistic alternative for a custodial sentence. Through subsequent custom and practice, the order has come to be regarded as a sentence in its own right.'

In a recent attempt to make the order appear much more punitive and credible than it is, and justify the introduction of national standards for the administration and enforcement of the order (for further details see Chapters 5 and 7), the Home Office (1988g) avoids any direct reference to the community service order as an alternative to custody. However, it still manages to say something about the confused status of the order stating that it serves three main purposes: punishment of the offender, reparation to the community and provision of work beneficial to the community. The 'by-product' of these aims, the Home Office states, may be a 'positive and stimulating experience which may help to reintegrate [offenders] into the community' (Home Office, 1988g: 2). It then goes on to state, in rather hesitant and uncertain terms, that the community service order was meant to be an alternative, but that it is not. Nonetheless, it adds, many probation areas are trying hard to use it as an alternative! The Home Office (1988g: 2) cannot find anything new or encouraging to say about the status of the order and is forced to reproduce — almost word for word — the statement made in a previous publication (Home Office, 1986: 41):

> When Parliament accepted the proposal for the introduction of the CS order, it was seen as a penal sanction which made serious demands on the offender and could thus be regarded as a realistic alternative for a custodial sentence. There continues to be much debate about the standing of CS as a sentence in its own right. The schemes provided by many probation committees, however, are already demanding and tightly supervised in order to cater for offenders who would otherwise go to prison.

In its efforts to establish more credible alternatives to custody in the community, the Home Office is willing to equate 'serious demands on the offender' with a sentence being an alternative to custody. That is, what is interesting about the above uncertain stance and the push towards 'punishment' is that suddenly it is not the gravity of the offence or the intentions of the courts (that is whether they regard an offender and his or her offence as culpable enough to merit a custodial sentence) which should be detailed or considered before choosing to divert an offender from custody to a community penal measure. Rather, it introduces a worrying and confusing notion that the *harsher the punishment, and the more stringent its administration in the community, the higher the probability that the community penal measure is a credible alternative to custody*. This is, as I argue in Chapter 7, muddled and confused thinking which creates new risks and puts efforts to clarify the position of the order (and other alternatives to custody) in disrepute. For instance, if that clumsy philosophy prevails, one could still have petty offenders, who would never have received a custodial sentence, being regarded as deep end (that is to say, high-risk) offenders by virtue of their participation in a so-called 'tightly supervised' community service scheme. Their true status in terms of the gravity of the offence committed, circumstances, and their true position in relation to custody (and other penal measures) may be lost under the guise that a punitive scheme houses only deep end offenders who have been spared the ultimate punishment of imprisonment. In short, their involvement in a scheme which prides itself on its ability to deliver harsh punishment or 'tight supervision' may place such offenders higher up the tariff system, and may send false signals to sentencers that any failures or lapses by those people should be met with a swift and punitive response by courts. That could mean that by virtue of a label, many offenders could run the risk of experiencing harsher treatment (possibly incarceration) in courts for subsequent appearances (either for violations of conditions of the order or for other offences) than would have been the case had they not been given community service in the first instance.

The above possibility is given credence by the fact that the majority of offenders placed under a community service order are by and large those committing 'minor' offences. Although there have been a few variations in the type of offenders sentenced to community service in the last 10 years or so, for instance an increase in the number of offenders convicted for burglary since 1977, in general little has changed since the inception of the order in 1972. Between 1979 and 1986 the proportionate use of community service for indictable offences went up from approximately 3 percent to approximately 8 percent. But really serious crime among those given orders is a fairly atypical event (Home Office, 1988a; Vass and Menzies, 1989). In terms of 'culpability' as measured by the previous criminal record of those commencing community service, in 1981 about 40 percent (ranging from 27 to 57 percent in different parts of the country) of offenders had served custodial sentences. In the same year, on average 10 percent (ranging from 5 to 21 percent across the country) of orders were made on individuals without a previous criminal record. In 1986, persons commencing community service orders by known previous criminal record had thus: custodial sentences, 37 percent; wholly suspended sentences, 1 percent; community service, 6 percent; probation or supervision, 17 percent; fine, 18 percent; other sentence or order, 3 percent; and no previous convictions, 13 percent (NAPO, 1988a: 16).

Of course, it is difficult to gauge from such figures how many offenders would have received custody in the absence of community service, particularly when many of those are imprisoned for property offences. In many respects, the very fact that quite a considerable number of those given community service have previous custodial convictions may lead to the positive interpretation that despite its flaws, the order may be diverting some offenders from custody. However, that the majority of those offenders who are given community service do not appear to be so 'culpable' (especially in view of the fact that a sizeable proportion of the community service population is made up of first-time offenders and of offenders whose only previous sentence is usually a small fine, or a supervision order, or a probation order), raises questions about whether the order is working as an alternative to custody. Indeed, right from the early start of the scheme in the early 1970s, research has cast doubt on the ability of the order to act as a true alternative. For instance, a study by Pease et al. (1975) of the records of 757 offenders showed that over 57 percent of offenders had no previous custodial experience and 21 percent had no more than one previous custodial sentence, and many others had fairly minor offences and 'light' sanctions. In looking at this aspect and in conjunction with other matters (for instance, recommendations made by probation officers and the way in which courts responded to those recommendations), Pease et al. (1975: 26), concluded thus: 'Taking the evidence together, then, it appears that sentencers in many cases seem to regard community service as an alternative to non-custodial sentences at least as much as, and possibly more than, an alternative to custodial sentences . . .'.

Pease et al. (1977) followed up the previous findings and by using a number of techniques to find out whether community service was being used as an alternative to custody concluded on a pessimistic note that at best the order diverts about 47–58 percent of offenders from custody, suggesting that many of those who are given community service are diverted from other non-custodial penal measures. Similar findings are reported in other studies (e.g. Vass, 1981, 1984; Willis, 1977; Young, 1979). Young (1979: 124), for instance, in his account of the variations in the administration of community service in five areas — Suffolk, Kent, Nottinghamshire, Bedfordshire and Cambridgeshire — states that 'there were ... many examples of the community service order being used for trivial offences and for offenders with minor criminal records; cases where imprisonment would have been highly unlikely.' And, further on, he (1979: 140) adds:

> the hope that the community service order would divert a substantial number of offenders from custodial sentences may have been unduly optimistic . . . It might have been hoped that, in the courts which made greater use of imprisonment there would have been more scope for the use of the community service order as an alternative to it; in fact, in general the reverse was true.

A time-trend analysis of sentencing in England (cf. Bottoms, 1987; Vass, 1981) is, as Bottoms (1987: 192) puts it, 'if anything, less encouraging'. Despite the expansion of the order there has been no evidence of any reduction in the proportion of offenders sent to prison. Indeed, as I have already pointed out in previous chapters of this book, the rise in the rate of incarceration continues unabated. Of course, it is not clear whether, in the community service order's absence, the rate of incarceration would not be even higher, or whether its popularity has more to do with taking away offenders from other non-custodial penal measures or acting as a sentence in its own right. If the latter is true, then the question becomes whether it accelerates, reduces, or plays no part at all in the process of incarceration. If one assumes some diversion, given the above estimates, then it has some effect in halting bigger increases in the prison population. This is counteracted by the order's regular use as an alternative to other non-custodial sentences. If one accepts that possibility as fact, then the order may have the tendency of sucking into its meshes shallow end offenders (that is to say, low-risk offenders) who are later incarcerated not because of the gravity of their crimes or lapses but because their position (higher up the penal ladder according to risk of custody) has been redefined and restated by their experience of community service. This assumed reality, and failure of alternatives to act as true alternatives, has prompted the National Association of Probation Officers to react to current penal policy and intentions to expand the range of alternatives to custody in negative terms. They state (NAPO, 1988b: 6):

> the Home Office has chosen to ignore the history of recent attempts to reduce sentencers' reliance on custody by offering ... alternatives. Research ... has suggested that suspended sentences were used at least as much to replace other non-custodial measures as terms of immediate imprisonment: a finding apparently supported by the Home Office which rejected calls to reinstate suspended sentences for young adult offenders (removed in 1982) because they feared they would be used when immediate imprisonment

would not be . . . The evidence of the use made of community service is depressingly similar. Although it has proved popular with sentencers . . . research has suggested that it has been used about as much to replace other non-custodial penalties as to replace custody . . . and has failed to produce a drop in the proportionate use of custody. By 1987, the suspended sentence and community service accounted for 19% of sentences passed on adult males but this has not prevented the use of immediate imprisonment for adult males rising from 15% in 1974 to 21% in 1987.

The use of statistics in the above manner may make sense if put in the general context of findings about the community service order and the suspended sentence, as well as other non-custodial penal measures. It is within this general context that Bottomley and Pease (1986: 107) suggest that suspended sentences of imprisonment, partly suspended sentences, supervised suspended sentences, probation orders with enforceable conditions, and community service (among others) have failed in their task to control the prison population and that none of these measures has been used exclusively as an alternative to custody. However, their analysis of official statistics directs the reader to consider the point that that assumed failure has to be understood in relation to other relevant factors. From Bottomley and Pease's analysis it is obvious that one needs to put that failure in the context of sentencing practices and the *type of offender* who should be diverted in order to allow for reductions in the prison population. By looking at the evidence in terms of the constitution of the prison population (short- and long-term prisoners) they argue that although 51 percent of receptions are short-term prisoners of up to six months, in reality they account for only 17 percent of the actual prison population. Bottomley and Pease point out that as those who receive shorter sentences (and who constitute only a small section of the prison population) are the 'obvious candidates for diversion from custody', it means that the effect of alternatives on the prison population is negligible. Indeed, they argue, even to attempt to reduce just 17 percent of the prison population, 'over half of the custodial decisions of the courts would have to be substituted by non-custodial decisions' (Bottomley and Pease, 1986: 107), meaning a drastic if not altogether complete change in current sentencing trends. But even with such a drastic change in sentencing policy, the overall effect in reducing the actual prison population will still be very small, once again the implication being that it is difficult to 'achieve substantial reductions in prison populations by the use of non-custodial alternatives'. Bottomley and Pease (1986: 107–8, italics in original) write:

> To achieve significant reductions of the prison population by diverting the most obvious groups, like fine defaulters, is truly a daunting proposition. This is in no way to suggest that less serious offenders should not be diverted

from prison. If they are, though, it should be on the basis of judgements that their offence is too trivial to deserve being locked up for. Nor are we denying that diversion from custody might achieve some relief for that part of the prison system under greatest pressure, namely local prisons. It is simply that one of the clear lessons of published prison statistics is the difficulty of making substantial inroads into the prison *population* by action to divert short-term prisoners.

In effect, though Bottomley and Pease fail to reach or state the most obvious conclusion arising from their own analysis, if one wants to reduce the prison population, *alternatives should be geared towards those who receive longer sentences.* One can infer from the analysis that it is not alternatives to custody which fail to divert offenders from prison. Rather, the point is that whether they have any real or positive effect may depend on *how they are handled by courts and how they are targeted at types of offenders.*

Therefore, when one considers statistics, as the above NAPO (1988b) report does, caution should be expressed when attempting to interpret the existence of relationships between custody and alternatives. For example, referring back to the interpretation reached by NAPO (1988b: 6), it may be true that immediate imprisonment for adult males has risen from 15 percent in 1974 to 21 percent in 1987. However, to hold alternatives to custody as being responsible for that increase or for failing to check the rise in the rate of incarceration is not a very credible interpretation. One way of challenging this is to suggest, as Bottomley and Pease (1986) find, that it is not that alternatives fail to divert from custody. Rather, that they are successful in diverting the *wrong* people — short-term prisoners. This concentration of alternatives on short-term prisoners may have, as Bottomley and Pease argue, a very negligible effect on the actual prison population — hence the rising statistics. Furthermore, by implication of their status, as those short-term prisoners who are diverted are also the ones who reappear in the criminal justice system particularly in prison statistics far more than long-term prisoners (Bottomley and Pease, 1986: 107), there can be little chance of seeing a reduction in the prison population. Altogether, in considering the assumed relationship between prison and alternatives by merely looking at statistical trends may lead someone to suggest that alternatives are not diverting when in fact they may be successful in doing so but with the problem that they are targeted — by courts and supervising officers — at the wrong offenders. Another possible alternative interpretation is that in the absence of those alternatives to custody the rate of incarceration and the proportion of adult males receiving immediate imprisonment could have been even higher. Although reservations could be raised about a more positive interpretation of the role of alternatives if that

interpretation is put into the context of 'time-trends in penal policy' (cf. Vass, 1981), there is nothing in the analysis of those 'time-trends' to suggest that such an interpretation of the more positive role played by alternatives is false or inaccurate.

The view that as the community service order (or any other alternative) rises in popularity the prison population should fall is a very crude and quite unrealistic assumption about a crude and possibly unrealistic relationship between prison and alternatives. First, too much importance or faith is placed on the relationship at the cost of other intervening variables. That is, even though the prison population is still rising, it does not necessarily follow that community service is not working as an alternative to custody. That is merely a *choice* of interpretation. A corresponding and equally feasible interpretation could be that in the absence of the community service order the rate of incarceration as well as the prison population itself could have been even higher. In short, the existence of the community service order (and other alternatives) may be acting as a barrier to more people being incarcerated, even though it is difficult if not impossible to measure the effects of that barrier in terms of numbers. The order may merely check the prison population but cannot do more than that in the absence of concerted government policy to stem the rising tide of imprisonment. Secondly, the criminal justice system is not a simple affair involving only a crude linear relationship between custody and the community service order (or any other alternative). To suggest that just because the prison population is rising despite a corresponding rise and expansion in the alternatives means that those alternatives are failing in their main task of challenging the prison establishment is an inaccurate perception and a misunderstanding of the complex multi-factorial nature of relationships within the criminal justice system. That system is a complex web of social relationships which take place at different levels of participation and in different contexts — from policy to sentencing to enforcement and back again. Each one of those relationships, decisions, levels of discourse, outcomes (anticipated and unanticipated), and choices, to mention but a few, is capable of creating a ripple effect within the whole system and setting in motion processes which nullify or distort intentions. As an impression or assumption, it reveals much about our ignorance and the poverty of our methods in understanding and measuring relationships between various penal measures but says little about the causal relationship between prison and alternatives. The fact is that there is no concrete and foolproof method of knowing exactly how to calculate the effects or lack of effects of one penal measure on another and what the status of one penal measure is in relation to another. For example, the expressed view that alternatives may increase the risk of imprisonment by putting offenders higher up the tariff and bringing them closer to the gates of prison establishments has been accepted as fact. Surprisingly, this association between alternatives and higher risk of imprisonment has never really received close attention and has never been properly tested in an empirical sense (Vass, 1986a: 107). Therefore, what one could confidently say is that the available evidence does not *appear* to support the view that alternatives to custody are fulfilling their objective of reducing the significance of imprisonment as a sanction. At the same time, such evidence does not prove that such penal measures are failing in their task of diverting some offenders from custody and checking in some way or another further and perhaps, in their absence, a more rapid expansion of the prison establishment.

Notwithstanding these qualifications which should be present in any form of assessment of the impact of alternatives to custody, the 'evidence' against alternatives stretches beyond national boundaries. Similar findings claiming that alternatives to custody do not act as real alternatives to incarceration and that they tend to widen the net of sanctions without any real benefits, have been reported in other countries too. For instance, variants of the community service order are available in the USA, Australia, New Zealand, Tasmania, Canada, Denmark and the Netherlands, among others. The findings reported in some of these countries concerning the effectiveness of community service in diverting offenders from custody are not positive. In Tasmania, the community service order, known as the 'work order', was introduced in 1972. It is regarded as an alternative to imprisonment and the offender is ordered to perform unpaid work every Saturday for up to 25 Saturdays. If the offenders do not comply with requirements they are liable to a term of imprisonment. It has been argued that not only is the work order not used as an alternative to custody (the diversion rate is estimated to be between 47 and 53 percent; see Pease, 1986), but also that it contributes to the process of incarceration (Hopkins et al., 1977; Varne, 1976). In summarising her findings, Varne (1976: 104–5) concludes that the work order 'is not a real alternative at all' and that 'Work orders are being offered to offenders in the courts as an alternative to a prison sentence . . . when in fact a prison sentence would not be appropriate'.

In Canada, research on community penal measures in general (cf. Chan and Ericson, 1981; Hylton, 1981a, 1981b, 1982; Solicitor General Canada, 1982) and on community service in particular (cf. Menzies and Vass, 1989; Polonoski, 1981; Vass and Menzies, 1989) fail to support the proposition that alternatives to custody act as genuine alternatives. In terms of the community service order, findings suggest that although the order was intended as an alternative to custody, it is given to low-risk offenders who would not otherwise have been sentenced to a term of incarceration. In reality, then, the order does not constitute an alternative to incarceration but in many respects another condition attached to the requirements under a probation order (Polonoski, 1981; Vass and Menzies, 1989). In terms of alternatives to custody in general, there is convincing evidence that such programmes may not undermine the supremacy of the prison and indeed may even assist the prison establishment in expanding further. Hylton (1981b), in a rare attempt to present empirical data on the 'expansion' hypothesis, offers evidence from the Canadian province of Saskatchewan. He finds that a detailed linear trend analysis of the province following expansion of alternatives to custody 'confirms that institutions are not being abandoned'. In the period of study, 1962 to 1979, instead of running down penal institutions in the advent of community penal measures, the province experienced an increase in prison admissions. He finds that 'the average daily count per 100 000 population in Saskatchewan institutions increased from 55.23 in 1962 to 84.87 in 1979 — an increase of some 53% in 18 years' (Hylton, 1981b: 19). In order to avoid possible errors arising from average daily counts, Hylton employed another method in examining the case. He looked at sentencing policy in relation to custodial sentences and found that the number of admissions per 100 000 population increased from 434.85 in 1962 to 688.72 in 1979. This, he says, constitutes an increase in the rate of incarceration by 58 percent. In view of the findings he concludes that custodial institutions are not being displaced by the 'alternatives'. In fact they are proliferating. Hylton (1981b: 19) writes:

> There is no evidence that institutions are being abandoned in Saskatchewan. The provincial prisons process more offenders now than at any other time in their history and they process a larger proportion of the total provincial population. The analysis also suggests that further increases can be expected in the future. Importantly, this expansion of institution-based strategies of social control occurred concomitantly with the expanded use of 'alternative' programs. While some might argue that community programs reduced the numbers which would have been institutionalized had no alternatives been available, it is clear that, in Saskatchewan, they have not replaced the institutions.

The above conclusion is supported by Hylton's analysis which tests the hypothesis that the end result of alternatives to custody may not be to reduce the size of the prison establishment but instead to expand the system of social control and surveillance. By analysing data on custodial institutions, and methods of supervision in the community (probation, community training residences, and the community service programme for fine defaulters — known as the Fine Option Program), he finds that the rate per 100 000 population under supervision (including custodial establishments) increased from 85.46 in 1962 to 321.99 in 1979. This constitutes a rise of 277 percent in 18 years. Hylton then looked at admissions to custodial establishments by relating them to admissions to probation and community service for fine defaulters. The analysis shows that the relationship between increases in community penal measures and increases in admissions to custodial establishments (hence an overall increase in the social control and surveillance in the system) is statistically significant. He reports that the number of admissions per 100 000 population to all types of supervision rose from 479.82 in 1962 to 1337.21 in 1979, a rise of 179 percent (Hylton, 1981b: 22, Table 3). He interprets the findings in this way (Hylton 1981b: 22):

> Convincing evidence of a steady increase in the size of the Saskatchewan correctional system has been presented. This finding obtained whether admission or daily average figures were employed and whether 'raw' data or rates per 100 000 population were used. The 'expansion hypothesis' has thus received strong support. Throughout the period under study, both the number of persons under supervision of the correctional system and the proportion of the total provincial population under supervision increased dramatically . . . There can be little question that the expanded use of community programs in Saskatchewan provided the means by which the correctional system expanded.

Identical arguments are reported in studies from the USA (cf. Callison, 1983; Clear and O'Leary, 1983; del Carmen and Trook-White, 1986; Doig, 1983; Lerman, 1982; Nimmer, 1974; Rutherford and McDermott, 1976; Scull, 1984). Although there appears to be a general acceptance of the moral that alternative forms of punishment outside the walls of custodial institutions may be one way of alleviating overcrowded prison conditions, in reality that view finds little support and it is argued that 'the movement to use alternatives has never taken hold on a serious scale, and those incursions that have been made have often produced ambiguous results' (Mullen, 1985: 40). For instance, Pease (1986) quotes studies from the USA which find that community service lies somewhere between 'incarceration and probation' and that by and large the order fails to act as an alternative to custody. The tendency is to use the order to 'deal predominantly or exclusively with offenders who are extremely unlikely to be incarcerated' (Pease, 1986: 3). Pease writes, as has already become evident, that: 'there is thus remarkable consensus, wherever the proposition has been put to the test, that community service orders do not replace custody in a clear majority of cases in which they are imposed, even where it is clearly stated that the order was introduced for such a purpose' (Pease, 1986: 4). In more general terms and in a different context, Harris (1985: 154), one of the authors quoted by Pease, concludes that attempts to reduce the number of people incarcerated by promoting alternatives to custody have met with serious failures, and evidence suggests that merely expanding alternatives to custody does not lead to an automatic or corresponding depletion of the prison establishment. Harris (1985: 154) writes:

> Experience with these strategies to increase the use of noncustodial penalties for offenders who otherwise would be incarcerated still is limited, and little evaluative information is available. Prison population reduction is not linked directly to many of these programs, and past experience suggests that even the most carefully designed and implemented programs generally have failed to avoid being used as add-on punishments for lesser offenders. As more states seeking ways to alleviate prison crowding consider such approaches, it would be wise to think carefully about a number of unresolved issues concerning the short- and long-run feasibility and desirability of [these] popular strategies.

Indeed, this warning about whether it is wise to expand such alternatives without examining their full implications (for which there is still scant empirical evidence but much hypothesising), appears to have had no influence on current policy in either the USA or in England where there is a search for new and more refined methods of punishment or supervision in the community. Other than an expansion of traditional or new methods of control in the community (such as refinements to the probation order or community service), there has been a push towards the innovation of techniques which rely on technological breakthroughs and which use highly sophisticated electronic modes of surveillance.

In England, building on the US experience of electronic monitoring (cf. Ball et al., 1988), the introduction of a pilot scheme in three cities in 1989 whereby non-violent offenders will be offered the option of remand in custody or bail with electronic surveillance is one such example (cf. Vass, 1989). It is intended that tagging will be used for different types of offenders (including football hooligans, thieves, burglars, drunks and vandals — cf. Johnson, 1989) as an alternative to custody once legislation has been passed. The introduction of electronic tagging is presented as a tough new approach to crime which may prove a more flexible and efficient method in controlling offenders who would otherwise be in prison (Home Office, 1988c: 12). However, neither this view, nor the experience in the USA, has considered the findings of research which suggest that there is something called 'reciprocity' in the organisation of relationships between offenders and those who attempt to control them. That is to say, as the system becomes more sophisticated in its attempts to keep, for example, burglars or robbers out or to make thieving difficult, offenders' organisations reciprocate by inventing new techniques or creating their own counter-armoury to overcome those new obstacles in 'doing the job' (cf. McIntosh, 1971). In an age when computer 'hackers' may introduce 'viruses' which can knock out entire computer systems; or may penetrate even the most guarded systems worldwide, including highly classified information kept in military establishments, it is not inconceivable to imagine a situation when, a few years from now, electronic tagging may prove a heaven for offenders as they innovate and invent their own 'jamming' devices or electronic systems which may continue to signal to the authorities that offenders are under house arrest while in fact they are out committing the perfect crime. A reliance on electronic tagging may create the perfect alibi, for how could an authority prove that Z had committed a burglary (or perhaps a serious crime against another person) when Z would vehemently contest the accusation by using the authorities themselves, and their computer data, as his main line of defence in proving that at the time of the commission of the crime he was confined (and there is official evidence to that) under house arrest? Notwithstanding such a possible scenario which will not only bring ridicule to the system but may also create havoc in court proceedings, there is the more practical and current problem of such new methods of surveillance as identified in the USA: that this new breed of modes of surveillance, like so many other types of alternatives to custody, may have become another means for widening the net of the criminal justice system. In the USA home detention as a means of dealing with young offenders without sending them to custodial establishments goes back to 1971. These were forms of intensive supervision. However, more recently there has been a movement towards putting adult offenders under house arrest as a means of diverting them from prison for the same reasons we have considered in earlier chapters: that home detention is cheaper; less stigmatising and more humane; reduces pressure on prison crowding; and offers a flexible approach to keeping offenders in the community.

Although the idea of using the 'electronic bracelet' in monitoring offenders was literally taken out of a comic book by a judge in New Mexico in 1983, the current interest in home arrest and electronic monitoring of offenders as an alternative to imprisonment has spread rapidly in both theoretical and practical terms; and has attracted attention by governments, academics, penologists and, no less important, companies which specialise in electronics. According to Ball et al. (1988: 35) by 1986 at least '30 states [in the USA] were implementing some form of house arrest ... with another dozen states planning programs to be implemented within one year'. In England support for this new proposed alternative to custody is led by the Home Office and firms specialising in the manufacture of electronic tags. The opposition for such a measure is led by such diverse groups as the National Association of Probation Officers, National Council for Civil Liberties, the Law Society, Howard League for Penal Reform, Association of Chief Officers of Probation, Prison Officers' Association, the Prison Reform Trust, the Police Federation, and the National Association for the Care and Resettlement of Offenders. At a recent international conference on electronic monitoring at Leicester Polytechnic in 1988, the supporters of the scheme accused the opposition of 'getting in the way of history' and that opposition to new methods of community control will leave the probation service in particular 'looking like King Canute'; that 'tagging is not irrelevant to the probation experience'; and that moral and ideological objections to the scheme have no place in the debate as this method of diversion is a tool to help offenders to rehabilitate. In the view of one of the participants and early explorers of the scheme in the USA, Professor Lilly, objections to electronic tagging are 'self-serving' rhetoric (Cork, 1989: 4–5). In support of the advocates, the *Guardian* (1988c) commented thus:

> There are, indeed, good reasons to be wary of the tag. Our criminal justice system already has more alternatives to custody than any other sentencing system in Western Europe . . . There is a serious risk of the tag being used as an alternative to an existing non-custodial sentence — like probation, community service order or fine — rather than prison . . . Even so, there could still be a role for the electronic tag . . . The argument should be about practicality not principle . . . It is nonsense for the penal reform groups to talk about the tag's intrusion into family life. It's not nearly as traumatic an intrusion as prison. It allows the offender to continue to work which, as the reform groups know, is one of the keys to going straight. Opposition from the probation service was understandable. They prefer to be helpers rather than controllers. They have always resisted being turned into 'screws on wheels'. But if more offenders are to be kept out, then more controllers will be needed.

It is not really true that the opposition is merely advancing rhetoric and ideology rather than practical and convincing arguments against the new alternative to custody. In the first place, it is odd that the opposition should be accused of being ideological and rhetorical when much of the argument put forward by advocates and proponents of the new measure does little else than play with ideological and rhetorical, old-fashioned and ageing epithets to describe the benefits of the new approach: we are told that the new alternative will be 'cheaper'; 'humane'; 'rehabilitative'; 'effective'; less 'traumatic'; will reduce the 'stigma' of imprisonment; will help offenders be 'self-supportive' by keeping to a job and being with their families. In the second place, interestingly enough, none of these desirable qualities of electronic tagging have yet come under serious support from available research nor has any research thus far looked closely at the personal, interpersonal, and group or community effects of this new method of surveillance.

It is easy to confuse 'self-serving' rhetoric and actual research findings. This is well illustrated by Lilly's charge that critics are obsessed with rhetoric and self-interest while in a different context (cf. Ball et al., 1988; Ball and Lilly, 1988) he appears to support the critics' worst fears that electronic tagging may widen the net of social control without reducing the prison population. From reported research findings advanced by Ball et al. (1988) it is not clear whether this form of alternative does actually reduce the prison population. There appears to be contradictory evidence. For instance, in Kenton County the objective that home incarceration would alleviate prison over-crowding was found to be lacking, and the evaluation concluded in rather ambiguous terms that 'home incarceration did not substantially reduce the jail's overcrowding', though it did prove to be cheaper than keeping someone in jail. An explanation for the failure of the scheme to reduce the jail population rested on the fact that too few offenders were sentenced to home arrest to have any real impact on the incarcerated population (Ball et al., 1988: 81–2). In another scheme, however, the statewide Florida project, there appear to be positive results. It is suggested that since 1983, nearly 10 000 offenders have been sentenced to the programme and the number of prison admissions has fallen by an average of 180 per month. Of those offenders, just over 1500 had their sentence revoked and were subsequently imprisoned. It is argued that approximately 85 percent of offenders placed in the programme are genuine diversions from custody (Ball et al., 1988: 91–2). However, the findings and arguments about the success of the scheme cannot be verified. The statements about the success of the Florida scheme rest on the limited and polemical account offered by the director of probation and parole for the Florida Department of Corrections whose expressed philosophy about such community penal measures is that they enhance democracy and enable offenders to realise their full potential by becoming self-reliant, learning the work ethic, and thus becoming independent subjects (Flynn, 1986). As there is a lack of information and independent research, such claims have to be treated with caution, for they may reflect the rhetoric of public pronounce-ments as opposed to the reality of the situation. We know very little or nothing of how those offenders are selected; what their socioeconomic background is; what role supervising officers, namely probation and parole officers, play in the process of establishing or reaching such favourable outcomes; how those supervising officers see their relation-ship to offenders; and what impact home confinement linked to electronic monitoring has on offenders, their family or the community.

On a more fundamental level, the above early advocates and proponents of such a policy have recently expressed serious anxieties and reservations about the misuse of the original ideas by 'bureaucrats' who, out of expediency, allow a practice to develop which departs from the original policy intentions in running such schemes. Thus, for instance, whereas the original intention of some of these advocates was to use volunteers to assist with the monitoring of offenders (Ball and Lilly, 1983), in practice monitoring is tightly reserved for agencies of the criminal justice system. Ball et al. (1988: 146), expressing a concern about the disjunction between policy intentions and actual practice, write:

> The fact is that new correctional policies are rarely carried out as originally envisioned. They tend to be caught in a common pattern involving a 'dialectic of reform', in which the established agents of social control who operate the criminal and juvenile systems on a day-to-day basis accept certain 'reforms', but only on their own terms . . . The eagerness to embrace electronic monitoring now suggests that those operating the criminal and juvenile systems may be more interested in maintaining tight, bureaucratic control over offenders than in opening supervision programs to the public.

Of course, why the above authors should be so 'troubled' about such a disjunction between policy and practice and the fact that so-called community programmes rely less on the community and more on a traditional conception of professional responsibility is not clear because it is an issue which has been pointed out in the literature (cf. Sarason, 1974; see also the original intentions of the Advisory Council on the Penal System, 1970, with regard to community service, and subsequent developments as described in Vass, 1984). Also, why volunteers should make things better is not quite clear, unless the authors are implicitly advocating a move to 'informal justice' (cf. Holt, 1985; Matthews, 1988). Other than the theoretical and ideological troubles to which such an approach is prone, there are also pragmatic obstacles which relate to practice and the evaluation of outcomes (cf. Curtis, 1987; Downes, 1979; Hope and Shaw, 1988; Vass, 1986b). In practice, even where volunteers have been used to monitor offenders (cf. Vass and Menzies, 1989), they are found to be highly constrained and not acting of their own accord. As they are, in the main, used as 'para-civil servants' they become the subjects of control and influence by government officials. Also, the argument made by Ball et al. that employing volunteers works out cheaper than using probation officers may be true to a point if one accepts the official, simple and crude calculations based on per capita expenditure. As I have suggested, there are many hidden costs in supervising offenders in the community which are not amenable to proper investigation and make comparisons between the cost of penal measures and ways of supervising them difficult to attain. For instance, these para-civil servants may appear to be doing the job more cheaply by reducing the unit cost of providing a service — after all, they are paid substantially less than government officials. But in fact they may do the opposite: as they still need to be regulated, it means that new powers are given to government officials to do so; other officials are vested with the new responsibilities of implementing the new powers; others are employed to act as advisers; others are hired to supervise or inspect the administrators of the service, and so on. In short, rather than reducing bureaucracy and costs, volunteers may do just the opposite by expanding the net of social control services, and by bringing in more officialdom and regulation. Keeping the number of civil servants fairly constant by hiring the 'good services' of the community in the form of volunteers may make good political sense but how good it is economically, or in genuinely helping the process of diversion from custody, is an open question (cf. Vass and Menzies, 1989).

Indeed, it is also on this last note that home confinement and the use of electronic tagging faces serious challenge. Once again, even advocates of such a scheme have come of late to suggest, with expressed anxiety, that home confinement may not after all work as an alternative to custody and may be given to the wrong and unintended population of offenders; and thus may add to the plethora of other social and state control devices which widen the net of surveillance. Ball and Lilly (1988: 160) write with concern:

> Even in our earliest papers dealing with home incarceration, we expressed concern about the possibility of widening the net to include a greater percentage of the population and gave special attention to the 'Orwellian overtones' of electronic monitoring and the implications of home incarceration for the 'Anglo-American tradition of "home as castle" in which the private dwelling place is regarded as sacred ground off limits to the state except under extreme conditions . . .'. Developments since then have done nothing to reduce these concerns. In fact, we have become increasingly impressed by theoretical arguments such as those of Foucault . . . who maintains that there is a fundamental structural movement by which official control is extended in very subtle ways through a spiral of knowledge and power. As the state is able, especially through more effective technologies, to attain to greater knowledge of the private lives of its citizens, it is capable of extending its power in ways of considerable subtlety.

In their conclusion, Ball and Lilly (1988: 162–3) add the following:

> We do not accept the argument that the knowledge-power spiral is inevitable and that the individual is doomed to succumb to the increasing power of the state . . . Nevertheless, we are concerned that the panopticon mentality may be gaining ground, especially in view of the rapid developments in what has been termed 'the new surveillance' (Marx, 1985) . . . In any consideration of home incarceration, particularly with electronic

monitoring, we would urge that the scope of legal concern [and safeguards] . . . be widened further in order that the perceptions of those subjected to surveillance be taken into account and its impact upon them assessed . . . Foucault . . . may be wrong in his assertion that we are headed for the totally disciplined, 'carceral' society, but the spread of home incarceration with the use of electronic monitoring provides little hope for those who disagree with this dim view.

Even in Holland's 'mild penal climate' and where a 'prison sentence of six months is considered a rather long sentence which is not lightly imposed' (Junger-Tas, 1986b: 3), there appears to be some concern about whether alternatives to custody (as in the case of the community service order) really displace custodial sentences. In the first place, community service, for example, is virtually reserved for property offences and traffic offences. As in England, Junger-Tas argues, there is 'considerable reticence to impose it on violent offenders'. He writes that offenders are mainly young, poorly educated (one-third of them have no more than 'primary education' and more than half have only 'a little more'), and unemployed (88 percent living on social security payments). As similar experiences have been recorded in England and Canada (cf. Menzies and Vass, 1989; Vass and Menzies, 1989), all these facts make some of the ideological justifications for such penal measures (for example that they teach them self-discipline, or keep them in employment) lack credence. In addition, the main principle of enacting such measures, that of displacing custody, is challenged by the available evidence. Thus, again, referring to the Dutch community service order which has the explicit objective of replacing prison sentences up to a maximum of six months, Junger-Tas (1986b: 5) argues that 'there are still many uncertainties and questions. We still do not know whether there is real displacement of custodial sentences.' The best estimates of diversion that that author could offer (and which are regarded as 'hopeful') are in the districts of Groningen and Breda: 50 percent and 25 percent respectively. One may be tempted to question Junger-Tas's view that these figures are 'hopeful'. They are far from satisfactory for they beg the question of what type of offenders constitute the other 50 and 75 percent respectively. It may be assumed that in Holland, as in other countries, those offenders who fall outside the estimates of true diversion are by and large people who might not have experienced custody in the absence of community service. They are people who are diverted from other non-custodial penal measures, or accepting Hylton's (1981b) argument, those who might have escaped any formal or informal supervision in the community.

In conclusion to this section, there appears to be evidence that supports the thesis of the dispersal of social control and that alternatives widen the net of surveillance without inhibiting or challenging the supremacy of the prison. But as Bottoms (1983, 1987) recognises, there is a danger of exaggerating the adverse effects of alternatives to custody without recognising other, perhaps more positive, aspects. Bottoms (1987: 198–9) states:

A . . . theme much favoured by some critics has been that 'alternatives' to custody actually become additions to the system, and thus tend to increase both the total number of offenders in the system and the amount of social control intervention . . . There is undoubtedly some truth in this suggestion, as the earlier discussion in this paper has made clear; yet at the same time the thesis can be presented in an overstated manner, and should not be accepted uncritically . . .

An alternative view

In considering the evidence so far there appears to be very little chance of reaching the conclusion that one can be critical of the dispersal of discipline thesis or the view that alternatives are merely a Trojan horse. However, it is possible to criticise the belief that alternatives to custody only help to expand the system on both theoretical and practical grounds.

I have tried as far as possible to offer evidence from different countries and on different penal sanctions. But in the end much of what is known is still *limited* and *restricted* to a few studies, a few penal measures, and often not entirely comparable findings. Part of that problem is obviously explained by an author's lack of knowledge — indeed ignorance — of what happens elsewhere or indeed everywhere. Alternative or additional studies may be available, which expand the field of study and give further support or challenge to particular interpretations, but which are missed or unintentionally omitted. Of course, to assume that an author should be able to report all available evidence is an ideal situation and few people can claim such encyclopaedic knowledge. Another explanation for this limited and concentrated focus may be that much activity in the field of criminal justice and the way particular alternatives to custody work remains silent and unrecorded, thus preventing a proper and reliable assessment of the role of such measures in keeping people out of prison and having any positive or negative effects on participants, their immediate social circles and the community at large. This inevitable lack of 'total' knowledge about what exactly is happening at different times, in different situations, under different penal measures and by different people creates a problem of generalisation. That is to say, there is a serious question about whether one should be using particular examples or findings which have to do with particular pieces of legislation or means of controlling offenders as representative of the general, if not total and universal, experience of applying or deploying alternatives to custody. Thus in a basic way, though the spectre of net widening as a primarily negative development has its usefulness and may be valid to a point in demonstrating where policy *can* go wrong, it does nothing to understand or seriously examine the possibility that *some* alternatives for some *types* of offenders under certain conditions demonstrate their contribution in both keeping some offenders out of custody and helping them to experience fewer, not more, formal and coercive legal controls (cf. Matthews, 1987; Raynor, 1988; Vass, 1984).

According to one view (McConville, 1988) there are a number of alternatives to custody which have a 'decade of solid success behind them and are increasingly earning public and judicial respect'. He refers to the work of the National Center on Institutions and Alternatives (NCIA) and The Sentencing Project (TSP) which have developed refined approaches to diversion from custody by creating packages of 'individual sentencing schemes' that try to fit the punishment to the crime, the criminal, the victim and society. Judges are presented with a package of alternatives which takes account of deterrence, retribution and restitution. A typical package offers the court community service, employment, restitution, close or intensive supervision and the possibility of some time in prison, or a halfway house which may enable an offender to search for or keep a job. Before a recommendation is made to a court 'a score-sheet of factors, such as seriousness of offence, prior convictions and incarcerations' and whether the defendant is currently under any supervision (for instance, probation), or whether bail has been refused and why, is used to alert the authorities about the likelihood of the offender receiving a custodial sentence. Thus by considering a 'risk of custody scale' (for a similar UK attempt used in Cambridgeshire and gradually gaining ground in other probation areas, see Bale, 1987), only offenders who are regarded to be at the 'heavier' end of the 'market' receive attention and are included in the recommendations. As such, this emphasis on deep end offenders reduces the risk of giving alternatives to custody to offenders who would otherwise not have received a custodial sentence in any case. McConville (1988: 21) gives an illustration:

> An unemployed drug addict, for instance, facing four charges of burglary and with a prison record for drug offences was on his way to prison. His sentencing plan included a month-long drug treatment programme, followed by six months' residence in a halfway house. The offender also performed six hours' service per week for a year at a local charity for the destitute. He was referred [to] an employment bureau and was required to obtain and hold a full-time job. An agreed amount of restitution was to be paid to his victim . . . All this was supervised by the probation service.

Monthly reports were filed with the court, which constantly held out with the likelihood of imprisonment if the conditions were not met in full.

Of course, such a scheme or other alternatives to custody can never manage to satisfy the needs of all types of offenders and thus those of courts in dealing with very serious crimes including violent offenders and 'chronic recidivists'. But, for the majority of offenders whose crimes or criminal record appear to put them under the threat of imprisonment but who could be dealt with safely in the community, alternatives to custody may have a useful contribution to make in that sphere. Merely to reject such alternatives as widening the net without considering the possibility that they can be used, even if that means for a temporary period, as substitutes for incarceration, is not sufficient. This is well demonstrated by some of the achievements or 'successes' reported by various youth projects which have been set up to act as alternatives to custody and which work with serious and persistent offenders — for instance, those convicted of arson, robbery and indecent assault as well as multiple cases of dwelling-house burglary (cf. Children's Society Advisory Committee on Penal Custody and its Alternatives for Juveniles, 1988). Drawing attention to the lack of comparability among findings and the lack of standardised methods of monitoring alternatives to custody, the Children's Society Advisory Committee (1988: 15) writes:

> The provision of a successful community programme is not straightforward. The resource must be provided in such a way as to be acceptable to the courts; its use also has to be restricted to the target group of offenders. Community programmes have the potential to bring a wider group of young people into close supervision while the use of custody remains at the same level. It would be of great concern, for example, if new programmes drew offenders from those who would otherwise receive fines. Community programmes can be very intensive and involve reporting five days a week or more for several hours at a time over a number of months. Working with the wrong [shallow end] offenders would be neither cost effective nor just . . . Unlike penal custody, there are no nationally based monitoring or research studies on which to assess the effectiveness of community programmes which work with serious offenders. There are an increasing number of local studies from widely separated and varying parts of the country which show great reductions in the use of custody:
>
> > In Knowsley the custody rate dropped from 17% to 5% . . . In Ebbw Vale custody was reduced by 76% in the first year of operation and by 1987 was down to 1.8% of juveniles in court . . . In Kirklees the custody rate was cut by 80% . . . In South Birmingham the use of detention centres was cut by 88% . . . Surrey has a custody rate below 2% . . . Basingstoke has been custody free for two years . . .

The above claims may be accepted or rejected depending on one's perspective. If you believe in the diversion process you probably find them appropriate and exciting. If you do not believe in the diversion process and you are in sympathy with claims that alternatives widen the net of social control without challenging the supremacy of the prison, then you may brush them aside as mere rhetoric. If you have an open mind you may look at them with incredulity but may ask for more information to guide you through the maze of reaching those outcomes. You may ask to know, for instance, what types of offender, what age group, what tasks or relationships, and what type of supervision may be conducive or inhibitive to such good results. In short, you may think that statistics have no value unless they are interpreted. Also, one cannot interpret those claims unless detailed information is given to the reader about the interactions and processes leading to such positive outcomes. Notwithstanding these observations, what the above claims suggest without any doubt is how limited and restricted our knowledge is about what type of activities which offer alternatives to prison, are available across the country, at the local and national level. That is, there may be many local and innovative projects which use alternatives in novel ways — far away from popular awareness — which help many offenders to remain in the community as opposed to experiencing custody. For example, whereas Rutherford recognises the risk arising from alternatives in that 'there is disturbing evidence that sanctions which are supposedly alternatives to custody have the result of supplementing rather than replacing custody' (Rutherford, 1984: 157, 1986; Rutherford and McDermott, 1976), he also offers examples of projects which demonstrate positive outcomes and lead to a genuine process of diversion. Among others, he details the experiences and work of the 'Woodlands Centre' in Basingstoke, Hampshire.

The centre deals with older adolescents and confines its attention to those young people who are at risk of receiving custodial sentences. According to the author, the 'Woodlands Centre adamantly refused to paddle safely in the "shallow end" and opted for the tougher challenges of the "deep end"' with the objective of stopping altogether the number of custodial sentences in the juvenile court in the area (Rutherford, 1986: 138). The centre is situated in a housing estate and operates on weekday evenings. It provides both a formal and informal atmosphere which offers 'firm and clearly articulated requirements' and the programme evolves around the needs of different types of offender. The 'high intensity' programme, which is intended for those who are at risk of receiving a long sentence of detention at a young offender institution, 'consists of 280 hours of attendance over a period of twelve months'. For others who might receive shorter custodial sentences, a 'medium intensity' programme of 100 hours of attendance for six months is offered as an alternative to incarceration. Although much of the programme is based at the Woodlands Centre, part of the time is allowed for a 'community placement serving as a means of reparation for the offence, not to the individual victim but to the community as a whole' (Rutherford, 1986: 141). The centre, though 'closely aligned to the court its approach bears little resemblance to the punishment approach; nor do notions of treatment and welfare provide a useful framework for assessing its contribution' (Rutherford, 1986: 145). Rather, the team aims at guiding and showing young offenders the way out of trouble, and the objective is to 'bind the young person with the locality'. The centre claims some remarkable successes in diverting offenders from custody and for bringing about positive changes within the local criminal justice process. Rutherford (1986: 144) writes:

> The impact of Woodlands on the local criminal justice process is of considerable significance. In 1980 eighteen juveniles were sentenced to the prison system. In 1982, the first operational year for Woodlands, there were five custodial sentences. In 1983 there were two. This remarkable transformation in sentencing practice was largely achieved as a result of the Woodlands Centre assuming a gatekeeping role at the point when a custodial sentence or an alternative disposition at that level of the tariff is being considered. In the period 1981–3 some thirty youngsters were received at Woodlands on orders from the court. Another fifteen to twenty were assessed by the programme. Remarkably, these youngsters were refused not because they were too difficult to handle but because their offences were not high enough on the tariff. That is to say, in the view of the Woodlands staff, the case did not merit a custodial sentence, and the young people were diverted to lower-tariff sentences.

It is obvious that, as Rutherford points out, the importance and effect of Woodlands as well as the significance of other similar local projects (see for instance Longley, 1985; Pitts, 1988: 74–82; Smith et al., 1972) goes beyond local criminal justice arrangements. Although local and unpublicised, they show that alternatives to custody, when properly used and deployed by taking into account type of offenders, seriousness of offence, risk of custody and building on a network of social relations including probation officers, police, magistrates and other community agencies, not only do not widen the net but can act as genuine substitutes for imprisonment (see also Musheno, 1982; Quay and Love, 1977).

Furthermore, even though some of these projects may not be fully successful in keeping offenders out of trouble and may only help to postpone — rather than put a halt to — the process of incarceration, there may be a most significant difference between the interpretations attached to that experience by the participants themselves and a criminologist making a judgement on their behalf. For the criminologist, short-term diversion may mean only a temporary displacement of the problem of the prison. By implication, if alternatives are not successful in keeping offenders outside prison walls on a permanent basis, such alternatives may be seen as only assisting in the maintenance of that institution and in widening the net without any real benefits. But that stance is rather paternalistic and does not take into account the wishes or experiences of the offender. In short, in response to that view, it is worth reminding the criminologist of Stan Cohen's phrase here, 'it's alright for you to talk'! From the point of view of the recipient, the offender, even a short reprieve from the process of incarceration is far better and much to be preferred than immediate imprisonment. In addition they may also derive other social benefits from diversion such as guidance, friendships, or encouragement to mend relationships or find employment (see for instance Flegg, 1976; Hil, 1986; Murray, 1986; Thorvaldson, 1978; Vass, 1984). As there may therefore be hidden benefits in the first instance and our knowledge may be limited in terms of the type and number of projects attempting to utilise specific types of alternatives to keep offenders in the community, it follows that any generalisations arising from the view that alternatives only help to expand the criminal justice system without challenging the prison establishment are suspect and should be treated with caution. For example, much has been said about the failure of the probation order with or without special requirements to act as a proper diversionary penal measure (cf. Walker and Beaumont, 1981, 1985). But there may be another view on the subject. When looked at closely, probation has its problems but at the same time it does appear — when used in a systematic and intensive way — to act as an alternative to custody. Raynor, in a detailed evaluation of a project in West Glamorgan which uses modified probation orders to provide an alternative to custody for young adult offenders, shows that it is possible to achieve reductions in custodial sentencing by resorting to such a penal measure. The study offers empirical evidence which suggests that offenders are not only diverted from custody but also receive useful help, and show some reduction in expected reconviction rates (Raynor, 1988).

When outcomes are considered in this positive light, even what seems a watertight argument, such as that advanced by Hylton (1981b) begins to look insecure. As the reader may remember, I have referred to the study as being an empirical verification of the proposition that alternatives to custody widen the net of social control. However, in view of the points raised thus far, even correlational evidence needs to be considered with some caution. For example, the measurement is between two variables: prison population statistics and alternatives to custody statistics. But, as I have already suggested, the assumed causal relationship which is established between those variables is both simple and crude. Correlational evidence shows the *possibility* of a relationship. But it does not and cannot *confirm* the existence of an association for too much is left to chance and too little taken into account. For instance, my argument that the criminal justice system is a web of complex social relationships and intervening social variables is totally ignored by correlational evidence. Any one of those factors (known or unknown) could be capable of challenging or nullifying the assumed but crude and simplistic correlational evidence presented as confirmation of the proposition that alternatives are a monster in disguise. Furthermore, correlational evidence cannot account for the fact that some alternatives do help to divert; that they may work better for some types of offenders than others; and that it may not be, after all, that alternatives are failing in their task. On the contrary, some of them may be doing, or are capable of doing, a perfect job if only they could be targeted at the right offenders. For example, the deep end offenders as Rutherford's illustration above shows, or those given or running the risk of being given long sentences of imprisonment, as Bottomley and Pease (1986), suggest. As Matthews (1987) argues, much of the idea of net widening, and the failure of 'decarceration and deinstitutionalisation' policies, is based on false or misunderstood premises. Close examination of the effects of alternatives to custody reveals that rather than being 'failures', such policies may have, as he puts it (Matthews, 1987: 55–66) 'impacted upon different populations in significantly different ways, and have been associated with a fundamental reorganisation and reconstruction of the penal population . . .'. He suggests that by rejecting those alternatives and by ignoring their 'successes' we have condemned them 'to a premature burial'.

Matthews's critique (though at times marred by his failure to conceptualise his terms clearly, for instance he assumes that 'alternatives to custody' as a concept is simply explained by placing it within the ambit of 'decarceration' policies) echoes reservations which have already been raised. He suggests that the dispersal of discipline thesis suffers from three pervasive flaws: globalism, empiricism and impossibilism. Globalism is the tendency to overgeneralise from the particular. There is a tendency to use specific unrepresentative and idiosyncratic samples, studies, offender or other 'deviant' populations, or particular contexts as the means to 'globalising' findings without at the same time expressing a concern that such a 'blurring of the categories of analysis and lumping together of diverse groups into an undifferentiated whole' can be an overblown distortion of reality. He argues, for example, that the thesis adopts a stance which works on the principle that social control practices are the product of 'well-orchestrated decision-making processes, managed and manipulated by the "ruling class" or the "powerful" '. He suggests that modes of social control and changing patterns of control can also be a 'reflection of demands from below, forged through social and class struggles, or they may reflect institutional tensions and contradictions' (Matthews, 1987: 43; see also Cain, 1985).

Although Matthews's argument is feasible and certainly correct, it misses a very significant point about the power of the state and its political machinery to *engineer* interest in the introduction of particular policies (as, for instance, an expansion in community sanctions) and thus develop a public consciousness of an event or intention. In return, that public consciousness can then be expressed in terms of a debate or occasionally in terms of demands made by affected groups for the government and its policy machinery to do something about their predicament or plight. This activity (and a good example is the current publicity of government intentions and rationale in expanding alternatives to custody, cf. Home Office, 1988b, 1988c, 1988d) is part of the process of legitimation which creates, and at the same time derives support from, a public awareness of particular problems, explanations of their causes, and means which are promoted for combating those causes. Nonetheless, this criticism should not deflect attention from Matthews's attempt to remind us of the fact that expansion of controls or specific types of modes of surveillance can often be a reactive response to demands from below rather than mere exertion of power from above. An addendum to Matthews's point would be that discussions about social control and the widening of the net thesis often ignore historical evidence that those on the receiving end (particularly working-class families) are capable of displaying resistance to state (including welfare) control (cf. Van Krieken, 1986). More serious than that, there is some evidence that particular social groups (again working-class families) may develop their own 'ideology' which is used to socialise and constrain their own members from going beyond their own class boundaries and effectively making them accept their social position as fair and just (P. Willis, 1977); or that working-class families may also actively try to use ' "bourgeois" welfare institutions to socialise and constrain their own members' (Rodger, 1988: 566; see also Philips, 1977; Tholfensen, 1976; Van Krieken, 1986).

Matthews (1987: 45) is suspicious of the Orwellian overtones of the net widening thesis and suggests that contrary to the idea that it is a negative development, net widening may have its positive sides. He writes:

Much of what parades under the heading of 'net widening' may be constructive and progressive. Social workers, community workers, youth workers and the like are not simply 'agents of social control', nor are they just 'clearing up after capitalism' or 'papering over the cracks', for if nothing else these agents have undoubtedly brought much needed resources into deprived areas.

More importantly, the blunt assumption that alternatives help to disperse and widen the means of social control, fails to take into account what has already been pointed out in earlier parts of this book — but see in particular the next chapter for detail: that usually there is a serious disjunction between intended policy and actual practice. That is to say, penal measures have a public face (political and legislative intentions) and a private one (the way they are administered and applied by those entrusted with the task). When the two are examined one finds that the so-called 'coercive social worker' or 'probation officer' (cf. Handler, 1973), who is often vested with the responsibility to apply sanctions, becomes his or her own policy maker in miniature. The officer invents new informal means of social control which may expand the informal networks of control still further but also help to protect and shield offenders from the more coercive formal channels of the law. Those new informal modes of control which contradict and often challenge, evade or distort formal discipline, help to nullify official policy, and modify and negotiate disciplinarian regimes (cf. Vass, 1984).

The second main source of criticism levelled against the net widening thesis by Matthews is 'the widespread adoption of a methodology which relies upon generalisations gleaned from collections of untheorised "facts": namely empiricism' (Matthews, 1987: 47). As we have seen with reference to the presentation of statistics and outcomes and the crude associations established between a rising prison population and an expanding system of alternatives to custody, this sort of empiricism 'constructs a twin mystification'. Matthews (1987: 47) explains: 'On one side it observes the simultaneous expansion of community corrections and incarceration and uses one to explain the other. On the other hand it employs similar techniques to "demonstrate" that the various diversion and deinstitutionalisation strategies are not working effectively by evaluating them primarily in terms of their associated rates of recidivism.'

Matthews's statement requires further elaboration. As I have shown in Chapter 3 it is not true that alternatives are evaluated only in terms of their failures. Indeed, much of their expansion has taken place against a background of official rhetoric haphazardly supported by pseudo-empirical manifestations of 'success'. For instance, the success rate of probation orders and community service has been a major tool of propaganda in the hands of managers of the probation service and the Home Office. Therefore, it is not only failure that is mystified in the above crude exercise. Success can also be distorted and mystified by resort to the same method. Either way, it has already been suggested that this crude technique of reaching interpretations about the relationship between custody and alternatives may ignore other intervening social factors affecting the levels of both incarceration and alternatives to custody and the effectiveness of the latter to control the former. To add to the factors which have already been referred to, one needs to pay attention to the growth of serious crime, the changing incidence and distribution of crime and to theorise about the relations among the many factors involved. Matthews suggests that 'it is not the absolute size of the prison population which should be our primary point of reference but the *relationship* between the imprisonment rate, the crime rate and the growth of community corrections' (Matthews, 1987: 49, emphasis in original; see also Box, 1987; Box and Hale, 1986). Matthews's list is too modest. I would add a plethora of other factors which should be seen in relation to the above three variables. For instance, changes in policing tactics, legislative changes, sentencing practices, offender populations and type of offenders given alternatives to custody, length of prison sentences, how supervisors enforce sanctions in the community, the differential nature of intervention (cf. Bayer, 1981) and the diverse types and backgrounds of supervisors, the social characteristics of offenders, differences between type of alternatives, economic factors, changes in the ratio of women and men, and ethnic groups given prison sentences, to name but a few. In sum, the relationship between prison and alternatives is not always a simple mathematical calculation. The critics of alternatives to custody tend to look at quantity (that is, whether alternatives reduce or do not reduce the prison population) at the cost of neglecting other relevant factors and at the cost of some more close-up snapshots of the relationships between participants and the processes by which those participants make sense of their activities and reach outcomes. As I show in Chapter 6, day centres may not be allowed to act fully as true alternatives to custody because *courts* choose to restrict the number of deep end offenders who are diverted to day centres. In other words, the courts themselves may be 'diverting' offenders *from* alternatives *to* prison establishments, therefore limiting those measures' impact on the rates of imprisonment and undermining their credibility as alternatives to custody.

There are also other problems with the conclusions reached by many of the critics. By merely looking at the expanding public face of the social control apparatus without asking questions about other aspects of relations in the criminal justice system and questions about 'the subjects involved in such relationships and their consciousness and capacity to change what is administratively and politically established' (Rodger, 1988: 569), conclusions reached are both theoretically and empirically suspect. They lead to false impressions about the complex nature, types, means and ends of social control. First, behind the crude statistics there may lie qualitative issues which remain untapped and unknown (cf. Smith, 1987; Vass, 1988b). For instance, one should be able to say something about the social context within which outcomes emerge, about social relationships in the making, and understand whether any social and personal benefits are accrued by participants which may not be amenable to quantitative measurement. Examples of this area of concern are those personal aspects and effects of interaction which remain largely unnoticed or unknown to outsiders but which are observed, experienced and well recognised — often just as impressions — by those directly involved in the encounters. Secondly, the dispersal of discipline thesis may be confusing mere expansion of penal sanctions with an inevitable increase in surveillance and control. The thesis assumes that as the system expands, inevitably more people are or ought to be caught up in its wider net. Although it is true that there has been an expansion of penal options in most western states, it does not necessarily follow that more people are falling victims to that expansion and are caught in the expanded net. Indeed, that is exactly what still remains to be empirically demonstrated. Furthermore, as Downes (1986: 311) suggests, trends in *informal* controls are completely ignored and though formal controls may be expanding, they 'may be makeshifts for net reductions' elsewhere. In addition, accepting that the 'growth of the machinery of regulation is real enough', Downes (1988: 64) also points out important flaws and omissions in the thesis. He states that:

> There are, however, many respects in which this awesome machinery of control limps behind the growth of phenomena which it can barely chart, let alone constrain: the informal economy, tax evasion, corporate crime and occupational deviance are tolerated more because of the dispersal of their victimization than its magnitude ... It sometimes seems as if the only people in gaol, apart from the occasional spectacular gangster, are those unemployed or marginal workers who lack routinized access to occupational crime.

One must, of course, draw attention to the possibility that Downes's argument about reductions in informal means of control may have its own flaws. As in the case of formal controls, any reductions in that sphere have to be demonstrated. Indeed, one can say that there is expansion, not reduction, in *some* spheres of informal control activity (cf. Curtis, 1987; Hope and Shaw, 1988; Matthews, 1988; Wright and Galaway, 1989). In fact, Downes's (1986) illustration that there may be reductions in informal family controls may be quite inaccurate. There may be an assumed reduction (because of rediscovered theories about, say, hooliganism and political pressure towards reinstating the 'good old British way of life' — cf. Pearson, 1983), but in reality this may be part of the legitimation process of promoting and enacting new criminal laws. Thus, in England, there is now a push, by the present government, towards the idea that the family should play a more fundamental role in the control of its members. In order to enforce that ideology, the government has expressed the intention of introducing legislation which will make parents liable to prosecution for failing to prevent their children from committing crime (Winstour, 1989).

Finally, the term 'impossibilism' is used by Matthews to draw attention to a most serious and pervasive aspect of the dispersal of discipline thesis. In its extreme version, the thesis fosters the belief that 'nothing works' and that every new effort to do something about the prison system by expanding means of community controls will inevitably fail. As Matthews (1987: 51) puts it: 'This is the impossibilist impasse in a nutshell. Prisons are a disaster, community corrections are invariably worse, realistic reform cannot be achieved without a "fundamental transformation of the social structure", which is unlikely to occur in the foreseeable future, so there is nothing that can be done.'

Once again, this view distorts what may actually be happening in practice. It overinflates the failures of attempts to 'destructure' the prison establishment and gives no credit to the often-genuine efforts made by those working in the field to offer more constructive and less damaging alternatives to offenders than the experience of imprisonment. Furthermore, it falls in the trap of generalising from particular experiences to the general field of activity within the criminal justice system, without bothering to clarify that in certain cases and circumstances certain alternatives to custody appear to be fulfilling their obligations in diverting deep end offenders from custody.

Conclusion

In sum, though there is evidence for net widening in some spheres (e.g. Bottoms, 1987; Hylton, 1981b; Pratt, 1986), it may not altogether follow that more people are caught up in the expanding net, or that the mere expansion of community penal sanctions leads later to more people becoming imprisoned. In effect, much of what is said about alternatives and the assumptions made about their negative nature in building or expanding an 'evil empire' from within, are based on ideological and personal values rather than on any serious and detached assessment of the workings of such penal measures. Despite much rhetoric we still know very little about what exactly those alternatives are and how they are administered, what the real effects of such measures are on the criminal justice system and those who experience them, and what their true relationship is to custody. The dispersal of discipline thesis, or as Stan Cohen has characterised alternatives to custody, the Trojan horse of the criminal justice system, has gained such widespread approval that some of its major flaws and lapses have been allowed to go unnoticed or have remained unquestioned. Its beguiling attraction — mythologised by the writings of people such as Foucault — has created a culture of professionals and academics who are too quick to reject new developments out of hand, as if we have all been conditioned to react with despondency and total negativism on every occasion when governments introduce 'new methods of treatment', 'diversion', 'humane treatment', 'alternatives to custody', or, as the new terminology goes, 'punishment in the community'. Penal measures are too often rejected on ideological grounds — the same grounds which are often deployed for the introduction of those measures — without much real thought and careful assessment of their means and ends. Those penal measures are rejected and usually mocked at the moment of their inception or infancy and well before those developments have had a fair chance to prove or disprove themselves and their worth in practice (cf. Pease, 1983). We cannot offer such developments a fair chance unless we also try to find out how those developments fare in practice, at the local and national level.

The metaphor of the Trojan horse (which describes alternatives to custody as a monster in disguise) is useful in that it draws our attention to developments which ought to be critically evaluated and some of their worst scenarios kept under close scrutiny. But it can also be a dangerous thesis if we accept it without questioning its credibility. It can lead to impasse and a paralysis of inventive thought and praxis. It may encourage pessimism and idleness and can undermine or even discourage any attempts to do something about the growing prison population. It can inhibit as well as prohibit the development of more acceptable and constructive ways of dealing with offenders than dumping, segregating and keeping them in the squalor of prison. The view that Box (1987: 109–10, emphasis in original) expresses in support of the thesis is worth noting:

> There is nothing in Britain . . . or Canada . . . or the USA . . . to support the idea that 'decarceration', 'diversion' and 'decriminalisation' had led to its social control network shrinking. Indeed, behind the rhetoric of these 'alternatives to prison' is the harsh reality of more state control. Not only does the network of control agencies expand *physically*, but it also expands

territorially. Persons not previously part of its domain now find themselves increasingly caught up in its machinations.

'Nothing in Britain . . . or Canada . . . or the USA . . .'? 'Persons . . . caught up in its machinations'? The above paragraph epitomises what is really wrong and problematic with the metaphor of the Trojan horse, and the dispersal of discipline thesis. 'Nothing . . .'? I hope that the present chapter has shown the reader that there may be *something* after all in both theoretical and empirical terms to justify and invite a fresh and more critical look at the metaphor.

5 Community service as a process of tolerance

In previous chapters I argued that one cannot even begin to understand alternatives to custody, their organisational aspects and their means and ends (and thus outcomes) unless some knowledge of *process* — the transactional aspects of relationships between supervisors and offenders — is available. I offered illustrations about how, for instance, arguments about successful alternatives to custody (community service, probation, and parole) can be shown to hide the influential role played by supervising officers in socially constructing, thus engineering, outcomes through expediency (as in negotiating organisational constraints) and by interpreting rules, expectations and goals according to their world view. This, I suggested, is part of a natural process to be found in any type of social organisation, including prisons, which involves regulation and the application of sanctions. This process introduces routinisation, evasion and distortion of formal rules and expectations into relationships. This chapter follows through the concept of 'process' by offering an illustrative example of how it operates in the context of one alternative to custody — the community service order.

My aim is to concentrate on the ways in which supervising officers[1] attempt to enforce the order and regulate offenders. The purpose is to suggest what kind of possible problems, means and ends emerge in the context of having to supervise offenders in the community and, in that sense, administering and enforcing alternatives to custody. Reference to substantive details about what is actually happening 'on site', that is to say, while offenders are performing tasks for the community; accounts of court proceedings; illustrative material from official records; statistical evidence; and direct information or quotations from participants among other aspects of the process under consideration are omitted and the reader is invited, if need be, to consult the original studies on the subject (see below) as well as others (for instance Pease, 1980; Pease et al., 1975, 1977; Varah, 1987; Young, 1979). In addition, I do not make any references to the order's position in relation to custody. This has already been discussed in previous chapters. Finally, as the discussion is based on the findings of my own research into community service, all non-attributed information with regard to sources refers to the citations listed below.

The research background to the discussion

The discussion which follows, albeit brief and in some ways circumspect, is based on empirical findings and a broader argument which I have detailed elsewhere (cf. Vass, 1984) and which I have explored in terms of its consequences in a number of other publications (see for example Menzies and Vass, 1989; Vass, 1980, 1981, 1986a, 1988a; Vass and Menzies, 1989).

In the main, the original empirical work which subsequently led to further investigations was carried out between 1978 and 1980 (cf. Vass, 1980, 1982b, 1984). This research was a participant observation study of community service in two areas of the probation service. It entailed the actual completion of 220 hours of community service in the company of offenders and under the guidance of supervising officers. The tasks which I performed under a community service order, and in my capacity as researcher, involved the following: the construction of a children's playground, roof laying and repairs, burning rubbish, window cleaning, escorting and assisting mentally handicapped children, demolition tasks, painting and decorating, felling trees, sweeping leaves and clearing roads, clearing woodlands, moving ballast, scraping benches, moving cement and stones, gardening, construction of a footpath, restoration work, bricklaying, concreting, earth removal, hedge cutting, looking after elderly couples, hospital work (collecting dirty linen, cleaning wards, entertaining patients) among others.

In the course of those tasks, I was treated as an 'offender'. As I was instructed to carry out particular duties, my attendance and perform- ance, with a few exceptions, were monitored, evaluated and hours were credited by supervising officers as though I was under a real court order.

In addition to participant observation, I acted as an observer in disciplinary proceedings, observed encounters between supervising officers and offenders in the course of disciplinary interviews, observed many hours of court proceedings against defaulters, accompanied supervising officers on their visits to absentees, examined and analysed official files, offenders' records, and statistical data, interviewed offenders, supervising officers, magistrates and clerks to the justices, attended regular staff meetings, and socialised outside community service hours with offenders. In that respect, the empirical work was a combination of a number of research techniques which offered reliable findings and accounts about community service, and generated new knowledge about legal, organisational, personal and interpersonal relationships (for further details, see Vass, 1982b).

Forms of dissociation from community service

The starting point in the enforcement of community service orders is the pre-sentence report. The court is obliged to request a report from the probation service concerning the suitability of offenders for community service. Once that is accepted, and an order made, the court duty officer (who represents the probation service) furnishes offenders with a copy of the order and issues instructions to them to report for an initial interview with the community service organiser.

At the initial interview the officer explains and reiterates the requirements of the order. Offenders are reminded that they have *consented* to the order and that the order is thus a *contract*. In that respect, the offenders' attention is drawn to the risks (including the possibility of imprisonment) should they violate the contract. Before the interview is over, offenders should normally appreciate the 'informal' and unwritten *code of conduct* in community service. First, that if they keep to expectations, they will receive a sympathetic response from their officers in case of difficulties. Secondly, that officers expect no more or less than any other employer regarding attendance, punctuality, standards of work and behaviour. Thirdly, that both officers and offenders should live in peace and that neither side should do anything to rock the boat.

The idea of consent embedded in the court order constitutes no evidence that offenders are eager or willing to perform unpaid work for the community. Consent is one way of avoiding an unknown risk. Rather than risk anything far worse (a harsh fine for instance, or custody) offenders offer their agreement to serve under a community service order because that is the rational thing to do under the circumstances. In court, they are given to understand that the alternative could be imprisonment. However, they do not actually know whether they would be made the subject of a custodial sentence or face a fine, a suspended sentence, a probation order, or a conditional discharge order. With the exception of a very few cases where offenders may refuse that offer and thus challenge the court's invitation to consent to an order, most offenders are quick to accept community service. However, in accepting the contract they also recognise that the order is a distinct form of punishment. They know that they are obliged to labour for the community; to do things which they may not particularly like; to keep in touch and be under surveillance; to be punished and penalised further still for non-compliance. Thus, after a brief spell, and having overcome the immediate euphoria of having narrowly escaped imprisonment, reality sets in. They find that far from being let off easily, they are now subject to fairly long hours of leisure controls and at any given time they could be liable to further penalties if they default on their order.

Under those circumstances, the order is perceived as essentially antithetical to offenders' interests. They find ways in which they attempt to neutralise or minimise the constraints and restraints imposed on them. They invent and develop at some point certain idiosyncrasies — that is to say, 'personality traits' — which they use to legitimately excuse themselves from doing much work. For instance, some allow themselves to be seen and understood as 'lazy', 'incapable', or 'morons' which, in the theory of their supervising officers, explains the offenders' lack of motivation. Such offenders become, in the vocabulary of their supervisors, the 'no-good-for-nothing-Jack'. As they are what they are it would be futile to try to push them harder.

If, though, offenders do not like the label and the role of a 'moron', they turn to an alternative trait. They assume the identity of someone who is perpetually 'unwell'. They have the 'sick-John-syndrome'. They are observed arriving at community service projects feeling miserable, sniffing and groaning and telling everybody that they should be in bed. They develop an image of being hypochondriacs and when they are warned by their supervisors about their lapses and poor work record, they tell those supervisors in distressed voices, 'We can't help it. We are sick men'. In the process, they manage to accrue an impressive list of ailments which are triggered, like allergies, by coming in contact with anything which denotes 'work'. On the other hand, they may not like that stereotype either. They can choose instead to be the 'all-too-eager' types who want to do everything and be everywhere but who constantly remain idle, complaining that there is nothing much to do. When they are reprimanded for their casual attitude to community service, they tell their officers, 'Don't blame us! Give us the right tools guv'!'

They may, of course, choose none of those traits because they fall short of their own expectations, vanity and impressions of their self-concept. These are usually the 'wise guys', who also happen to be the masculine type, and whose self-publicised reputation as irresistible womanisers often leads them to telling numerous stories of sexual exploits and other great deeds for the benefit of the less fortunate members. Their 'wise guy' character occasionally demoralises officers and threatens the existing order and pattern of relationships. When they are told that disciplinary measures may be taken against them, they incite other offenders to engage in mutiny while tending themselves, in private and in the presence of their supervisors, to be full of apologies.

The above choices and methods of neutralisation (the list is not exhaustive) are often attributed by supervisors to the personal characteristics and traits of individual offenders. However, they are, in many respects, instrumental adjustments, that is solutions, to the constraints of community service organisation. Although offenders may report personal benefits which they derive from the experience of community service, at the same time they complain that the experience fails to inspire them. In particular, they often complain (especially when they are working in groups and doing work which is not immediately recognisable in their minds as 'community') that they cannot think of any useful and tangible — other than completion of order — short- or long-term rewards for their labour. They usually measure rewards in material terms. When material terms are absent, labouring for the community is seen as a form of oppression. Inventing various means of relaxation and avoidance of what is alien to them becomes an essential part of their involvement in community service.

The main, and most frequent as well as most serious, form of dissociation from the work and values of community service organisation is *absenteeism* (cf. Devon Probation and After-care Service, 1980: 3; Durham County Probation and After-care Service, 1975: 37–8; Home Office, 1988g, 1988i; McWilliams and Murphy, 1980; Murphy, 1979; Richards, 1979; South West London Probation and After-care Service, 1981: 4; Sussex, 1974; Vass, 1984: 115–50; Young, 1979: 66–7). Absenteeism, that is failure to attend work without a reasonable excuse, is an explicit failure to satisfactorily perform duties and tasks and thus a failure to comply with the law. In that sense, offenders are in breach of their community service requirements and are liable to face prosecution. Absenteeism is not only an endemic feature of community service which occasionally may run at an average rate of one-quarter of all attendances per month, but also many — as much as half — of those absences are due to reasons considered as unsatisfactory or unreasonable by supervisors. By and large, 'legitimate' reasons advanced by offenders are in relation to 'sickness', 'family illness', and 'employment' — in that order. Many of those 'legitimate' reasons are usually 'uncertified' (see Home Office, 1988g, 1988i, for an attempt to clarify and define appropriate procedure in this area, and my critique in Chapter 7).

Modes of control and surveillance

Violations of the law, as in the case of absenteeism without an acceptable or reasonable excuse and other dissociations such as disruptive behaviour 'on site', are expected by the formal rules to be dealt with in a resolute and firm manner. The regulations stipulate that supervising officers are expected to react to such a breach of requirements in a swift and unequivocal manner by punishing defaulters. Such punishment for failure to comply with requirements of order should normally be administered through the courts. In other words, breaches should be prosecuted (Home Office, 1988i).

However, breach proceedings as an instrument for exerting pressure on offenders and forcing them to comply with community service requirements are used as a last resort by supervising officers. It emerges that the most common methods preferred and used by officers in controlling offenders take the shape of alternative, less authoritative, measures. In the main, these are postal communications, home visits, and disciplinary interviews.

Table 5.1 depicts this aspect of law enforcement by offering an empirical example of the way in which infractions of community service by offenders were dealt with by supervising officers in two areas of the probation service. A total of 103 offenders were followed through their community service career between November 1978 and October 1979 and their relationships with supervising officers were closely observed and monitored in the period (cf. Vass, 1984: 115–50). In addition, the offenders' official records were examined in respect of their absences in that period. That is to say, each offender's attendance record, form *Part D*, and record of contacts with their supervising officer(s), form *Part C*, were painstakingly analysed. With the exception of only 15 offenders who showed no absences, the rest of the group ($n=88$) showed various degrees of persistent absenteeism. A total of 599 absences were recorded against the 88 offenders in the period, giving, on average, 7 absences per offender (with a range of 1 to 35). The analysis of all contacts between supervising officers and offenders revealed that those offenders' failures to conform to requirements were dealt with by both formal and informal techniques. The informal and less authoritative techniques — postal communications, home visits and disciplinary interviews — constituted the main mode of control exerted on offenders, whereas breach proceedings (prosecutions) remained the least used method in enforcing the order of the court (see Table 5.1).

Postal Communications
In the social world of community service the code of conduct is defined in terms of two basic rules. First, offenders should contact the relevant officer if they are unable to report for work. Preferably, this should occur on the day of the absence — by telephone — as that denotes a measure of personal involvement and responsibility. Secondly, offenders should convey a satisfactory excuse for non-attendance. In return, supervisors maintain their side of the 'unspoken bargain' by

Table 5.1   *Type and frequency of controls applied on offenders (n=88) following unauthorised absences between November 1978 and October 1979*

No. of offenders dealt with	All offenders with absences %	Types of control applied	Frequency of controls No.	All controls %
75	85.2	Warning letters	370	74.8
37	42.1	Home visits	64	13.0
24	27.3	Interviews	31	6.3
19	21.6	Prosecutions	21	4.3
6	6.8	No action	6	1.2
2	2.3	Other	2	0.4
		All controls	494	100

Source: Vass (1984, Tables 16 and 18 combined).

by remaining flexible and exercising their discretion, thus avoiding the need to invoke the law. Preservation of and adherence to that code of conduct is seen as establishing a dialogue between consenting and rational individuals who share a common concern — the successful completion of order — and which leads to the formation of mutual feelings of trust. The principle of *trust*, therefore, becomes the pivot on which supervisors' perceptions of and reactions to offenders are determined and structured.

When offenders do not subscribe to that principle of trust, supervisors take the initiative of contacting them via postal communications in an attempt both to satisfy themselves that the offenders are still active participants (holding on to the contract) and to re-establish the process of interaction before it is allowed to disintegrate any further. An example of such a communication process is the following letter:

Official Warning Notice

To:

Date:

On the above date you did not report for work as instructed and failed to contact the Department to explain your absence. Failure to contact the Department on the day you are instructed to report is an offence which places you in breach of your order and will automatically be dealt with by official warning notices regardless of any circumstances that you may subsequently communicate to the Department. On the first occasion you will receive a yellow notice, on the second occasion a blue notice, on the third occasion a pink notice.

A warrant will automatically be applied for in all cases where pink notices are issued. The colour of this paper will indicate your present situation.

You are advised that in cases of Breach the court has the power to impose a fine ... and order the completion of your Community Service Order; or in more serious cases the court may revoke your Community Service Order and commit you to prison.

Recorded Delivery Post

This particular way of controlling offenders who fail to comply with their order has obvious overtones of debt collection (Rock, 1973). The scaling of notices to reflect a particular stage in the career of offenders and the presentation of colour as a visual cue associated with sanctions are well-established and regularly employed features in any situation where bills run into arrears. Each of those warning letters is a preparation for something worse to come if defaulters refuse to comply with requirements.

In practice, though, succeeding stages do not only fail to occur at such a rapid rate, but also the threatened sanctions do not always materialise. In cases where offenders do not respond, supervisors, faced wtih the choice of breach proceedings, or further attempts to enrol the cooperation of offenders, will opt for the latter. More often than not, the threatened breach proceedings are constantly being postponed to allow more time for officers to explore other avenues in securing a response from offenders. The more articulate offenders — those who appreciate their position in this bargaining process — tend to reinforce the code of conduct by avoiding, as far as possible, consecutive absences. In other words, their absenteeism is made to look irregular. This pre-empts any coercive reactions from their supervisors and increases their chances of claiming 'reasonable excuses' should they be faced with the prospect of a prosecution.

In this process of establishing a dialogue and an exchange of views through postal communications, offenders are allowed to remain as active participants in community service and are thus reprieved from any immediate and direct penalties.

Home visits
Home visits increase the pressure on offenders as they involve, where successful, face-to-face contact. Therefore, they serve literally to act as a 'push' factor, by exerting pressure on offenders to attend work. However, they serve other functions too. First, they act as a means of protecting offenders from breach proceedings. Home visits tend to defer the process of prosecution and through this method of control, the chances are that some offenders are assisted in successfully completing their hours of community service. Secondly, they supplement or supersede postal communications by offering closer surveillance. Thirdly, home visits enable supervisors to enquire about offenders' immediate physical and social surroundings by noting any irregularities which could be vital in forming a more refined 'theory'

about whether those offenders should be trusted or not. Such clues help officers to build a model of offenders' character, personal qualities or disabilities. As such, supervisors begin to place offenders into either an 'all right' or a 'risk' category. If they are put in a risk category, offenders undergo closer and more rigid surveillance in terms of tasks performed, attendance record, and general attitude to supervisors and others. An example of the type of encounter which may develop and the type of impressions gained by supervisors are the following three extracts from official records (cf. Vass, 1984: 154–5) concerning the encounters between supervising officers and offenders.

Case 1   Fifth letter to ZA pointing out that the letter was a final warning for him to fulfil his community service or be returned to court . . . It stressed that he had to report on Sundays for the Department was no longer prepared to pull him out of bed and bend over backwards to help him.
    ZA failed to attend again. A home visit was made. He came to the door looking very sorry for himself stating that he had attended a party and had eaten some strange food, which made him feel unwell. He was going to the doctor who is apparently open on Sundays. At 5 that evening he drove past me in a car. He stopped. I asked him where he was going. He said that he had just been to the doctor's but he was closed and he was on his way home. However, the road he was on meant that there was no way he was on his way home; he was therefore told to get a medical certificate because he was getting himself in deeper and deeper trouble with his excuses.

Case 2   I called at [Y's] house and found him at home. He refused to accompany me to the site for Community Service as he said his wife had disappeared and left the house in a mess . . . I said that it would be in his interests to attend for Community Service today as he had missed the last two occasions and a summons might be imminent. He said he welcomed this as he would like a heavy fine instead. I warned him that Community Service is an alternative to imprisonment and that in view of the previous breach action a custodial sentence is a distinct possibility.

Case 3   I called at his house and spoke to his sister . . . I told her that he has not reported for Community Service since 20 May, and although he had informed us that he was sick, no medical certificates had been submitted to cover absences . . . I was not asked into the house and I waited at the door while his sister spoke to his mother. She returned to say that her mother was going to the doctor's this morning to pick up medical certificates. I asked where Z was. I got no answer. I gained the impression that the whole family were 'banding together' to save his neck. I fear a return to court will be inevitable.

On many occasions, home visits as a direct means of surveillance and a way of forcing offenders to participate in activities prove to be of limited value. Offenders do not always answer the door, thus rendering the visit quite fruitless. On such occasions, as the supervisors cannot be entirely sure whether offenders are in (claiming to be sick, for instance) or out (claiming to be in paid employment), the principle of the 'benefit of the doubt' emerges in social interaction. It leads supervisors to ignore infractions and to turn a blind eye until they are in a position to confirm the whereabouts of defaulters and consider what other appropriate action they should take to remedy the situation.

Disciplinary interviews

If offenders fail to respond to verbal or written warnings and show successive failures to comply with their order without any signs that they intend to reconsider their position in the light of those warnings, the enforcement process moves up to a more personal and inter-personal level and takes the shape of a disciplinary interview. The following extracts from official reports offer examples of the type of encounter which takes place in the course of disciplinary interviews (cf. Vass, 1984: 142–59).

> *Case 1*   He came to the office to discuss his absences . . . He immediately apologised for his absences . . . I put to Mr . . . that we both shared a common purpose in getting him through his Community Service Order as soon as possible. He agreed. I said that he was a smart and presentable lad and there was no reason why we could not organise an individual placement for him. He is agreeable to this.

> *Case 2*   He reported for interview as instructed. I told him off for his arrogance. He agreed that he had been messing us about and let us down badly over his attendance. He would give no real reason for this except that he didn't fancy getting out of bed after working hard on Saturday. He was told that his performance must be improved drastically or he would be returned to court for breach.

> *Case 3*   He attended for interview as instructed in the presence of the senior probation officer. When he was asked about being sent home from the job he explained that he was in an argumentative mood and had been so for some time. He agreed that no supervisor had provoked him and that he realised the fault was entirely his own. He now realised he was unreasonable and put it down to his general state. He offered to apologise personally to the supervisors. To sum up it seems that the past few weeks were the culmination of many unconnected problems and at present he is in quite a poor state. Due to his obviously poor health he was returned home and not sent out to work for the rest of the day.

The interview acts as a reaffirmation of supervisors' powers and status as an authority above the offenders and aims to demonstrate the inviolability of the code of conduct broken by those offenders. The face-to-face interaction of the interview poses a fair amount of strain on offenders. They cannot any longer get their next of kin, or others, to convey excuses on their behalf by telephone or by someone else answering the door for them. They do not have time to reflect on warnings and weigh up the 'reasonableness' of their excuses, nor can they hide their emotions and other non-verbal cues. The way in which offenders manage the interview and the conviction of their answers become the testing ground for their chances of either remaining within the organisation of community service or being threatened with ejection. On the whole, most disciplinary interviews end on a happy note if offenders admit guilt and agree that they have acted irresponsibly. The following example drawn from official records (cf. Vass, 1984: 159) shows what happens when offenders do not admit guilt and reject offers of help from probation officers.

Case 1   She was called for interview so that she could discuss her problems particularly with regards to her Community Service obligations . . . She presents as a short, stocky girl dressed in a masculine manner wearing an Army Combat jacket, jeans and flat masculine shoes, has short cropped hair. She was sulky and not very forthcoming. She claimed that there was little work for her to do at the project and she claimed on occasions when there was work it was of a boring nature . . . She left the meeting without further comment and I felt that I had achieved little in getting to the bottom of the problem.

The interaction which takes place in an interview passes through a number of phases. It starts and runs along a continuum of formal gestures during which each party, constrained by their role-related functions and thus power, embarks on what is essentially a process of 'social stroking'. That is to say, they theorise about each other's expectations and intentions and try to reduce their social distance. Although the two parties find themselves socially distant from each other at that early stage, they are closely related by conscious efforts to bridge the gap and establish the foundations of some common ground.

Inevitably, the emergent common ground which establishes some consensus of opinion is completion of order. Supervisors suggest to offenders that unless they recognise their responsibilities, completion of the order will be impossible, in which case they will have to face the dire consequences of a return to court. Offenders typically agree that they need to complete their hours of community service and suggest in return that they have acted in an unwarranted manner. Following this realisation of common objectives, the scene is set for a more relaxed mode of interaction. The interview moves towards a general discussion about community service, work, family, and other relevant issues which serve to provide a picture about possible reasons for the offenders' failure to comply with requirements. A successful negotiation of this stage quickly leads to open informality which brings the interview to a happy end. When that stage is reached, both parties reaffirm their mutual obligations and their common desire to cooperate towards a successful completion of order. Indeed, even in those circumstances where offenders adopt an uncooperative posture, supervisors still try to find a way out of the dilemma of having to initiate breach proceedings by excusing offenders' unrepentance in terms of defective personality or low intelligence. This degradation of status helps supervisors to rationalise and explain their subsequent actions (in not initiating breach proceedings against offenders) in the sense that offenders require help or pity, not punishment. For example, the case of offender A offers a clear illustration of how that process works (cf. Vass, 1984: 159).

> *Case 1*   A came for interview. He is a lad of medium height and build with dark bushy hair. He is of pale complexion and has dark eyes of 'wild appearance' and tends to look permanently unshaven. It was clear from the commencement of his order that he was a 'lost soul' and would need extra vigilance . . . His work has deteriorated and he has begun to work rather spasmodically and it is obvious that he will require supervision for the remainder of his order . . . As he is of poor intelligence, it would be difficult to say just how effective this will be in helping him to face reality.

In retrospect, the interview, where possible, is not allowed to become coercive enough to create schisms between the two parties. Any discomfort produced by the face-to-face interaction is quickly countered by resort to anecdotes or by dropping or replacing language codes which are found too formal or coercive in order to establish the appropriate and desirable type of response on a more informal level of information exchange. The interview can be both abrasive and patronising but at the same time supportive to offenders. For supervisors, a successful negotiation of their differences with offenders means personal feelings of worthiness (in the sense that they have helped someone in need, and practised their counselling skills) and offers them a welcome reprieve from formally having to replace their role of probation officers with that of prosecutors (see Vass, 1980, 1984). For offenders, the interview and its successful negotiation means a reprieve from pending court proceedings.

Breach proceedings

In the main, supervisors use prosecutions as a last resort. They only activate their legal powers when every alternative way of enforcing the order has been exhausted. Prosecution of defaulters is not initiated necessarily because of breach of requirements, but, rather, because the act is measured against the overall attitude of offenders towards their supervisors, and in particular how far they retain or violate the code of conduct governing their relationships. When supervisors begin to experience an erosion of their authority, feelings of discontent and loss of self-esteem, they resort to breach proceedings against offenders who seemingly pose a threat to the organisation of community service and the fraternisation process between supervisors and offenders.

However, even at this stage of the enforcement process, supervisors are searching for mitigating circumstances (such as personal, inter-personal, familial, or other reasons) which could be usefully employed to explain offenders' failure to respond to requirements. In most cases, supervisors do not resort to breach proceedings as a means of excluding, rejecting or ejecting offenders from the social organisation of community service. When they do occur, prosecutions are in the main 'disciplinary'. Supervisors prosecute but their action is intended as a sharp reprimand or reminder to offenders of their standing obligations. Far from being coercive, supervisors still aim at accom-modating offenders and in so doing they resolve some of their own personal and professional dilemmas, such as seeing the process of breach proceedings as being antithetical to their personal and organisational culture of 'social work' (cf. Vass, 1980, 1986a, 1988a; Vass and Menzies, 1989). But there are also other reasons why supervisors try to avoid or postpone breach proceedings and still find ways of negotiating differences with offenders. For instance, the law itself as well as courts allow and encourage flexibility in the encounters between supervisors and offenders. The law is ambiguous and allows supervising officers considerable powers of discretion in the way in which they manage community service. The onus is on officers to prove guilt by resort to the argument that offenders do not offer 'reasonable excuses' (Powers of Criminal Courts Act 1973, Section 16(3)). In effect, what this really means is that supervising officers are expected to allow the law to be broken on a number of occasions and to gather evidence before breach is proved. Also, prosecution of defaulters is an expensive and arduous process involving time, resources, gathering of information, and finding witnesses where necessary. The problem of witnesses is of particular significance here. Credible witnesses are usually drawn from the ranks of employees, such as sessional supervisors, or from recipients of the service. However, this process is resisted as far as possible because of its obvious implications. It is one matter to employ sessional staff to assist in the organisation of community service, and another to use them as witnesses for the prosecution. It is one matter to ask community organisations, individuals or groups to offer work for offenders serving under a community service order, and another to allow or force those recipients to be caught up in the alien business (for them) of breach proceedings. Such action runs the risk of leading to unwarranted publicity, and creating less cooperative sessional supervisors and recipients of the service. These and other personal and organisational pressures make the choice of avoiding or delaying breach proceedings an end in itself.

In sum, the act of controlling offenders by alternative and less authoritative means — the letter, the visit and the interview — helps to postpone or in most cases immobilise the process of administering formal sanctions by courts. Those alternative modes of control create for participants in the context of community service a sense of security, and in that respect they are seen by such participants as rational and legitimate means in organising their relationships around the common goal of successful completion of the court order.

National standards for community service orders

In an attempt to regulate the way in which the community service is enforced and to limit discretion, the Home Office has drawn up national standards for the operation of community service orders (Home Office, 1988i). The statutory rules, which took effect from April 1989, focus on the following main areas of concern:

1 *Making the order appear harsh punishment.* Thus, every offender serving an order of 60 hours or more should spend at least 21 hours in a group placement. People who are physically or mentally unsuited to work in a group, who might disrupt work or be a bad influence, those who need to travel at least two hours in each direction in order to attend a group placement, and those who have special domestic responsibilities (for upbringing of children for example) and need to travel at least one hour in each direction in order to attend a group placement, are exempted.

2 *Exercising more control over offenders' choices and structuring working arrangements.* Community service should not be performed at the convenience of offenders. Offenders must be given clear instructions and a leaflet which sets out the requirements of the order. They must attend for the first work session within 10 days of notification of the order being received by the probation service unless there are legitimate delays or because of offenders' health or other exceptional circumstances. Community service schemes should aim to ensure a work rate of a minimum of five hours per week throughout the order. Generally no offenders should be allowed to work more than 21 hours in a week, unless previous absences make this necessary to complete the order within 12 months. Only work done at the time and place specified counts towards the community service order. Offenders who report for

work without an appointment should not be allowed to work. Travelling time does not count towards the completion of an order, except when offenders are travelling under the supervision of community service staff (see Vass, 1984, for an appreciation of this issue and its effects on the hours credited to offenders). In addition to other requirements, lunch breaks which count towards the completion of an order must not last longer than half an hour. If other breaks are allowed, these must not last longer than ten minutes and any excess should not be counted towards completion of an order. Offenders should not be allowed to leave the site unless authorised to do so by the supervising officer. In bad weather, which may necessitate cancellation of work, no more than one hour can be credited to the work record of offenders for any one session, for time lost.

3   *Enforcing discipline and required standards of work.* If offenders fail to meet the stated required standards of performance and behaviour, the reasons for that should be identified, and those offenders should be warned of the possible consequences. If unsatisfactory work or behaviour continues, offenders should be reported and be liable to be sent home, and treated as if they had failed to attend (including forfeiture of any hours worked on that day). If offenders are late in arriving for work without a reasonable excuse, they are liable to be sent home and a failure to attend should be recorded. Those who are more than half an hour late, without a reasonable excuse, should not be allowed to work on that day. When offenders fail to attend work appointments or behave or work unsatisfactorily, action by supervising officers should be taken within two days. First, an explanation must be sought for each failure to comply with the requirements of the order. Secondly, action taken must be recorded. Thirdly, the offenders' explanation for those failures to comply with the requirements of the order must be recorded as either acceptable or unacceptable. Fourthly, if explanations are accepted, that choice must be clarified. Acceptable reasons for failure to attend are medical grounds, family or religious responsibilities, requirements of usual paid employment and educational or training commitments, and circumstances beyond the control of offenders. Where medical reasons are accepted, these must be supported by a certificate signed by a doctor. If frequent absences are recorded on grounds of ill-health, further evidence should be obtained about offenders' state of health, and if necessary by requiring offenders to undergo an independent medical examination at the expense of the probation service.

After the first instance of a failure to attend or unsatisfactory performance without an acceptable explanation, offenders should either be taken to court or be warned in writing that further breaches of the order will make them liable to court proceedings. After the second such instance, the case should be referred to the senior probation officer who must decide the next appropriate action. Breach proceedings should normally be started following no more than three instances of unacceptable absence, work or behaviour.

Conclusion

Whether the national standards will work or their requirements will be followed and enforced by supervising officers is an open question. I deal with this matter, the rationale of those statutory rules, and their possible consequences in Chapter 7.

However, as the effect of those statutory rules will not be known for some time and until there is more empirical work on the subject, the preceding discussion should be regarded as a factual representation of current activity. The introduction of the statutory rules by the Home Office, and the latter's determination to structure activity, is a direct recognition and confirmation of the validity of the findings reported in this chapter and the reliability of the analysis.

In sum, in this brief account of the interactions between supervisors and offenders in the context of community service, I have attempted to show that in organising and enforcing this alternative to custody, supervisors play a crucial role in the process of defining and determining, among other issues, the outcomes of their supervision of offenders. In advocating alternative means of control to either supplement or supersede the authoritative sanctions installed by law, officers evolve a screening process which is characterised by a degree of *tolerance* for technical infractions of the law. This principle of tolerance remains operative, for the majority of offenders, at the *cautioning* level without advancing against such offenders any special or severe penalties. By expanding the sanctions and scaling them against a background of pressures, officers manage to determine the rate of successful completions of orders. This process indirectly promotes in public the value of community service as an effective penal measure, and in private protects many offenders from re-entering the criminal justice system as defaulters of their order. In essence, that tolerance expressed by those officers and their elastic responses to infractions of the order, may be *instrumental in expanding the opportunities open to offenders to remain in the community and outside the walls of prison establishments*. In other words, by using formal sanctions as a last resort and focusing instead on methods which allow a protracted process of negotiation, those officers may in fact, without realising it, be promoting the basic and fundamental justification for providing and running *alternatives* to custody. In some circles (for instance overzealous politicians or managers of the probation service who are divorced from practice) this tolerance, informal exchanges, and means of enforcing an order may appear to represent an abdication of professional responsibility and an attempt to downgrade or indeed violate the spirit of the court order. They are quite wrong. What is happening in community service, in an unofficial capacity, is not so different to the officially promoted and condoned policy of 'police cautioning' of juveniles in an attempt to divert them from courts. Hard as it may seem, tolerance of some rule-breaking, and, overall, some discretion and elasticity in the way offenders are treated, are necessary and integral parts of the administration, organisation and enforcement of laws; for the preservation of stability in social relationships; and for keeping prison populations down. The statutory rules discussed earlier are in contradiction to that principle of tolerance and if successful in their aims, they may well structure community service but they will not destructure the prison.

Note

1 'Supervising officers' refers to both probation officers and unqualified staff (ancillaries) employed to administer and enforce the order. For a detailed analysis of the social structure of community service, how the different social groups involved in it relate to each other, and what their main tasks and duties are, see Vass (1984, 1988a; Vass and Menzies, 1989).

6 Probation day centres as an alternative to custody

The objective of this chapter is to consider and examine another alternative to custody to offer further understanding of the way in which alternatives to custody may take different shapes and forms, and what role they play in the criminal justice system. In addition, I focus on this second type of alternative in the hope of informing others about an area of practice which is still relatively new; and whose future, though it remains unknown and unpredictable (Bottoms, 1987: 195), promises further expansion as it falls within the government's policy of 'punishment in the community' (see Chapter 2; Home Office, 1988c). The discussion is based on various findings and views about probation day centres (hereafter 'day centres') and the local experiences of a day centre as defined under the provisions of the Criminal Justice Act 1982, Schedule XI 4(B).[1]

Background to day centres

'Probation with special conditions' usually sparks a very lively if not heated discussion on issues of 'care and control'. The word 'conditions' has become a buzzword which triggers a negative signal which in turn sets off a reflex response from your audience. Before you know it, you may even be accused of espousing a philosophy of punishment and surveillance and attempting to poison the social work roots of the probation service. This may sound far-fetched or mildly anecdotal, but the introduction of day centres has not been an easy and smooth affair. Day centres have led to suspicion and fear among many probation officers that the service is experiencing a drift towards tougher community penal measures which could force on to it new methods of working with offenders which contradict its basic social character and culture as a social work agency. That is to say, the fear has been that compassion for clients could change into aggressive enforcement and control of their lives. Thus, instead of working *with* offenders (denoting choice, togetherness, negotiation, and allowing some power to 'clients') the concern has been that probation officers would have to adopt new ways of working *against* offenders.

These fears are not imaginary, nor are they the product of the probation officers' own 'deviant imagination'. Their inner suspicions and private fears were given an outlet and were reinforced by academics and practitioners who contributed to the debate in the early 1980s and who wrote or spoke publicly on the 'changing functions of the probation service' (Vass, 1985). These changing functions assumed, in the late 1970s and early 1980s, a new significance in that they were perceived to be drifting into more overt and refined areas of control, establishing the probation service as another policing institution in disguise (cf. Drakeford, 1983; Griffiths, 1982; Jordan, 1983; Lacey et al., 1983; Vass, 1982a; Willis, 1983). For example, in response to a particular early 'experiment', Kent's controversial Close Support Unit, for juveniles, and the Probation Control Unit, for adults, which brought the debate about care and control to the fore (cf. Ely et al., 1983, 1987; Kent Probation Service, 1983; Ralphs, 1986), the National Association of Probation Officers at their Annual General Meeting in 1981, stated its opposition to the units as contradicting the basic values of the service. Instead, it called for more money for the expansion of day centres which centred on the principle of voluntarism, compassion and help. In the context of that Annual General Meeting, the Association stated its opposition to the enforced and structured requirements characteristic of the Kent units thus:

> This AGM opposes practices which increase the control and surveillance role of the Probation Service, and calls for changes in the law to prevent such developments. In particular, the close support probation and control unit in Kent are examples of developments which necessitate clients degrading themselves by relinquishing normal rights as citizens. This AGM believes that existing alternatives such as Day Training Centres and voluntary Day Centres have already begun the task of diverting offenders from custody. Therefore, this Association calls for the provision of extra resources for Day Centres and other alternatives at attempting to promote change for the benefit of both clients and society through willing co-operation. Accordingly, it calls upon members not to co-operate with such practices as the close support and control unit and to inform the Association of developments in this area throughout the country.

Vanstone (1985: 21-2) captured those concerns expressed above when he wrote about day centres and the general climate of opinion at the time: 'Are day centres to be the probation service's "big guns" in the march towards "getting tough" and increased state coercion or are they to be concerned with the setting up of a social environment and a pattern of incarceration in which relevant helping programmes can be offered in response to client choice?'

The reply has yet to come. For at present the same concerns are expressed (see for instance Chapter 4 on the reactions to tagging) and although in public pronouncements there appears to be some unity between Chief Officers of Probation, Senior Probation Officers, and the National Association of Probation Officers, there are clear divisions among and within each group to the new types of tasks expected of the service (cf. Edwards, 1987; Griffiths, 1982; Lacey et al., 1983; Scarborough et al., 1987; Ralphs, 1986; Spencer and Edwards, 1986; Vanstone, 1985). Edwards (1987), for instance, calls for change, but is critical of the new directions in penal policy, for they are taking probation into the wrong type of work. He calls for a crusade to keep the service independent and at the same time to defend itself against two related enemies: a repressive society, and attempts to push probation into becoming part and parcel of that repressive system. Edwards (1987: 82) writes:

> The Probation Service has to operate in a society which feels more repressive and where climate of opinion appears to be against a humanitarian approach to crime and offenders . . . Whilst we need to continue to try to contribute to the reduction of the prison population by the ways in which we work with courts — and particularly what we offer in terms of the simple probation order — there is also a need to try to tackle at every opportunity the sentencing climate which is an over-punitive one . . . There is a desire to see all the agencies and institutions in the criminal justice system working more closely together and whilst this has many positives it is very necessary that the Service retains its separate and distinct identity and particularly that we resist any moves to establish us as a community correctional agency.

On the other hand, Griffiths (1982) and to a lesser extent Ralphs (1986), though recognising the challenge, see more structure and new methods of working with offenders in the community as a way forward. Lacey et al. (1983) and Vass (1982a) are quite scathing about Griffiths's call for the probation service to develop a 'powerful sense of purpose' by seeing itself within the criminal justice system as a system of unadulterated punishment, and where 'containment would become the unambiguous objective of supervision' (Griffiths, 1982: 514). Lacey et al. (1983), in a challenging mood, bombard Griffiths with three sermons about what the values of the probation service are and should remain. All three sermons come down to the point that the probation service exists to help clients at the personal level (as they are victims of an unequal and oppressive society) and to assist those clients by acting as a social change agent, thus promoting structural changes in society. Lacey et al. (1983: 120) state:

> People matter. At their highest they are capable of sublimity, creativity and spontaneity; at their lowest, they can be mechanistic, measurable and amenable to containment, often the result of constraints, both biological and structural, which do not encourage the realisation of their true potential. Probation Officers are in the business of developing, not

containing, human potential. They do have a special focus for their work which is that wrongs must be righted and grievances remedied. The practical expression of their belief that people matter is to help in making good the harm that has been done.

It is not clear how this concern and debate has arisen, particularly with respect to offenders being required to attend a day centre as an alternative to custody where, according to one view, they are subjected to pressure and control, while from another perspective they are offered help, assistance, structure in their lives, 'life skills', and a reprieve from the ravaging effects of imprisonment. It is not possible to pinpoint the exact period in which the idea took off as a viable proposition and may not even be useful, for our purposes, to attempt such a lengthy task. However, a brief reference to the possible origins of day centres in England may help to put current developments in context.

The first time the idea of a 'training centre' which could operate for several evenings a week over a specified period offering boys aged 12 to 19 counselling, education and skills was proposed by the Magistrates' Association in their submission to the Advisory Council on the Treatment of Offenders in 1961. They did not recommend acceptance of the proposal. A slightly modified proposal was put by the Magistrates' Association to the Advisory Council on the Penal System (Wootton Committee) in 1970. At the same time, Priestley (1970: 3), in discussing the problems of short-term prisoners and ways of keeping them in the community, suggested that they are placed on 'probation with a condition that they attend as directed at a non-residential Community Training Centre'. Although this idea was already somewhat in operation by the creation of voluntary centres (for instance, the Barbican in Gloucester and Sherbourne House in London, cf. Vanstone, 1985: 22), such centres lacked statutory powers. On consideration of the proposals, reservations were raised by the Advisory Council on the Penal System mainly on the grounds that there would be problems in finding 'suitable premises', and that there would be a problem in finding well-trained people to supervise such centres. In addition, the Advisory Council expressed doubts about the 'applicability of non-custodial training . . . to offenders aged 17 and over' (Advisory Council on the Penal System, 1970: 41). However, they did recommend that if resources could be found for 'experiments in this direction' to aim 'for centres providing extra-mural activities as well as indoor training', combined with 'periodic detention work' on the lines of the New Zealand 'periodic detention work centres' (Advisory Council on the Penal System, 1970: 41, 54). The recommendations of the Advisory Council were not enacted but in their place the government introduced a new condition under a probation order, attendance at a 'day training centre' which not only provided a new approach to dealing with offenders in the community, but also legitimated the existing voluntary and informal practices.

Probation with special statutory conditions requiring offenders to attend at a day centre was introduced under section 20 of the Criminal Justice Act 1972. The aim was to offer training in social and personal skills to certain types of offenders (such as the unemployed) on a daily basis for up to 60 working days. The intention was that these probation orders with day training centre provisions would act as a diversionary penal measure for socially inadequate and petty offenders. Indeed, the intentions of the scheme were made quite clear in the course of parliamentary debates on the subject. *Hansard* (HC. Standing Committee G, 10 February 1972, Col. 533), states what sort of offender would be diverted from custody through attendance at a day centre: 'the socially inadequate petty recidivist — the sort of person with a bad work record, who repeatedly returns to prison for minor crimes and [is] basically socially incapable, when left on his own, of coping in society without getting involved in petty crime.'

The establishment of day training centres left too much to the imagination of the probation service in terms of the focus of work, means and ends. Unsurprisingly, this ambivalence and lack of direction (not an unusual feature of criminal justice intentions or legislation, cf. Lewis and Mair, 1988; Vass, 1984, 1986a; Young, 1979) permeated into the workings of the four experimental projects set up to test the viability of the measure. Four day training centres were set up in Liverpool, London, Sheffield and Pontypridd, initially for an experimental period of two years but they remained in existence, in that state of experimental status, for nine years. The Home Office monitoring exercise (whose findings have never been fully presented) revealed considerable differences in the activities and programmes offered by the four centres. For instance, the Sheffield centre put more emphasis on educational issues and its programmes reflected that by trying to train offenders in 'life skills'. The Inner London centre was geared to a more therapeutic model in an effort to work at character formation, leading to self-knowledge, social relations and acceptable behaviour. In Pontypridd, the emphasis was more on expressive and analytic techniques and less on practical skills. Finally, in Liverpool the centre preferred a structured programme based on contracts which were rooted in behaviour modification techniques (Payne, 1977). Referrals proved to be unreliable and erratic partly because of lack of knowledge among probation officers about the purpose of those centres, and partly because of their resistance (as at present, cf. Bullock and Tidesley, 1984) to conditions attached to probation orders (Smith, 1982; Vanstone, 1985). On the other hand, the take-up rate of recommendations made to courts was, according to Smith (1982: 35), quite promising. As an illustration, Table 6.1 shows total referrals, offenders 'screened' and found suitable, and the take-up rate by courts.

Table 6.1 *Offenders referred to day training centres, number found suitable and take-up rate by courts from 1972 to 1975*

Centre	Referrals	Offenders found suitable		Take-up rate	
		No.	%	No.	%
Sheffield	209	146	70	103	71
Pontypridd	106	96	91	78	87
Liverpool	185	131	71	111	85
Inner London	226	143	63	128	90

Source: table constructed from figures supplied in Smith (1982: 35).

The trainees, whose average age was 19 in Liverpool and 28 in other areas, were persistent offenders, with an average (median) number of previous convictions ranging from 6 in Liverpool to 12 in London. The 'mean range of previous custodial sentences [varied] from just over two in Liverpool to just over six in London' (Smith, 1982: 36).

Interestingly, in terms of referrals to courts with a recommendation by probation officers for the making of a probation order with day training centre provisions, the main justification offered by courts for not fully accepting all recommendations was that they 'judged that a custodial sentence was more appropriate and/or necessary' in those cases than probation with day training centre conditions (Smith, 1982: 36). This could imply two things. First, that those given orders were indeed high up the penal tariff and therefore the making of a day training centre order implied a true diversion from custody. Also, it suggests that if courts accepted all recommendations the rate of diversion would be genuine as we already know that the majority of those who were refused probation with day training centre requirements were subsequently incarcerated. Secondly, the interpretation could be less complimentary. Courts diverted individuals who would not have been given custodial sentences in the first instance and effectively refused to divert those who faced a real risk of custody and who, in the end, did receive a custodial sentence. However, according to interpretations reached by researchers and commentators on the workings of day training centres, despite the differences in means recorded earlier, day training centres appeared to focus on people who ran the risk of imprisonment (Fairhead and Wilkinson-Grey, 1981; Vanstone and Raynor, 1981). Indeed, Vanstone and Raynor (1981) suggested that day centres appeared to fare better than the community service order as an alternative to custody. Whereas the community service order's intention to divert was neutralised by the emphasis on less serious offenders, in contrast, the authors argued, day centres catered for deep end offenders.

Contrary to expectation or criticism that day training centres would dehumanise their subjects and remove their basic rights as citizens, trainees appeared to express the view that they benefited from the experience and 'reported [that] personal problems diminished over the training period' (Smith, 1982: 36). However, there were problems of attendance and recidivism. According to Smith (1982) the 'drop-out' rate varied between 10 and 26 percent. This was mainly due to further offending, illness, or non-compliance with attendance and requirements. Between 7 and 20 percent of trainees reoffended during the 60-day period of attendance, most offences being against property (theft and burglary the most common). One year reconviction rates varied between 40 and 65 percent. These problems and others (cf. Bottoms, 1987: 194), particularly their high operational costs, meant that these day training centres remained more at the level of intention and experimentation than reality. As I have suggested in previous chapters, the idea that alternatives to custody are cheap, or cheaper than institutions, or that they all share similar low costs, is not particularly convincing. In the case of day training centres, their operational costs almost equalled those of a prison. Therefore, centres operating below full capacity were unattractive to the government. Smith (1982: 37) states:

> The nature of the intensive training provided has necessarily involved a high staff-client ratio and also the provision of special premises; hence DTCs have proved to be expensive when compared with other non-custodial disposals. In 1980 each 60 day order cost from three to seven times the cost of a probation order running for a full year and from four to ten times the cost of a community service order for a full year. In 1981 the cost of a completed 60 day attendance was £1250 at the most economically run centre and £3000 (nearly as expensive as the cost of imprisonment) at the most expensive.

In those circumstances, the case for expanding the experiment and establishing it on a nationwide basis was not very strong. Nonetheless, despite the failure of the experiments and reservations about their ability to offer effective 'treatment', as well as the growing suspicions of probation officers, the experience of offering something more than just individual 'supervision' led to change. It became apparent that by converting day training centres into just 'day centres', offering more flexibility to different types of clients and more choices to courts, the service could begin to innovate new and exciting ways of working with offenders. The experiences arising from day training centres prompted the probation service in many areas to begin to introduce a number of complementary, non-statutory (though at the time thinking that they were statutory) day centre facilities to probation under various 'titles, with various aims, styles of operation and management structures . . . some emerging almost spontaneously and others after long deliberations' (Fairhead and Wilkinson-Grey, 1981: 1). According to Hil (1982), by 1979 there was some sort of day care provision in 28 out of all 56 probation areas in England and that in the latter part of 1979 new centres were mushrooming at the rate of one a month (Burney, 1980). These day centres were found to have diverse aims and objectives: as alternatives to custody; alternatives to traditional probation methods; training centres for the 'employability' of offenders; educational centres; and as centres for the resocialisation of offenders where they would be helped to recognise personal failures, redefine their relationships, and accept responsibility for their actions. In short, they were to be taught how to conform to society's expectations. Day centres were also seen as offering containment — they were there to provide users with a place to be, thus limiting their opportunities for committing crimes while wandering aimlessly outside on the streets. The conclusion reached by the Home Office researchers (Fairhead and Wilkinson-Grey, 1981: 26) who enquired into these developments was that:

> day centres can constitute a direct alternative to prison, perhaps via statutory orders, where a structured and formal programme is possible. This may often be regarded as appropriate in dealing with younger offenders and others who have maintained their place in the community. There is also an important role for day centres in keeping persistent petty offenders out of prison, although it is an indirect effect and one which the courts may not immediately recognise.

Given these intentions, probation areas began to offer day centre activities as alternatives to custody and courts began to add new requirements to probation orders. Hil (1982), in his study of one such day centre, Centre 81, on the outskirts of Southampton city centre, finds that clients in general 'felt that the centre had at least taught them to control and develop aspects of their social behaviour' (Hil, 1982: 39). He quotes one 'former borstal inmate' as saying (Hil, 1982: 39): 'I've learnt to be a bit more patient and to talk to people. I don't fly off the handle anymore . . . That might help me to keep out of trouble . . . who knows? Once I leave here I'm in a different world — the world of the streets and unemployment.'

Hil argues that despite the feeling that the day centre may have helped to 'suspend rather than displace a life "on the streets"', most clients saw the centre as a positive development and described officers as 'caring', 'warm' and 'friendly'. Some saw the centre as a convenient means of control but in contrast with the experience in a custodial establishment, the day centre was rated as a place where something useful and constructive was on offer and where there was always someone to 'talk to', and 'help'. In addition, they placed importance on the centre's capacity to allow them to experience punishment but still be treated 'with dignity as individuals'. One of Hil's respondents, with seven years prison experience, is quoted as saying (Hil, 1982: 39): 'When I came to the centre I began to feel like an individual, a person people were prepared to listen to and take seriously . . . That's a novelty I can tell you . . . In prison I was a number and nothing but a "trouble maker" . . . No-one ever cared or bothered about you . . .'.

These comments may suggest satisfaction or preference in comparison with the experiences of imprisonment, but one must not accept such statements without some caution. For example, as I found in my study of community service orders (Vass, 1984), comments are usually linked to some instrumental reason and occasionally they just fit the situation or context and are common rationalisations of one's position in a social structure. Just to offer an illustration of how the context and the structure may force people to make exactly contradictory statements, is the finding from another study of prisoners' perceptions of the prison disciplinary system (Ditchfield and Duncan, 1987). These authors find that prisoners, when given a choice, do not ask for alternatives but want more privileges and improved conditions in prisons, not outside.

With regard to the question of whether the day centre worked as an alternative to custody, Hil (1982) is less optimistic, though later (Hil, 1986) does appear to modify his views and suggest that they may after all be working, as alternatives. In his earlier article he states (Hil, 1982: 39): 'the impact [of day centres] in terms of actually diverting offenders is negligible. Indeed, it is difficult to estimate how many of the 5000 or so offenders in day care would have gone to prison had day care not been available.' Although Hil may draw attention to the problematic nature of knowing what is an alternative and how exactly one can measure the rate of diversion if any, he does not offer any explanation as to how he had reached his conclusion, first with regard to his case study, and secondly, and more seriously, with regard to his *generalisation* about *all* centres. This is exactly the point I have made earlier, in Chapter 4, about generalising from the very specific (particularly when data on a particular case or example are also limited in scope and depth) to more global interpretations and conclusions.

One particular example of day centre activity which attracted attention and controversy was the Kent Close Support Unit and the Probation Control Unit which operated between 1979 and 1984. The first catered for juveniles. It was a co-joint venture with Kent Social Services which funded the project and probation officers organised and supervised activities. The project, which ended in 1984, partly due to financial reasons, political pressure, and falling numbers of referrals as the number of juveniles prosecuted in the Medway towns declined, was aimed at young people of 14 to 17 years of age (Kent Probation Service, 1983). The Close Support Unit provided a programme of 90 days Intermediate Treatment of 12 hours' supervision per day for five days a week, and involved, in addition, community work tasks from 9am to 4pm on Saturdays. Furthermore, each evening, following return home after 9pm, trainees had to remain under 'orders of curfew' until the next morning. A member of the Unit staff would telephone parents or guardians to check their safe arrival, and investigate failure to abide by requirements with an immediate visit or search. Staff also made random checks and visits to homes (about once a week) to see that 'curfews' were observed by both parents and trainees. During term time, daily contacts between Unit staff and schools discouraged absconding. Finally, local magistrates were also involved in the Unit by monitoring progress (Ely et al., 1983, 1987). The Probation Control Unit shared a similar structured environment and catered for adults and was absorbed, that is the title was dropped (though not necessarily the methods, see Spencer and Edwards, 1986), into the general day centre programme available within the county from January 1986.

The main concept of the Close Support and Probation Control Unit was that 'for serious offenders more structure was required but within that structure the activities should be positive, and as far as possible within a group setting, focused on the individual' (Ralphs, 1986: 154). According to Ralphs, the then Chief Probation Officer of Kent, the regime of the Unit was highly structured in order to convince the courts that 'the probation service meant business' and to 'take those [offenders] who would need structure to hold them in the community without offending'. It was this structure and emphasis on control and surveillance which embroiled the Kent Unit in controversy. On the one hand, there was a suspicion expressed by some people that the Kent Unit was 'all talk but no action': that is to say, the regime, in its private domain, was not coercive or rigid. On the other, it was alleged that its operations mistreated offenders' human rights, that it was a 'day prison' and that it symbolised 'the unacceptable deprivation of liberty' (Ralphs, 1986: 155). Ely et al. (1983) investigated the effect of the availability of the Unit on the courts' sentencing trends in the five years before the Unit was established with developments in the three subsequent years after operation. Although not clear from the reported findings what type of scales and other measures were used to compare trends, the team reported thus (Ely et al., 1983: 43): 'custodial sentences declined proportionately by some 50 percent compared with the level obtaining before the Unit was established. Magistrates and Clerks indicated, however, that they had considerable difficulty in considering the Unit only as an alternative to custody . . . The Court would have preferred to use the Unit more extensively as a sentence in its own right.'

In the team's view, offenders placed in the Unit would have gone into custody or care if that alternative disposal had not been available. Thus it would appear, given this limited information, that the Unit met its primary aim of diverting high-risk offenders in danger of going into custody. However, its other main and basic aim of stopping offending and keeping offenders out of trouble was not met. There was no evidence that the centre decreased reoffending after termination of orders (Ely et al., 1983; Ralphs, 1986). Indeed, despite the assumed rigid structure and surveillance, nearly a quarter of trainees had reoffended during the programme (Ely et al., 1987). In keeping with predictions that the more rigid and coercive the structure, the more the antagonism from clients, as demonstrated in various studies including research on the community service order (Vass, 1984), Ely et al. find that considerable disruption and troublesome behaviour was manifest (from their participant observation) in the Unit. The authors write (Ely et al. 1983: 43–4):

> Virtually full attendance at school, work, or the Unit was maintained in all cases save one. Proceedings for breach of supervision order were only taken for one boy, suggesting that the problem of keeping order within the project was not such as to inflate the numbers receiving a more serious sentence, as has happened with 'alternatives' elsewhere ... But bad behaviour in the Unit probably influenced the bench in dealing with re-offenders . . . Some 23 percent of trainees re-offended during the ninety-days' period, though only a small proportion of these were then sentenced to custody.

In parallel with previous findings on the cost of day training centres, Ely et al. found the Unit to be quite expensive to run. Although cheaper on a daily basis than the cost of a detention centre order, over a full 90-day programme (allowing for the savings to accrue from remission of sentence for good behaviour in a detention centre which was not possible in the Unit), the Unit proved to cost more than a comparable detention centre order (Ely et al., 1983: 44, 1987).

The proliferation of day centre activity and the willingness of the probation service and courts to add day centre requirements to probation orders was challenged in the Court of Appeal. The activity was found to be unlawful (*Cullen v. Rogers 1982*). This led to impasse and confusion until day centres were legitimated in the same year under the provisions of the new Criminal Justice Act. Schedule XI 4(A) and 4(B) of the Criminal Justice Act 1982 gave a legal basis to the establishment of probation orders which could oblige offenders to participate in special activities at day centres for up to 60 days.

Under the provisions of the Act, such day centres must be approved by local probation committees; that courts know of the activities offered; and that offenders, as well as supervisors, consent to the requirements attached to the order. The two sections 4(A) and 4(B) refer basically to two types of probation orders with requirements: the former allows, as in the past, informal arrangements for or requirements on probationers or others (that is to say, considerable discretion is left to the probation officer to determine how the order should run); the second is a more formal and structured approach to requirements for probationers and where a court distinctly specifies attendance at a day centre. In general, therefore, the latter type of order is seen as a 'heavy end' alternative to custodial sentences.

Day centres in general

The probation service's entitlement, under the Criminal Justice Act 1982, to offer day centres, exemplified the notion that compulsory attendance at a day centre is deprivation of liberty of another kind based on 'leisure controls' and subject to further penalties including further curtailment of offenders' rights should they fail to comply with requirements. The legislation did little to suppress fears that the probation service was coming under political pressure to modify its methods of work and change its character from a social service to a policing institution. Even at the present time, the polarised debate over care and control has been continuing unabated. For instance, the Audit Commission (1989) has recently suggested that the probation service is not doing enough to promote the government's new policy to punish offenders in the community and thus reduce the prison population (Sharrock, 1989: 4). In response, the National Association of Probation Officers dismissed the findings of the Audit Commission as 'partial and simplistic'. As Vanstone (1985: 24) puts the case in respect of the role of day centres in this debate:

> In a ten year period there has been a shift from the situation in which day centre innovations occurred in an atmosphere of faith and liberal concern towards offenders who were experiencing social problems, to a situation in which day centres, it would be argued, are being set up as a response to the growing political pressure on the service to be seen to be containing offenders effectively.

The above concerns appear to be partially verified by Parker et al. (1987: 26). The authors analysed data from a national survey of the probation service and found that most of those who responded said that they 'had recently produced new or revised policy statements' to accord with current developments on the basis that new developments 'provide genuine opportunities for alternatives to custody'. At the same time, the same probation areas also viewed current developments with a jaundiced eye. They saw them as an unwelcome extension of their role as a community control agency through the practice of social work. Nonetheless, despite the concerns, including financial constraints and lack of adequate referrals from main grade officers, there has been a proliferation of day centre activity carried forward by a large measure of agreement between areas that day centres are 'high tariff disposals which are alternatives to custody, primarily for 17–25 year olds' (Parker et al., 1987: 34).

Thus by 1984, 3 percent of probation orders carried day centre provisions (Parker et al., 1987: 38). By 1987, nearly 5 percent of probation orders (n=42 216) had day centre conditions (Home Office, 1988h). However, are they acting as alternatives to custody? Parker et al. (1987) suggest that day centres may be another illustration (for instance, see the previous chapter on community service orders) of individual control shifting towards 'more collective forms of control' (cf. Mathiesen, 1983) directed particularly at the 'young, mainly male, unemployed offenders' (Parker et al., 1987: 41). Although the authors appear to be cautious in accepting the 'dispersal of discipline thesis' and offer examples of local projects which if used with care can be successful in reducing local custody rates (though they recognise that because projects are local their effect on the national custody rate is minimal), they argue that despite the expansion of day centres and other community packages, their chances of reducing the prison population are not good. They also appear to support the notion, as previously stated, that these new methods of containing offenders may increase the risk of 'social work agencies' engaging in more social control of their clients. Parker et al. (1987: 41) write: 'the prospects for cutting custody rates significantly are not good. The development of new community supervision packages in this context clearly runs the risk of involving social work agencies in the escalation of control particularly in relation to the younger unemployed. [But, they add] . . . this does not necessarily require the conclusion that the "new orders" should be totally resisted.' They should not be 'totally resisted' because despite their flaws, day centres may offer more benefits to certain types of offenders (particularly the unemployed) than traditional forms of casework (Parker et al., 1987: 41).

Hil (1986) and Vanstone (1986) support the above views, first in the sense that offenders, though critical of some aspects of day centre activity, in the main report positive experiences and a preference for day centres in comparison to other sanctions, particularly prison (see also Walker, 1987). Hil is sceptical about their effectiveness as alternatives to custody but writes that his account of the day centre is based 'on the informed assumption that offenders would probably be committed to custody if Day Centres did not exist, such facilities thereby serving as alternatives . . .' (Hil, 1986: 71). He then concludes (Hil, 1986: 90):

> Day Centres could become a credible and effective alternative to custody. For this to happen on a sufficiently wide scale, a financial investment comparable to that currently being made in the building of new prisons is needed. Moreover, on the ideological front, a campaign against the continuing use (and misuse) of prisons is needed, directed towards both sentencers and the public. Clearly a much more active championing of such alternatives is required of the probation service . . .

Vanstone (1986), however, in referring to the experiences of another day centre, is quite clear about the centres' position on the penal ladder. He writes that day centres can and are working as alternatives to custody. A study conducted by Willis (1979) on the Pontypridd day training centre (prior to the Criminal Justice Act 1982 and the subsequent reconstitution of those centres into 'day centres'), and comparisons with imprisoned offenders drawn from the national prison population, found that the possibility of imprisonment for those sent to the centre was high and that the centre did help to displace offenders from custody. Vanstone (1986) reinforces those findings and writes that the 'profile of the people who have attended the Centre since it was established' continues to be one of deep end offenders. Approximately 76 percent of offenders have six or more previous convictions and 81 percent have previous custodial experiences. In addition, where recommendations are made by probation officers for day centre activity and are not taken up by courts, custodial sentence is the result in the majority of cases.

In the most recent, and most detailed study of day centres to date, Mair (1988) reaches several conclusions about day centres and their place in the criminal justice system. Mair (1988) investigated 44 centres between 1986 and 1987 through questionnaires and case studies (visits to six centres which appeared to exhibit different characteristics). In his study, there were 867 offenders participating in the centres examined. Of those participants, 519 attended day centres under Schedule XI (4B) of the Criminal Justice Act 1982. Many variations are revealed by the study in terms of organisational and procedural matters which raise serious questions about consistency of operation and equitable treatment of offenders. Mair (1988: 31) concludes:

> The major conclusion of this study must be to emphasise the great differences which exist amongst day centres. It is clear that such disparities do not lead to equitable treatment for offenders; and they also raise serious issues concerning the efficiency, effectiveness and economy of day centres . . . [C]entres sprang up without any clear thought being given to aims and objectives, and how these might be realised in practice; with little consideration being given to the relationship between clientele, staffing,

aims, organisation, premises, and activities; without considering the inequities for clients of providing centres with differing hours, days of operation, and length of orders; and without considering the question what to do with employed offenders.

In terms of hours offenders are expected to attend, Mair's study shows that these may range from under 10 to over 41, with most of the day centres focusing on 21 to 40 hours. Allocation of resources differs from centre to centre. Involvement of professional staff is minimal, and as in the case of community service orders (cf. Vass, 1988a; Vass and Menzies, 1989) many of those who run activities are essentially probation ancillaries; others are hired or used 'purely on a sessional basis'; and quite a high number of volunteers are also employed in supervising activities.

As regards activities there appears to be little uniformity of operation and little consistency in the aims to be achieved through those activities. In effect activities appear to be justified in terms of often-idealistic and ambiguous aims: diverting offenders from custody; meeting clients' needs; breaking the cycle of offending; bringing clients into contact with non-offenders and the community in general; broadening 'horizons' and improving clients' skills. Despite the variation in activities, those activities tend to fall under major categories. Mair (1988: 11–12) writes:

> social/life skills (e.g. communication, self-image, relationships, offending behaviour), health/welfare activities (e.g. job search, DHSS benefits, health, alcohol, budgeting), art/craft work (e.g. art, pottery, woodwork, mechanics, gardening, cooking) and sport (football, weight-training, swimming). Such sessions are focused on specific topics, but there is also time spent on group social work and work with individuals. Visits can be made to places of interest, and this is one area where day centres differ from attendance centres, as at the latter offenders cannot be taken off the premises. At some centres lunch is part of the day, prepared by those attending the centre and taken communally. At most centres a few sessions are compulsory for all those attending as a result of a 4(B) order, and there is a degree of choice in other classes.

The study does not say much about the offender population but what it does say appears to support some of the worst fears of critics of alternatives to custody: that day centres assist in the expansion of the social control network and the inclusion of individuals who would previously not have been subject to those controls. Day centres appear to boost numbers of clients by absorbing not only those who are required to attend under a 4(B) order, but others too who are there on a voluntary basis and on the advice or direction of probation officers. Indeed, three day centres which were specifically set up to meet the requirements of the Criminal Justice Act 1982 were found to have no

4(B)s at all; and of all the centres examined, almost half of them had less than 50 percent of offenders who were there with a 4(B) order (Mair, 1988: 9–10).

Of those who attended day centres 43 percent were under the age of 21, and 41 percent were between 21 and 30. Male offenders comprised 94 percent of attenders; and 87 percent of all attenders were unemployed. Furthermore, out of the 519 (60 percent of all attenders at centres, n=867) attending under 4(B), only 3 percent were female; and overall, 4(B) offenders were younger than those attending on a voluntary basis: 88 percent of those subject to 4(B) conditions were under the age of 30, compared to 77 percent of voluntary attenders. In the main, the offences committed by these individuals were burglary and theft (together constituting 67 percent of all offences); followed by violence against the person (8 percent); motoring (7 percent); and criminal damage (4 percent). Few were there for drug or sexual offences. Mair suggests that the distribution of offences does not support the view that day centres are effective alternatives to custodial sentences (Mair, 1988: 16). However, this initial conclusion is counteracted by his analysis of previous offences committed by people attending day centres. This reveals that only 4 percent had no previous convictions (a significant figure when compared to, say, community service orders where on average about 12 percent of offenders are without previous convictions); that more than 41 percent had had a previous experience of custody; that 34 percent of those people had had six or more previous convictions (Mair, 1988: 16–17); and that those attending under 4(B) were much higher up the penological ladder in terms of previous criminal history than those attending voluntarily who were, in general, shallow end offenders. More than 50 percent of the 4(B)s had had a previous custodial sentence compared to 26 percent of the others. Indeed, over 40 percent of the 4(B)s had had six or more previous convictions compared to 21 percent of those attending voluntarily (Mair, 1988: 17). The analysis leads Mair (1988: 17) to conclude that:

> . . . day centres may indeed be playing a part as an alternative to custody for those who are given 4(B) orders. They may even be doing so more effectively than community service; in 1985 36 per cent of those commencing a community service order had had a previous custodial sentence (Probation Statistics, 1985), whereas this was the case for 51 per cent of offenders who had a 4(B) order.

Cedar Hall day centre: An illustration

The Cedar Hall Probation Day Centre of the Hertfordshire Probation Service operates under Schedule XI 4(B) of the Criminal Justice Act

1982. Before a probation order with a day centre requirement can be imposed, the Court needs the agreement of the offender and the probation service. The first step is a written referral form which should be completed by the referring probation officer in consultation with the offender. This referral is also accompanied by the most recent social inquiry report and details of previous convictions. The next stage is for the probation officer and the offender to attend Cedar Hall for an interview which lasts between 60 and 90 minutes. Basically, this process takes the form of an interview in a group situation with referring probation officers and staff from the project. Offenders are given direct information on the following:

1   What the probation order with specific requirements means and for how long they would be expected to attend at a day centre. This covers the terms of the order and clear information that offenders have to attend as directed. If unemployed (or doing casual work) they are expected to attend on three days a week for eight weeks. If they are in employment, they are expected to attend for three evenings for eight weeks. The pressures of such a busy schedule are emphasised and offenders are asked to consider the implications for themselves and with their partners, friends, parents and others before committing themselves.

2   Offenders are told why they are being considered under Schedule XI 4(B): that a court will only make the condition if in their case there is a high risk of imprisonment.

3   An explanation about the activities at the centre. A lot of time offenders will be in a room with other people who have also been in trouble, participating in specified structured or unstructured programmes. They are also told that they will be expected to participate in educational programmes and sport, that at times they will be working on their own in programmes specifically designed to suit their own needs and at other times doing things in groups. That they may have the chance to meet and discuss their experiences with magistrates, clerks to justices, drugs/alcohol workers, victims of crime, the police and others.

4   Inviting offenders to consider their own reasons for accepting or rejecting the option offered to attend at a day centre: if they are unsure or not willing to accept the need for change, they are advised not to agree to the condition.

5   A clear message about attendance on time and their participation in activities; that no violence is tolerated; that no drugs or alcohol or glue are allowed; that if they are confused or have problems they should discuss those matters with staff.

6   Finally that in the course of their attendance they receive food; help

in its preparation; carry out cleaning tasks; have their travelling expenses paid; that staff are there to offer them help, advice, and that it is up to them to offer themselves a chance to break out of their criminal careers.

Part of the assessment is to discuss and identify other viable penal options available to the court before an offender is considered for a 4(B) order. In that way the offender's risk of custody is put into context and what is more reasonable or appropriate is recommended. For that matter, as the emphasis is on consent and understanding of what is expected, offenders are not asked to decide at the initial interview whether they want to participate in the day centre, and generally would be expected to contact the referring probation officer the next day before committing themselves to a decision. In that way, offenders are given some choice and power in deciding their own options. Thus though the order becomes binding after acceptance and a contract whose violation may constitute a serious matter is set up, prior to that offenders have the opportunity to decide whether to enter that contract or to stay out.

As an illustration of that choice, in January 1987 to June 1988, 234 offenders were referred to Cedar Hall. Of these, 24 were not recommended as being suitable for the programme. The majority of these offenders actually turned down the day centre recommendation for they decided that they could not participate in those activities and indeed suggested that going to prison was an easier and often quicker solution to their predicament. This aspect of negotiation and the fact that offenders *are* given a chance to consider and reconsider their options shows that consent to a day centre attendance (though it may be part of the social engineering of authority — cf. Vass, 1984: ch. 3) can succeed in drawing a balance between care and control. It can also reconcile restrictions of liberty and perhaps civil rights with those of offering a chance to offenders to stay out of prison and receive help in their personal or interpersonal relationships. That is to say, the question of how offenders may be compelled to attend a day centre without curtailing some of their basic rights of knowing what the choices are can be answered by having a programme structure which involves 'a joint assessment process' which leads to understood choices for offenders — and thus some bargaining or compromises 'hammered out' (Vanstone, 1985: 26).

Activities: Structured and unstructured groups
The idea of participating in specified activities over a period of 60 days may sound an easy option. However, when translated into hours of work or attendance the true impact of that order on offenders' time

becomes evident. Even a comparatively short programme such as the one run by Cedar Hall — 24 days/nights spread over eight weeks — works out at 144 hours for the day and 72 for the night. Compared to a well-managed ordinary probation order where a probation officer may see a client for one hour a week — giving around 52 hours in a full year — the day centre activity places officers and offenders under a potentially 'heavy burden' for relatively long and highly intensive periods of activity. For staff that means they have to work long, as well as anti-social, hours; and spend much time in constant face-to-face interaction with offenders. Their conditions of service (in terms of career structure) are far from satisfactory, meaning that there are difficulties in recruiting probation officers on a voluntary basis and particularly seniors to organise activities. Those who do work in centres do so in conditions which can only be described as inadequate, and offer poorly maintained services which are financially starved of resources (cf. Parker et al., 1987: 33). In addition, they experience as do their colleagues in community service (cf. Menzies and Vass, 1989; Vass 1980, 1986a, 1988a; Vass and Menzies, 1989) marginality and isolation. This marginality leads them to experience status dilemmas and social conflicts with colleagues — ancillaries working in day centres and professional colleagues who remain detached from day centre activities.

As in community service, officers employed to run day centres and supervise offenders who are subject to a requirement to attend such centres are the poor relations of the service. Consequently, but not so evidently as in community service, the pressures create a demoralised force of employees who feel used and neglected by the service and its management. This leads to a high turnover of staff and, more seriously, to some industrial deviance in the course of enforcing conditions. As in community service, though again not so marked, there is some flexibility in the way offenders, particularly those who violate requirements (as by non-attendance) are treated. It is common that absences are deemed 'reasonable' or 'unreasonable', and decisions to prosecute defaulters are only taken as a last resort and not before other means (such as warning letters or interviews) are deployed to resolve differences. For offenders, a day centre means that they become the subject of 'leisure' controls and surveillance for a considerable number of hours per week and at the same time have to contend with the demands and expectations of officers and to participate in activities which occasionally may not be desirable or attractive to them. Indeed, when one compares the hours spent by offenders participating in specified activities in a day centre with work done under a community service order, the day centre expectation (in view of the intensity of the activities and the shorter time allowed for

Table 6.2 *Schedule XI day programme – Cedar Hall day centre*

	Monday	Tuesday	Wednesday
10.00 am	good news/bad news	good news/bad news	
10.15 am	unstructured session	unstructured session	
11.15 am	coffee	coffee	sport
11.30 am	focused session	focused session	
12.30 pm	lunch	lunch	lunch
	group prepare/cook and clear away	group prepare/cook and clear away	group prepare/cook and clear away
1.30 pm	focused session	focused session	focused session
2.45 pm	coffee	coffee	coffee
3.00 pm	focused session	focused session	focused session
	unstructured session	unstructured session	unstructured session
4.00 pm	end of programme		

Table 6.3 *Schedule XI evening programme – Cedar Hall day centre*

	Monday	Tuesday	Wednesday
6.00 pm	tea prepared by group	tea prepared by group	tea prepared by group
6.30 pm	focused session	focused session	focused session
7.30 pm	coffee	coffee	coffee
7.45 pm	focused session	focused session	focused session
8.30 pm	unstructured session	unstructured session	unstructured session
9.00 pm	end of programme		

completion of requirements) appears to impose much higher demands on participants than the community service order. Table 6.1 shows the distribution of activities in the day and Table 6.3 shows activities in the evenings.

The day programme, lasting for eight weeks and about 144 hours, starts at 10 am and finishes at 4pm. Once the programme starts, no new members are admitted until completion of the programme. The day begins with 'good news/bad news' where offenders' feelings are expressed before any other activities are allowed to take place. The intention behind this is to allow anyone with any burning personal or interpersonal issues to have them acknowledged or explored by the group; it also acts as a safety valve allowing anger or apprehension to be aired, thus helping offenders to concentrate on more focused educational activities later in the day.

Unstructured sessions provide an opportunity for the group members to focus either on events in their lives which they find hard to cope with or behaviours which have negative effects on their personal and interpersonal relationships. In this context, matters such as drugs, alcohol, offending and other related issues are discussed. Alternatively they are encouraged to express their emotions towards others in the group, and through giving and receiving feedback, they learn how to resolve conflicts in relationships without resort to violence; how to deal with anxiety and fear; sustain friendships; face the reality of their actions through challenges by other group members; and how to take responsibility for their actions.

Focused sessions largely provide participants with social skills education and are more intensive in that they look at specific areas of life or behaviour. In each programme there are specific sessions on: offending behaviour; risk and costs to offenders; the victims' perspective; authority, the courts, police and probation; dealing with emotions such as hate, love, violence; relationships — what goes wrong and why; drugs and their effects; alcohol and its effects; health education (for example contraception, AIDS, etc); sport, art or drama. In addition to these activities, specialist areas identified by offenders as being important to them receive attention, such as stress control and financial pressures.

Unfocused sessions are intended to offer flexibility, create the right environment for relaxed relationships and offer opportunities in consolidating the aims of the structured sessions.

Lunch is considered as part of the process of sharing and building trust. Staff and offenders take turns to prepare and clear away food. Often, in these in-between activities, offenders will seek out members of staff to confide in or ask for more personalised help.

Sport is used to introduce relaxation at the end of the week, to improve physical health and build confidence through association. In addition, it provides opportunities for informal personal and inter-personal counselling.

The evening programme is predominantly for offenders who are in employment. The 8-week programme involves them in 72 hours of group work. The various activities follow the aims and patterns of the day programme, though discussions and activities are organised to take account of the shorter length of time available.

Referrals, outcomes and diversion from custody

Between January 1987 and June 1988, there were 234 referrals to the day centre. Of these 24 (10 percent) failed to attend for interview or turned down the option; 24 (10 percent) were found unsuitable and an alternative sanction was recommended. In total, 186 (80 percent of referrals) were accepted for day centre training as a condition of their probation order. The take-up rate of those recommendations by the courts was 41 percent ($n=77$). In the same period, 53 of those offenders (69 percent) successfully completed their day centre requirements; 13

(18 percent) were prosecuted for breach of their requirements; 4 (5 percent) were taken into custody for other offences after starting the programme; and 7 (9 percent) had their conditions suspended pending amendments to the probation order, or for a postponement of starting date.

In terms of recidivism, the picture is not better or worse than any other penal measure. According to available information to November 1988, of the 53 offenders who completed programmes between January 1987 and June 1988, 29 (54 percent) had not reoffended; the 24 offenders who had reoffended either had been processed through the courts or were, at the time, awaiting trial. This finding that day centres do not appear to reduce or change criminal behaviour is a general feature recognised in other research studies (see for instance Ely et al., 1983, 1987; Mair, 1988; Ralphs, 1986; Vanstone, 1985, 1986). Indeed, Vanstone (1986: 104) suggests that 'Any claims about the effectiveness of the programme for changing criminal behaviour must be treated with caution'.

This realisation that centres do not decrease reoffending, particularly after termination of orders, prompted Ralphs (1986: 155) to recommend that day centres should not be used as a general deterrent; nor should they be expected to reduce offending behaviour effectively other than by perhaps helping offenders to lead a more 'constructive and responsible life'.

However, behind these statistics, there lies an encouraging view from offenders: that 'had it not been for the programme they would have been sent to prison, and they viewed the programme as infinitely better than any custodial experience' (McCormack, 1988: 115; see also Ely et al., 1983, 1987; Hil, 1986; Murray, 1986; Parker et al., 1987; Ralphs, 1986; Spencer and Edwards, 1986). Parker et al. (1987: 41) write:

> The dilemmas for those engaged in running 'packages' or day centre programmes clearly remain. If such requirements in Orders are not being accepted as clear alternatives to custody, can they be justified? One view is clearly, that they cannot. On the other hand, it can be argued that the forms of social work involved in these schemes (e.g. group work, skills training) are actually of more relevance to unemployed youth than traditional forms of one-to-one casework.

In a similar vein, Vanstone (1986: 105), in response to an analysis of offenders' evaluation of their experiences at Pontypridd day centre, states:

> Working in the Centre has led staff to the view that if social workers can successfully extricate themselves from the straitjacket of the treatment model and its incumbent theoretical assumptions, then they will become more effective as social workers. By enabling clients to make informed

choices, they are better able to give help pertaining to those problems which are most important to clients. Within the Day Centre setting, it has been possible to help people improve, among other things, their levels of literacy, their confidence and their ability to form social relationships . . .

For some, the day centre temporarily fills a social vacuum, relieves chronic stress, and restores a measure of self-respect particularly for those who experience long-term unemployment. It gives others a renewed sense of identity and for those who complete the programme a sense of achievement. Several offenders are known to have found work with the help of staff; some have made dramatic changes in drug and alcohol use. Many others have shown changes in their appearance, presenting themselves with more confidence and attempting to alter their lifestyles. As a worker has commented, '. . . to see someone manage to go without drinking for three days a week and actually feel good at achieving it is a very strong motivation to keep workers trying'. Some offenders do have their negative views too. It has been reported that they view day centre regimes, activities and organisation, reminiscent of the authority and subordination relationships which they experienced in school, and which 'they associated with failure, rejection and pointless regimentation' (McCormack, 1988: 115). Vanstone (1986: 101–2) also finds that some offenders are critical of staff in the way they attempt to exercise authority. It is interesting here to draw a comparison with the experiences of offenders in community service. Offenders report that certain supervisors exhibit tendencies which they regard as 'power mad' (Vass, 1984: 117, emphasis in original):

Offenders consider that courts should punish wrongdoers; that community service is better than being in the 'nick'; that certain offences are real offences (murder, rape or serious assault) and that they ought to be punished accordingly; that the officers who supervise them are in the main 'alright' and 'fair'. If there is obvious animosity expressed, this is directed against officers who, in their zeal to enforce the order in a Napoleonic fashion, are likened to the presumably dictatorial and oppressive regimes associated with prison and policing institutions. On these occasions, the officers become the 'Hitlers', the 'screws on wheels', and the 'pigs' of this world. Dissociation becomes, in that instance, alienation from *particular* rather than general methods of control.

In a similar fashion, Vanstone (1986: 101–2) quotes one offender as saying:

I would not recommend this place. This place has messed me up. Of all the institutions I've been in I would not like to come to this place again if it were not for the threat of prison. There are too many personal discussions and so much distrust. It's very strenuous — you have to make an effort to control your behaviour. I'm up against authority here. I can't stand it. I'm anti-authority. It's not heavy but you still feel it.

The point that the above offender is making about *choosing* to consent to a probation order with day centre conditions as an alternative to custody, is important. He may not like what is going on in that day centre, but he prefers it to being in prison. As I have already indicated, much of that choice may be part of the process of the social engineering of authority (for full discussion of this see Vass, 1984: ch. 3). It is possible that consent is given because the offender *is made to believe (as opposed to the reality of risk of imprisonment) that he or she may be incarcerated if consent is not forthcoming* — hence compliance is gained by resort to covert threats about the implied risk of imprisonment when in fact imprisonment might not be one of the options considered by the court. However, from the available evidence, it appears that in the majority of cases offenders who attend day centres under Schedule XI 4(B) of the Criminal Justice Act 1982 are high-risk offenders who are displaced from custody. A similar picture emerges from an analysis of the workings of the Cedar Hall day centre.

As in the national survey (Mair, 1988), the majority of offenders are referred to Cedar Hall for offences involving burglary and theft, that is 'opportunistic' crimes. However, behind these opportunistic crimes lies a long history of offending. For instance, one offender — with heroin/alcohol dependency — had made 15 court appearances and had received the following sanctions, among others: three prison sentences, three community service orders, and two probation orders. A broader look at the background of the 53 offenders who successfully completed the activities at the day centre between January 1987 and June 1988, shows that between them they had recorded 94 custodial sentences, including 12 suspended and seven borstal sentences prior to their attendance at the day centre; 23 of those offenders also had, between them, 37 community service orders and eight of them had been prosecuted for breach of requirements of their community service. Seven of those prosecutions resulted in custodial sentences being imposed on defaulters.

Furthermore, information available on how courts deal with offenders who are not given 4(B) orders, reveals that the *vast majority receive custodial sentences generally of fairly considerable lengths*, which adds weight to the argument that the 'pool' of offenders who are referred to day centres for assessment and consideration of suitability are deep end offenders who run a high risk of receiving — in the absence of a day centre option — prison sentences. Thus, looking at a 12-month period between January and December 1987, there were 156 referrals to the centre for consideration under Schedule XI 4(B). Of these, 132 were recommended to the courts. Just over 40 percent ($n=53$) of recommendations were taken up by the courts. The rest ($n=79$) were dealt with in the following manner:

44 (55.7%)   received prison sentences, 32 of which were for periods exceeding 6 months;

13 (16.5%)   received community service orders;

9 (11.4%)   received suspended sentences of imprisonment;

4 (5.1%)   received probation orders; one contained a condition of attendance at an alcohol education programme;

3 (3.8%)   were fined;

1 (1.3%)   was given a deferred sentence;

5 (6.3%)   alternative sentence unknown.

The above characteristics of offenders with regard to their previous criminal history, and the sentences passed by courts for those who are not ordered to participate in day centre activities, suggest that the day centre does work on the principle of dealing with high-risk offenders and as such may be regarded as meeting its primary aim of diverting offenders from prison establishments. However, they are not allowed to satisfy that aim in full because they appear to face serious opposition by the *courts*. For instance, 44 (33 percent) of those offenders found suitable and recommended to courts (*n*=132) were not diverted as recommended by probation officers but given immediate imprisonment by courts. Therefore, the question that one should raise does not concern the activities of those who run alternatives to custody but *the activities of the judiciary*. In the above case diversion from custody would have been a remarkable achievement had *the courts accepted recommendations and made the 44 who were incarcerated the subject of a 4(B) order. Given that the 40 percent of offenders (n=53) who were made the subject of such an order were high up the tariff scale in terms of risk of custody, one could suggest that had the courts followed recommendations, the overall rate of true diversion would have been in the region of 70 percent or more.* The question posed here, arising from the experiences of the day centre, is not whether alternatives to custody act as true alternatives but *whether courts encourage them or allow them to be true and effective alternatives.*

This finding raises serious questions about the rigid statistical comparisons which are often made (see Chapter 4) to reach possibly false conclusions that alternatives to custody do not divert or have no real effect in reducing the prison population. As I have argued, such comparisons fail to take into account a host of known and unknown factors, and it seems that the persistent refusal of courts to accept community penal measures as alternatives to custody, may be a major variable in determining the success or failure of such measures. Furthermore, as has already been shown from a number of studies, such measures can work only if sentencers are persuaded to use them. For example, Smith et al. (1984) found that sentencers are not optimistic about the scope for reducing the prison population. But, if the results of the 'Hampshire experiment' — which involved ways of using alternatives to reduce custodial sentences through the coopera- tion of the probation service and courts — are to be taken as a faithful outcome of those intentions, then the conclusion which may be drawn is not dissimilar to the one which I have stated earlier. Smith et al. find that the pessimism was due more to magistrates' intransigence in changing their sentencing practices than to the failure of alternatives to effectively reduce the prison population. They find that magistrates were more willing to use alternatives to custody for less serious offenders and in many respects as sentences in their own right, rather than as means of diverting deep end offenders from custodial establishments. The exception was the Crown Court where a noticeable *reduction* in the overall rate of incarceration in Hampshire was noted. The study offers further support to my earlier contention that when alternatives are used to divert offenders from custody in a determined but careful way (by ensuring that only those who run a high risk of receiving custodial sentences are given alternatives to custody), they can be successful in checking if not reducing the prison population. Smith et al. (1984: 53–4) conclude thus:

> If changes of the magnitude which occurred in Hampshire during this project could, by whatever means, be replicated nationwide, they could have a substantial effect on the prison population — of the order of 5000 less in prison . . . the Hampshire results show that it is at least conceptually possible for appreciable reductions in the prison population to flow from decisions of the sentencers alone and to be achieved without significant additional provision for non-custodial disposals. . .

Further evidence about the role of sentencers in determining outcomes and how community sanctions are used in relation to imprisonment is offered by Ely et al. (1983, 1987). The authors found that the Kent Close Support Unit did demonstrate its effectiveness in reducing custodial sentences in the Medway region by nearly 50 percent compared with the number of such sentences prior to the establishment of that Unit. However, what perhaps the authors missed in their evaluation of outcomes was their significant, but largely ignored, statement that 'The Court would have preferred to use the Unit more extensively as a sentence in its own right' (Ely et al., 1983: 43). Such a statement is revealing because it appears to nullify the rationale of having *alternatives* to custody as opposed to simply expanding the pool of penal sanctions in general. That is, courts appear to be more interested in having more choice of sanctions rather than sanctions which are restricted to a few offenders. The repercussion of such an ambition or wish (and probably practice) expressed by courts is that if an alternative to custody *is* used as a sentence in its own right (see for instance the problems arising from this in respect of the community service order) then its status as a true alternative is watered down. As a result, instead of genuinely diverting from custody, such penal measures may tend to suck into their mesh individuals lower down the tariff scale who should not be there. In effect, if there is any net widening arising from alternatives to custody it may not necessarily arise from the ill-informed decisions of those who make recommendations to courts, or from the inability of alternatives to challenge prison establishments. Rather, much depends on how courts choose to use such penal measures. As Rhys et al. (1989: 53) also suggest, in considering recommendations and take-up by courts for day centres and hostels, it is 'revealing that [of those people] who were not put on [day centres or hostels] received immediate custodial sentences'. This finding leads them to conclude in this manner: 'Given that those who are unsuccessfully recommended for probation orders with conditions of hostel residence or day centre attendance almost invariably receive custodial sentences, it is clear that probation officers are very successfully pinpointing people at risk of custody when making these recommendations.'

The authors ponder on the lack of knowledge and the possible factors 'which make recommendations more likely to be successful', but fail to realise that a possible factor affecting the acceptance of recommendations is sentencers' intransigence in modifying their sentencing practices. Courts appear to erect barriers against the proper and effective use of certain community penal measures as genuine alternatives to custody. Although it is in their powers to use them as true alternatives (cf. Smith et al., 1984), they appear unwilling to lower the tariff they apply. By implication, they thus allow or encourage the size of the prison population to continue rising.

In sum, from what is known of the workings of the day centre in Cedar Hall, and in conjunction with similar findings by Mair (1988) day centres do appear to act as alternatives to custody for those who are given 4(B) orders. Of course, this interpretation should be regarded as a tentative conclusion for further work is needed to ascertain its validity. For instance, among many other intervening factors, we need to have more detailed information on those offenders, prior to, during and after completion of day centre attendance and the position, activities and ideology of sentencers. This is particularly important in view of the wide variations in sentencing practice which exist across the country (see Chapter 2): what may be deemed to be serious offences and deep end offenders in one context, and which may attract tough sentences including prison in the hands of specific benches, may merely attract lenient responses and non-custodial alternatives in another. Notwithstanding these qualifications, the interpretation calls for a serious consideration that day centres can and do act as an alternative to custody for specific types of offenders.

Criticisms: Age, gender and race

If serious criticisms are to be made of day centres and perhaps other non-custodial penal measures they are that, first, there appears to be an emphasis on young offenders, and this may pose serious questions about equitable justice. In Cedar Hall the offender group mainly consisted of offenders in the age group 17–25, though flexibility was applied to the upper limit depending on the type of offender under consideration. This predominance of young offenders in day centre activity is a national phenomenon. In Mair's study, 43 percent ($n=867$) of offenders attending day centres were under 21; 41 percent were between 21 and 30. Although this emphasis may serve a good purpose in the sense that this is the age group most at risk of imprisonment, it must also raise questions about the lack of opportunities offered to older offenders. Thus this distinction between age bands and the almost total exclusion of certain age groups may not be helpful in applying the justice principle of offering alternatives to custody to all suitable offenders. Secondly, as in the case of the national context, the majority of referrals are white males. This may reflect demographic and social characteristics of the Mid-North and Eastern region of Hertfordshire but serious thought must also be given to the possibility that as in the case of other non-custodial penal measures, ethnic groups appear (though the evidence is far from clear) to be underrepresented in alternatives to custody and overrepresented in prison establishments (see for instance Crow, 1987; Home Office, 1987a; Mair, 1986; NACRO, 1988).

The same dilemma exists with regard to female offenders. As in community service (cf. Dominelli, 1984; Menzies and Vass, 1989; Pease et al., 1977; Vass, 1984: 33–4; Vass and Menzies, 1979; Young, 1979), day centres appear to be reserved for men. In 1987, 2094 probation orders with day centre conditions were made in England. Of these only 6 percent were given to women (Home Office, 1988h). In the same year, of the 156 referrals to Cedar Hall day centre, only 12 (8 percent) were female, and less than half of those referred ($n=5$) actually received orders. Four of those who were not given orders by the courts following recommendation were sentenced to immediate imprisonment: two for more than six months and two for less than six months. Of those offenders who successfully completed requirements ($n=53$) between January 1987 and June 1988, 45 were white male offenders; eight were white female offenders; and none were from ethnic minority groups.

Race and gender issues need to be addressed by the probation service which must identify possible reasons for this poor representation of ethnic minority groups and female offenders in both *referrals* and actual *take-up* rate of recommendations by courts (cf. Mair and Brockington, 1988). In 1987, 26 045 males were given probation in magistrates' courts, and 1174 (4.5 percent) of these were with day centre requirements. This contrasts with 7925 orders given to female offenders with only 84 (1 percent) of orders relating to day centre requirements. In the Crown Court, 6567 males were given probation orders, of which 794 (12 percent) had day centre requirements. With regard to females, 1679 orders were made, with 42 of these (2.5 percent) requiring day centre attendance. If probation orders with day centre attendance are deemed to be alternatives to custody, the low distribution of such orders among female offenders in comparison to male offenders creates a considerable problem for women. At a time when the rate of incarceration and length of imprisonment are both increasing (Home Office, 1987b, 1988f), one would expect that courts would make more use of opportunities offered by alternatives to custody to limit the use of prison sentences. If, as it appears, a higher proportion of males are favoured for such penal measures, the conclusion one is forced to reach is that current sentencing practice does not work on just principles, and restricts women's chances of being kept out of prison.

The same problem may exist with respect to ethnic minority groups. Given the discussion in Chapter 2, and the rising number of ethnic minority groups in prison establishments, the tendency to under-use alternatives to custody to displace such offenders from custodial sentences may create similar inconsistencies and unjust practices in the course of sentencing policy. It is also surprising that the first national study by the Home Office (Mair, 1988) has shown an abysmal disregard for the issue of race: not a single reference is made to this difficult area of concern. If day centres are to be seen to be an alternative to custody, then there ought to be a real concern about their failure to accommodate or divert offenders who, though they may have comparable offences and criminal records to white offenders, appear to experience a higher risk of custody. This is not just a problem for courts in terms of differential treatment and inconsistent practices. Rather, it extends outside the courts to probation officers who are not exempt from the same charge that they fail to practise a non-racist and non-sexist approach to their clients. Although available findings are relatively sparse and inconsistent in their methods and interpretations, and should be treated with caution when generalising, various local studies appear to suggest that in making recommendations, probation officers favour white Europeans for non-custodial penal measures and disfavour black Afro-Caribbean offenders. For instance, in one study it was found that of the reports analysed, 45 percent of white Europeans were recommended for alternatives to custody as against 25 percent of black Afro-Caribbean origin. Indeed, 25 percent of reports on the latter group had no recommendation whatsoever compared to 8 percent of reports on white Europeans (for a review of the literature, see NACRO, 1988).

Conclusion

In this chapter, I attempted a critical review of probation day centres as an alternative to custody and offered an account of the workings of one such day centre. The discussion and findings lead to tentative conclusions. First, that day centres may work as alternatives to custody if properly organised and administered. In that respect, the assumption that alternatives to custody have nothing to offer offenders; that they merely make things worse; and that they expand surveillance and control in the community and as such they are complementary to prisons rather than real alternatives is, as already argued in Chapter 4, quite unwarranted. Secondly, that sentencers may play a crucial role in attempts to establish penal sanctions as alternatives to custody. Their decisions and choices appear to determine to a great extent the status of day centres in relation to imprisonment. Thirdly, the discussion has brought to light factual information about the issue of costs. Although it was not possible to offer information on the cost of running Cedar Hall day centre (as such information was unavailable at the time), the experience of running day centres in general points to the realisation that under proper investment, day centres are not found to be cheap or cheaper than custodial establishments. The argument, therefore, which is put forward in favour of alternatives to custody that *all* community penal measures are cheap or cheaper than custodial establishments may not be valid. Costs may vary among penal measures, thus there must be some differentiation between types of alternatives according to cost. Notwithstanding this qualification, the example which is set by day centres to those interested in comparing the cost of community versus custodial institutions is that, when properly funded, such community penal measures can be as expensive if not more expensive than prisons.

Finally, the discussion has also pointed to a serious professional matter. The analysis suggests that one should not underestimate or doubt the real *moral* dilemma confronting probation officers and others who supervise offenders in the community. The dilemma, as Parker et al. (1987) put it, about how those professionals wrestle with their consciences in seeing themselves as exercising social policing rather than 'social work' remain. However, one could argue, alternatives to custody, properly managed and applied, can draw a balance between care and control, and offer a viable and humane way of ensuring that some people at least are prevented from experiencing custody and instead have the opportunity of receiving help in the community. For that matter, if day centres are to become and remain a viable alternative to custody, every effort should be made to ensure that only people who would otherwise go to prison should be made subject to such requirements of day centre attendance. In conclusion, as Ralphs (1986: 155–6) suggests:

> Behind the concept of any kind of day centre is the idea that people can be helped as much in groups as they can in a one to one relationship . . . [High risk offenders] can be held successfully in the community, and that they need a well thought out programme of care and control, although we still have a long way to go before we can speak with any certainty about which type of offender will respond best to a particular programme.

Note

1 A co-joint article presenting some of the ideas raised in this chapter will appear in *British Journal of Criminology* (see Vass and Weston, 1990). Since this book was written, Hertfordshire Probation Service has reorganised and expanded its day centre provisions. Cedar Hall day centre has therefore been replaced by a broader and more ambitious project in trying to divert and keep offenders in the community.

7 Punishment in the community: Policy and prospects

'Mirror, mirror on the wall, who is the fairest of us all?', asks the evil Queen in the fairy-tale of Snow White and the Seven Dwarfs. In a similar fashion, and in a rare moment of total disarray, vainness, self-pity, and self-seeking salvation, the British government (Home Office, 1988c: 8) is captured admiring its own (policy) silhouette, and pondering on its achievements:

> There are over 50 000 people in custody in England and Wales, about one in every 1000 of the total population. Do they all need to be there? In 1978, the prison population was 41 800 and in 1968 it was 32 400. If past trends continue, the prison population can be expected to rise well over 60 000 and possibly 70 000 by the year 2000. The Government is committed to a substantial programme of building new prisons costing almost £1 billion and the recruitment of more prison officers.

As in the fairy-tale, the government then reflects in the mirror of its penal measures, and begs for confirmation of its resolute response to the problem of offenders and prison crises. It asks the reader (Home Office, 1988c: 9, emphasis in the original): *'Are we sending too many people to prison?'* The reader obliges: yes, you are. Be assured, your prisons are the fattest of them all. Your criminal justice 'policy' is indeed expansionist.

I have documented the expansion of the prison establishment and wider community controls in previous chapters. I have also looked at attempts to 'destructure' the prison establishment by various means especially through the provision of alternatives to custody. The discussion has pointed to many problems and unsatisfactory outcomes of that 'policy'. What is presented as a determined and well-thought-out policy by the government, turns out to be in disarray. *There is no clear policy for a reduction of the prison population.* On the contrary, the history of prisons and policies to destructure them are littered with empty promises, irregularity, drift, narrow-mindedness and dogma. Policy is an amalgam of rhetoric and confused praxis (wanting a reduction in the prison population but setting new, higher targets, for the number of people to be incarcerated — 70 000 by the year 2000), which is expressed in deeds which allow the capacity of the prison to grow in a relentless manner while at the same time allowing and encouraging a plethora of controls through various alternatives to custody in the community.

In this book I have attempted to look at the arguments for and against alternatives to custody, to offer an exegesis for their use and expansion and to identify both their merits and defects, as well as to separate fantasy from reality. What has become obvious from the discussion is that alternatives to custody cannot manage on their own — even where they demonstrate some effective diversion — to challenge the prison and check its rising population. Alternatives may have a place in the criminal justice system and may be desirable but their main flaw is their failure to show any clear effect on the prison establishment. That failure (though occasionally exaggerated) is not essentially the inherent property of those penal measures in that, as critics have suggested, they only disperse the means of control and act as complementary, not antithetical, sanctions to the prison. Rather, if one considers the arguments put together in this book (from the historical development of alternatives, characteristics of the 'prison crisis', sentencing practices, and government pronouncements or intentions, debates about prison and alternatives, to illustrations of the workings of specific alternatives to custody) there is clear evidence of the lack of any coherent *policy* for the reduction of the prison population. In short, there is, in England, a lack of concerted and planned action for a *criminal justice policy*. In that sense, the inability of alternatives to custody to work in an effective and persuasive way, by giving the appearance that all they achieve is an undesirable expansion of the net of social control, can be explained in part by the lack of policy. There is a need for a policy which directs and assists those in charge of administrating alternatives to custody to maintain and promote the fundamental principle behind such sanctions: the diversion of offenders from custody and, crucially, the reduction of the prison population. At the moment the lack of such direction and the absence of any systematic and rational understanding of what the purpose of prison, alternatives, and generally criminal justice *policy* should be leads to little more than a continuous escalation of the 'prison crisis' and the politics of punishment. 'Punishment', De Haan (1987: 20) writes, 'is no longer seen as a "necessary evil", but as a "normal" response to criminal behaviour'. As Rutherford (1984: 171) also states:

> Most contemporary prison systems are expanding through a combination of drift and design. Criminal justice administrators perpetuate the myth that the prison system is swept along by forces beyond their control or influence. The convenient conclusion is announced that, given increased rates of reported crime and court workloads, it inevitably follows that there is no

alternative other than for the prison system to expand further. Strategies which might shield the prison system from increases in persons processed by criminal justice have been disregarded and administrators have preferred to proceed as though policy choices do not exist. In large part, criminal justice administrators are the architects of the crisis with which they are now confronted . . . Most typically, expansion occurs in the absence of coherent policy . . .

Current government intentions in England

Rutherford's perception of the crisis is valid in its substantial point: that there is an absence of coherent policy, but what makes the above perception more relevant is that even at a time when there has been a drop in the recorded crime rate (with the exception of offences against the person and subject to the qualification that statistics may 'lie' and are socially constructed), the prison is enjoying one of the sharpest and fastest expansions in its history. At the same time, it may not be true that the government does not consider or propose *alternative* strategies for controlling the prison establishment's expansion. It is often the case that governments claim that a lot is being done to reduce the prison population and divert offenders from custody to more acceptable, desirable means of control in the community, and they use executive powers to keep that prison population under control (cf. Bottomley and Pease, 1986). What is significant is not the rejection of alternative choices to prison or that alternative choices are sometimes put forward or considered, but, rather, whether any of those choices are ever properly implemented or given enough scope and powers to keep people out of custody. It is in this context that the present government's 'policy' in *Punishment, Custody and the Community* (Home Office, 1988c) needs to be evaluated.[1]

The government's intentions (Home Office, 1988c) with regard to punishment in the community and its perceived means by which courts can be given tougher choices in dealing with offenders and encouraging a reduction in the prison population can be summarised in terms of three approaches.

1 To renovate existing orders or sentences and make them more demanding. The idea of introducing national standards for community service, or toughening up the probation order by expanding day centre provisions, are examples of this exercise to polish up the image of alternatives to custody as being real, and harsh community sanctions. The 'policy' here is to do away with flexibility and discretion, and provide instead more rigid regimes whose purpose is to engineer some structure into the lives of offenders and to guide, if not direct them, towards that end by strict

enforcement of rules and expectations and subjecting them to constraints and a policy of suspended rights.

2   To introduce new orders or sentences such as a 'supervision and restriction order' which will enable courts to make requirements which might simultaneously include a number of restrictions and requirements on offenders (see Home Office, 1988c: 9 for detail):

>   compensation to the victim
>   community service
>   residence at a hostel
>   prescribed activities at a day centre or elsewhere
>   curfew or house arrest
>   tracking an offender's whereabouts
>   other conditions (restrictions)

3   To enlarge the scope of supervision in the community by creating opportunities for the probation service to 'contract with other services, and private and voluntary organisations, to obtain some of the components of punishment in the community' (Home Office, 1988c: 17). Additionally, to provide opportunities for the development of new agencies to organise alternatives to custody, in particular offering a chance to non-statutory agencies to be engaged in the supervision of offenders in the community (see also Home Office, 1988b). In short, here we see a reference to the possibility of introducing market forces in the criminal justice system through a process of privatisation. Punishment for profit, by opening up opportunities for competition, contracting out services with private agencies, is seen as another way of making the system more efficient and finding new strategies for the control of offenders in the community and thus outside prison walls.

All these intentions are supposed to do a number of things for offenders and the community, which are expressed in an avalanche of rhetoric in Part I of *Punishment, Custody and the Community* (Home Office, 1988c: 1–2). Prison, it is suddenly realised (even though it is still allowed to expand on an unprecedented scale) reduces offenders' liberty and reduces their personal responsibilities. Alternatives can offer genuinely desirable outcomes, keeping many offenders out of that negative and destructive environment. In so doing, and in contrast to the alienating effects of the prison, alternatives are capable of offering, among others, the following benefits (see also Chapter 3):

>   reparation
>   self-discipline and self-reliance
>   opportunities to grow out of crime and become responsible citizens
>   choices
>   a sense of personal and social responsibility

guidance to offenders to exercise self-control
maintenance and mending of social relationships
work opportunities, training and education
reduction of public expenditure — they are cheaper.

All in all, so much gain and personal development can derive from being subject to community methods of control, that it makes one imagine that it is a good thing to be an offender these days: there is so much going for them in the community. Notwithstanding these assumed achievements, I shall concentrate on more concrete issues which may arise or fail to materialise from such 'policy' of *renovating, expanding and diversifying alternatives* to custody as a reaction to the prison crisis.

Harsher does not mean more efficient

In its new effort to establish alternatives as harsher regimes (that is to say, placing an emphasis on structure, control and enforcement) particularly with regard to community service (Home Office, 1988g; 1988i), the government is missing the point on a number of fronts. First, at both the abstract and practical level the new efforts will not make much difference to the way the schemes are currently run. It will be business as usual. At a recent Conference in London on community service (King's College, September 1988) most participants, from probation officers to Assistant Chief Probation Officers, agreed that the new standards have emerged out of a political necessity to demonstrate the government's tough approach to crime and offenders rather than out of any conviction that such intentions may have any practical significance either in terms of organising the schemes or reducing the prison population. There are reasons for this conclusion. As I have consistently argued in this book and elsewhere, policy is one thing. Putting into practice policy intentions (particularly when they go against findings which suggest that rigid enforcement is not always the best way to engineer compliance and exercise authority over offenders — cf. Vass, 1984; Chapter 5 of this book) is another matter. At that level, that is at the moment of applying rules and regulations, there is a lot of evasion, and distortion of expectations to make them applicable and relevant to the context and social relationships pertaining to the situation. Standards and structures are not merely the function of laws and governments' wishes under statutory rules. At the level of administration and enforcement, hence the interpretative and practical level, rules and expectations are applied by the 'on-the-spot' authorities according to prevailing organisational and personal needs in order to make those laws both manageable and workable. Therefore, attempts which aim at organising the various aspects and agencies of the criminal justice system, as in the case of alternatives to custody, to make them more rigid or coercive by eliminating overt opportunities for the practice of discretion and informality, can only succeed in making those distortions and evasions less visible and, perhaps, less desirable. The more the criminal justice process is allowed to become rigid and coercive in its posture, the more the fear of adverse publicity grows among those who administer and enforce such measures and thus the less obvious those distortions become. In such instances much of the distortion or 'rule-breaking' by officials is pushed downward and underground and is allowed to spring up in discreet and camouflaged places — far removed from the public eye — where it is less noticeable and less amenable to detection and check.

Secondly, it is interesting to note that much of the present push towards more structure and rigidity in the enforcement of alternatives to custody, such as the community service, and a move towards national standards (uniformity of operation) arises from findings and recommendations made by critics (cf. Vass, 1986a for a summary of major concerns and recommendations). However, the government has refused to heed advice that coerciveness and rigidity are not always conducive to compliance and the exercise of authority over offenders. For example, when my study of community service (Vass, 1984) was first published, a criticism made against it by officials was that the study focused too much on 'work parties' carrying out 'manual' work, thus neglecting the more profitable and constructive aspects of individualised placements. It is ironic that the government now shows a preference for manual work and menial tasks in order to persuade sentencers that community service is harsh punishment just falling short of the 'chain gang' image. What is more interesting and ironical is that my study showed that where much manual work was involved, offenders appeared to express more discontent, higher levels of defiance and violation of requirements than in cases where they could attach meaning to their work and understand who the beneficiary was — as in the case of individualised placements. At the same time, the study showed that accommodation (thus tolerance) of deviance in the context of community service helped to diffuse antagonism from offenders. It was observed that where attempts were made by officers to apply more rigid controls and structure, offenders reacted in more rebellious ways, used various techniques to sabotage those efforts, and were successful on more than one occasion in demoralising officers.

Given these findings, it is surprising that the government has retracted from the original concept of offering alternatives which are meaningful and give offenders a sense of personal worth by doing something useful and relevant for specific individuals in need or the community at large. The government's national standards in requiring, for instance, that offenders should spend at least 21 hours in a group placement ('working parties') and engage in 'manual work' (Home Office, 1988i: 8–9), in the belief that such experience will discipline offenders and establish the order's tough image as punishment in the community, are destined for trouble. Assuming that my first point above may prove wrong, and that such standards are not evaded or distorted and are applied in their unadulterated form by probation officers, the end result will be more trouble 'on site', more rebellion, and more failures. It will prove very taxing (in terms of resources, time and personnel) for officers to keep the peace and maintain order or induce compliance. Running an alternative to custody under strict orders is, in many respects, like sailing on the *Bounty*: offenders will react to what they will regard as further oppression and curtailment of their liberties and choices with counter-measures and mutiny. Instead of having stable and predictable social relationships (which are a common characteristic of a more lax and flexible regime which manages to accommodate certain deviations from both sides), participants will be led to a situation whereby instead of co-working towards coexistence and doing something constructive for the community, they end up being 'on edge', watching over their shoulders, and being on 'standby' for trouble.

Thirdly, the idea that by establishing alternatives to custody which are guided by structure, rigidity and quick, tough responses to breach of requirements creates credible and reliable penal measures is not convincing. The intention of keeping people out of prisons and at the same exercising punitive and inflexible power over them in the context of alternatives to custody is a contradiction in terms. If one follows the government's logic to its conclusion, then it is obvious that the idea of creating credible alternatives to custody is a fallacy because a credible alternative would imply a high level of swift enforcement (leading to prosecution) following breach of requirements, and a high risk of imprisonment on conviction. But keeping people out of prison (the reason for the alternatives) and exercising a rigid system of containment and law enforcement (the assumed hallmarks of credibility) are sometimes contradictory, for over-zealous control would undoubtedly *increase* the risk of imprisonment, not decrease it. Blind application of punishment as an institutionalised means of realising compliance is illogical. This is because the resources (social, economic and psychological) required for the exercise of containment and close, stiff surveillance are greater and far more costly than those required for the exercise of authority by elastic means of supervision. In a situation where the overall organisational objective is the completion of a 'contract' (satisfactory completion of order or sentence), and to enable an offender to achieve all or some of the above list of benefits of 'community' (self-reliance, finding work, establishing and sustaining personal relationships, exercising self-control, and so on), indiscriminate application of penalties and rigid enforcement can only prove to be detrimental to that goal. It will exclude the majority of offenders from any meaningful and constructive interaction with their officers, and will also prevent the majority of offenders from successfully discharging their obligations to the court and, to that extent, the community at large. In short, part of the problem with government 'policy', the rising prison population, and the punitiveness of the system as a whole, has to do with low levels of 'tolerance' (Downes, 1988). As I have argued in Chapter 5, tolerance *should* be a necessary precondition and an integral part of any attempts to destructure the prison establishment. In that respect, alternatives to custody can only function as real alternatives if they can demonstrate more flexibility and tolerance than is currently practised by the criminal justice process in general. By being expected to compromise that tolerance with harsher methods of supervision and a tough approach to offenders, the government is not heading for reductions in the prison population but for an escalation of the prison crisis.

Fourthly, the government is making another error by assuming that 'harshness' equals a 'real' alternative to custody. In its directions to the probation service and courts concerning the introduction of national standards for community service, the Home Office gives the impression that the more 'tightly supervised' an order, the more credible it will be as an alternative with the courts. However, this is a peculiar and naive suggestion and puts efforts to establish genuine alternatives into disrepute. Whether an order is applied in a lenient or harsh way has nothing to do with its status as an alternative. The Home Office is confusing the intentions of the courts at the moment of administering penalties with the way in which social workers enforce orders. The two things are not the same. One could still have petty offenders — who are unlikely to receive a prison sentence — sweating it out under a harsh order. But the existence of a tough regime may not imply that the order acts as a true alternative. Conversely, a deep end offender could be diverted from custody by being given an order, but have an easy time under a lax regime. In that case, it does not follow that because that scheme has a lax regime, it is not genuinely accommodating or diverting offenders from custody. Furthermore, the emphasis on harshness and tight supervision as hallmarks of the alternative may introduce its own injustices in the treatment of offenders. If this clumsy philosophy prevails, one could end up considering everybody on community service (especially those who would never have received prison sentences) as being deep end offenders by virtue of their participation in a so-called tightly supervised community penal measure. Their true status on the penal ladder, in terms of gravity of offence, previous convictions, circumstances and so forth, may be lost under the guise that a punitive community measure only deals with deep end, hard-core criminals. In short, it may mean that by virtue of the label — harsh community treatment as an alternative to custody — such offenders may run a higher risk of experiencing harsher treatment in courts for subsequent appearances.

Privatisation

The third intention of the government to expand the means of supervision by involving the private sector, thus diversifying the criminal justice system, will lead to further consequences for social relationships within that system (for details see Vass and Menzies, 1989). Here I shall summarise the main possibilities.

Productivity and expansion of the net

The criminal justice system will see an expansion of alternatives with a proliferation of activity. In both the public and private sector (profit or non-profit-making) there will be an encouragement to expand and sustain expansion, for neither of the two sectors will be able to remain in business if numbers of offenders, or 'clients', go down. It would be, in other words, unprofitable. In that respect, it is to be expected that the activity will lead to an expansion and widening of the net of surveillance and control.

Division of Labour

Profit making, whether financial in the case of private agencies or spiritual[2] in the case of voluntary organisations, is dependent on two things. First, a continuous flow of production — input and output at minimum cost — and secondly, stability in social (industrial) relationships. In that respect, the private or voluntary sector will *choose* to accept petty, shallow end offenders rather than hardened criminals. Hardened criminals are unpredictable and may require high security facilities: thus they may be costly both in financial and social terms. As 'punishment for profit' works on the principle of 'minimum security facilities' (cf. Borna, 1986; Ericson et al., 1987; Vass and Menzies, 1989) private agencies will 'specialise' in the main in supervising offenders who are lower down the tariff system. In effect, *privatisation may weaken, instead of strengthening, a penal measure's position in relation to prison*; that is to say, it may establish alternatives to custody as sentences in their own right or as substitutes for other non-custodial penal measures rather than as genuine alternatives to custody.

The more difficult offenders, or those who are really at risk of being sent to prison, will be dealt with by public agencies. This may increase pressures on statutory agencies (such as the probation service) and their predicament may be exacerbated by a lack of adequate resources. Resources will be limited because that which is available from the public purse may have to be divided between supervision of low-risk offenders (by private or voluntary agencies) and high-risk offenders (supervised by statutory agencies). Given that statutory agencies may be faced with higher risks and pressures arising from problems of compliance, security, and difficulties in maintaining stable relationships because of the personal and social characteristics of offenders supervised, the lack of resources may exacerbate those pressures and relationships and possibly lead to demoralisation and adverse publicity.

Mutual seduction

Once the process of privatisation is put into effect it will be difficult to stop. This is because there is a process of *mutual seduction* at work (Vass and Menzies, 1989). Each party, government and private or voluntary agencies, fall for each other because two ideologies are at work which join hands to lead to reciprocal ends: *privatisation* is the ideological bedrock of most western governments; '*publicisation*' is the ideological bedrock of private or voluntary agencies. Privatisation leads to contracts with such agencies; contracts lead to work, status, prestige and income for those agencies. This 'productivity' depends in the long term on publicity which extols the virtues of the work done and invites more contracts. In sum, privatisation *reinforces* publicisation, publicisation *legitimates* and in turn reinforces privatisation. Through this cycle of reinforcement and legitimation there is mutual dependency and an odd symbiotic existence between the public and private or voluntary sector. This cycle of relationships dictates that it is in the interest of both parties to praise the achievements of privatisation and the benefits derived from it for the community.

Costs

Part of the reason for offering alternatives to custody and opening up opportunities for private or voluntary sector involvement concerns saving money for the taxpayer. In theory, alternatives appear to be cheaper, but as I have argued earlier, in practice this may not be the case. This is even more relevant when prisons and community controls are expanding simultaneously. The taxpayer ends up paying for the maintenance of both systems and sees no reductions or savings in public expenditure. However, there are practical problems in justifying arguments that alternatives are cheaper. There are many hidden costs and unknown factors which are not taken into account when calculating expenditure. It is easier to offer information on the costs of prisons than of alternatives (see Chapter 3). It is argued that privatisation will be more efficient and cheaper, but it has been argued elsewhere (cf. Vass and Menzies, 1989) that privatisation may mean false savings. For instance, under privatisation, contrary to common belief, bureaucracy (involving para-civil and civil servants) grows and with it costs in terms of operation, regulation and organisation of the new schemes. In general, keeping the number of civil servants constant by hiring private contractors to run services may be good politics but how good it is economically is an open question (cf. Le Grand and Robinson, 1984; Roll, 1982; Vass and Menzies, 1989).

Poorer standards
In view of the mutual seduction process, monitoring of private or voluntary agencies will be less severe than that of public agencies. Accountability becomes blurred and intervention is avoided as far as possible. It has been shown, for instance, that enforcement of contracts and control of service delivery by private contractors is often difficult (Ascher, 1987); that privatisation of juvenile institutions appears to lead to low levels of accountability and blurred responsibilities (Lerman, 1984); and that when errors are discovered, it is easier for private or voluntary bodies to abdicate responsibility than for a statutory body; and that there are concerns that privatisation may make services and their quality far removed from popular awareness and thus less visible and accessible to public scrutiny (Earnshaw and Normandeau, 1987). Government action or intervention to monitor and expose malpractices will go against the 'public interest' of privatisation and the mutual seduction process. As such, though the government may have the power to exercise significant control over private and voluntary agencies (by threatening to cancel contracts, for example), such action will generally be avoided through a policy of benign neglect. The neglect will derive from the government's belief that contracting out alternatives to custody frees public resources and personnel for other work or leads to savings by cutting back on bureaucracy. The benign aspect derives from the government's trust that private or voluntary agencies will perform their tasks to satisfaction because they need to be seen as efficient and reliable in supervising offenders in the community, and thus ensure further contracts (Vass and Menzies, 1989).

Implications for social work

The question which has caused so much controversy is whether the push towards punishment in the community will convert probation officers (and other social workers involved in the criminal justice system) into a new breed of surveillance officers. So, would the new intentions of the government really have any effect on social work? The answer is a qualified yes. Developments even when they are rationally planned and controlled not to have specific effects often take off at some point, on their own. That is to say, they create their own momentum and their own unanticipated consequences. The intended changes in the criminal justice system will gradually instill into social work's consciousness a new way of understanding and conducting its business. In that sense, social work is both directly and indirectly under political pressure to accept new methods of work which may appear to contradict its traditional values. The new developments and the push towards more punishment in the community may increase the risk of social work agencies engaging in more formal and overt control over their clients (Parker et al., 1987). The current push towards punishment in the community is part of a general shift away from individual methods of control towards methods which survey larger populations and offer more 'collective methods of control' (Parker et al., 1987) based on leisure control and deprivation of liberty in the community (Vass, 1984). These measures are directed in the main against young, mainly male, unemployed offenders. Should these new measures be resisted? (cf. Inner London Probation Service, 1989; NAPO, 1988b; Vass, 1982a).

They cannot be resisted because the political climate does not permit that kind of activity. It is not wise to resist because resistance may mean the end of the probation service as a public, social work agency in courts. It will be disfigured and dismembered beyond recognition if it refuses to accept the current or intended policy of punishment in the community (cf. Vass, 1988a). On another level, they should not be resisted for ideological reasons alone and for the sake of demonstrating that probation officers are capable of running a counter-culture to the government's own. Such resistance may not be in the interests of 'clients' of the probation service. For some of those alternatives to custody — among them community service, probation with or without day centre restrictions — do help some offenders and do help to save a few from prison. As long as one recognises that behind the concept of 'punishment' there may exist a sense of social responsibility and an opportunity to *practise* what essentially lies at the heart of social work intervention — namely that people matter and can be helped as much in groups as they are in one-to-one relationships; and that social workers are in the business of developing, not blindly ordering or containing, human potential — then, whether the means of social work change or not, will make no difference to current practice or its ends. The emphasis may be different but the practice will remain essentially the same. That practice will, and should, still be a practical expression of the fact that probation officers 'have a special focus for their work which is that wrongs must be righted and grievances remedied' and the 'belief that [as people matter, the] task is to help in making good the harm that has been done' (Lacey et al., 1983: 120). It is also important to recognise that probation officers *are* important (and quite expensive) members of the criminal justice process and their tradition has always been rooted in the affirmation of the principle of supervising offenders in the community and keeping them out of prison. In that respect, they *are* an essential part in the process of offering alternatives to custody and they cannot continue to reaffirm the successes of their service in keeping people out of prison without demonstrating, in practical terms, a commitment to the basic, albeit confused (see below), intentions of the government to improve and expand non-custodial penal measures (Vanstone, 1985: 25; Vass, 1986a: 109–10). Whether, of course, the new intentions and 'policy' will have any real impact on the prison population is another matter. The next, and final, section of this chapter looks at the possibilities.

Alternatives v custody: Will they work this time?

The rationale behind the renovation, expansion and diversification of alternatives to custody and their administration or enforcement is, presumably, to reduce the prison population. However, contrary to this intention, the immediate effect of the measures is to expand the availability of sanctions for courts without any guarantees that the expansion will have any positive effect on the prison population or the rate of imprisonment. Although the 'dispersal of discipline thesis' has serious flaws, there is very little in the current intentions expressed by the government to allay fears that such alternatives to custody will not widen the net, with the result that more offenders may be filtered through to prison establishments. There is very little appreciation in those proposals of factors which may encourage a reduction or increase in the prison population; or which may merely nullify any minor but positive effects those measures may have, or be capable of generating, in keeping the number of people incarcerated in check.

The lesson from existing alternatives and from comparative research is clear. Either more construction and expansion of prison accommodation or a greater use of non-custodial penal measures, or both, may be needed to satisfy contemporary demands for more or better *punishment*. However, the construction of new prisons and an overall expansion of the prison establishment has failed, and will continue to fail, to resolve crowding until the problem is separately and explicitly addressed by concerted *policy* (see for instance Ashworth, 1983;

Bottomley, 1986; Downes, 1988; Evans Skovron, 1988; Rutherford, 1984). Similarly, an increased number of renovated, expanded and diversified alternative punishments is unlikely to be the answer unless it is also accompanied by other measures, stated in a coherent policy of intent and purposes, whose basic and genuine principle is to restrict the expansion of prison capacity and reduce its incarcerated populations. For such a statement on alternative choices and a defined policy, Rutherford (1984; see also Box, 1987) calls for a policy which encompasses a number of interrelated activities with the aim of establishing a criminal justice process based on a 'reductionist' rather than an expansionist line. He calls for a reduction in the 'physical capacity of the prison'; the maintenance and enforcement of minimum standards in prisons; the establishment of an 'optimal prison system staff-to-prisoner ratio'; the existence of 'early release mechanisms' to prevent overcrowding; the discretion enjoyed by sentencers to be curtailed; violation of alternatives to custody requirements not to be dealt with by imprisonment; the widening of non-imprisonable offences; and narrowing the scope of criminal law (Rutherford, 1984: 170–84).

Here I shall emphasise the main policy issues which emerge out of this book (particularly Chapter 2) and those which appear to be of particular and general relevance to keeping people out of institutions and retarding the expansion of the prison establishment.

Length of sentences and rate of incarceration
Bottomley (1986: 202, emphasis in original), in comparing England with the Netherlands, writes that 'bearing in mind that the two main factors that contribute to the size of a prison population are the *number* of persons committed to prison and the average *length of time* each spend in custody, the most important reason for the Netherlands' low rank order has always been its below average length of sentence' (see also Bottomley and Pease, 1986; Downes, 1988; Fitzmaurice and Pease, 1982). Given this realisation and the fact that too many people are sent to and kept in prison for far too long in this country, alternatives will have little impact on the size of the prison population unless there is a drastic shift in current practice towards fewer people being given prison sentences and reducing the length of sentence. If the government sincerely means to translate its own rhetoric into action by offering alternative choices to the courts, then a 'drastic shortening of sentences to custody is the major route' to that goal (Downes, 1988: 205). One must, of course, guard against an unanticipated consequence of shortening the length of sentences. Unless that policy is accompanied by an equal determination to *reduce* the number of people sent to custody, shortening of sentences could, in many ways, *increase* the

physical capacity of the prison (available space increases and is used more for shorter periods) thus creating a revolving-door policy whereby more people experience custody than previously but for shorter periods.

An argument against reducing the number of offenders sent to prison and shortening the time spent there is that the public may be endangered by an increased crime rate. This view is flawed. Comparative data, particularly with regard to states which have shorter sentences, do not support the proposition that fewer prisoners and shorter sentences lead to more crime. As Box (1987: 211) suggested, 'The public need not be endangered. It has been documented that the crime rate would not increase as a result of offenders being imprisoned for shorter periods, released earlier than at present, or diverted entirely into some alternative punitive scheme' (see also Inner London Probation Service, 1989b: 7).

Reducing prison capacity

As we have seen, despite promises of a reduction in the prison population and the expansion of alternatives to custody, the government takes pride in its ability to expand the physical capacity of the prison establishment and the high public expenditure which is currently going into refurbishing and constructing new prisons. This contradictory and 'narrow logic' (Downes, 1988: 202) does not assist in the process of achieving any reductions in the prison population, controlling the rate of imprisonment, or saving resources for more constructive alternatives. It has to be realised that expansion of capacity and the construction of more prisons is not a solution to the problem of incarceration and crowding. It merely encourages further misuses of available space. It reduces the social and psychological barrier of 'tolerance' and offers an easy and quick punitive response to many offenders who should, in normal circumstances, be diverted from custody. That is to say, an obstacle to the effective development and application of alternatives to custody is that the continuing expansion of the prison not only erodes any small gains or contributions made by such community penal measures, but also encourages sentencers, policy makers and the community at large to regard and expect the prison system to be capable of accommodating just about anyone who is deemed in need of deprivation of liberty. The prison in that sense 'provides an exceptionally convenient dumping place. Imprisonment [and its expanding physical capacity] reduces pressure to be vigorous and creative in consideration of alternative sanctions by sentencers and persons making recommendations to the courts, such as probation officers, hostel wardens and others . . . The prison system takes the individual immediately and completely, thereby effectively stifling incentives to seek less drastic forms of intervention' (Rutherford, 1984: 157–8).

Limiting the use of imprisonment for breach of
alternatives to custody
In a critique of diversion in *Justice of the Peace* (Vass, 1982a; 793, emphasis in original), I argued thus: 'It would make more sense if we begin to introduce new measures (if indeed we need any new measures) which *preclude* the risk of imprisonment. That is, measures which prevent the substitution of imprisonment for other [alternative] sanctions.' In short, if indeed there is a distinct and genuine desire to keep people out of prisons, imprisonment should not, for most offenders, be used as the penalty for punishing defaulters of alternative to custody sanctions. Eliminating the background sanction of imprisonment and substituting for it some other penalty or liability could be as effective in administering and enforcing requirements. Where consent by offenders is required (as in community service or probation) such consent would still be forthcoming even in the absence of the fear of imprisonment (cf. Vass, 1984: ch. 3, 1986a).

Targeting alternatives at the right offenders
Alternatives to custody should be given to people who would otherwise receive a prison sentence. That is to say, proper gatekeeping and screening of offenders and risk of custody, should be a priority and only those deemed to be deep end offenders should ever be considered for those penal sanctions.

In order to reinforce that policy and sustain a flow of true diversions from custody, and assuming that the background sanction of imprisonment is not withdrawn as suggested earlier, the current practice of not explaining in open court what the alternative is replacing (rarely do courts give the offender a clear understanding of what the alternative to custody is actually replacing — usually that could be another non-custodial penal measure and not necessarily imprisonment) should cease. I have argued elsewhere for a number of options (Vass, 1986a), of how to ensure that alternatives to custody are used for offenders who might otherwise be imprisoned. One of those options, which I shall briefly decribe here, is now in operation in the Republic of Ireland and from impressions gained the policy appears to be working in a satisfactory manner.[3] I argued that if a community service order is made, the court should be obliged to state, in open court, the alternative sentence which is replaced by the order, and then direct that the alternative sentence is registered for future reference. A written order issued to an offender to perform community service should also name the alternative sanction that is replaced by community service (Vass, 1986a; 108). I argued that applying this process of informing and registering the intended sanction which is replaced by the alternative to custody, increases the possibility that an order is restricted to those who are at risk of immediate custody, and offers the opportunity to courts and those recommending alternatives to custody to claim that their actions and sanctions genuinely divert offenders from custody.

The same principle can be introduced and applied to all alternatives to custody sanctions, not just the community service order. The principle of stating what sanction the alternative to custody replaces reduces hypocrisy, uncertainty and unjust inconsistencies and practices in sentencing. If, for instance, a non-custodial penal measure is made as a sentence in its own right this should be public and private knowledge for in any future lapses or breach of requirements leading to prosecution for failure to comply with the sentence, the individual could be treated for those lapses only and not under the false impression that his or her failures may merit a term of imprisonment when imprisonment was not even contemplated at the time of the original sentence. Equally, if an alternative measure is passed which genuinely replaces custody, then the offender, the court and subsequent courts, and his or her supervising officers (if any), should be aware of and be fully prepared for the possible consequences of any future lapses or breach of conditions of order or sentence. Furthermore, the principle of stating and registering the intended sentence may lead to more consistent practices in courts. For instance, if different courts are dealing with an offender who has served or breached a non-custodial penal measure those courts will at least have a clear understanding of the intentions of the previous court in passing sentence and act accordingly. Under current practice (and with the exception of the suspended sentence of imprisonment), this information is lacking, and subsequent court decisions are often based on assumptions and conjectures about the intentions of the previous court. Finally, no scheme is foolproof against difficulties and malpractices or unanticipated consequences (as the suspended sentence of imprisonment shows). Extra vigilance to restrict possible malpractices (for example suggesting that the intended alternative is custody when the reality is another non-custodial alternative) and promote proper and desirable practices must be enforced. However, this improper use of alternatives to custody could automatically be checked by the realisation that court decisions are subject to scrutiny and challenge. Any such act by courts, and given the material facts of the case, could be mitigated by the legal possibilities afforded to the defendant to appeal against the decision should that decision appear unreasonable or unrealistic or unduly harsh in relation to the offence, the circumstances of the commission of the offence, the circumstances of the offender and his or her criminal record. So, whatever the obstacles, including administrative inconvenience, the clarification of what alternatives are replacing at the time of sentence should offer some concrete and much-needed information about the true status of those alternatives to custody.

In targeting alternatives to custody at the right offenders there is also another matter raised by Bottomley and Pease (1986; see Chapters 3 and 4 in this book). They argue that offenders who are genuinely diverted from custody and are made subject to such penal measures are, by and large, offenders who would otherwise receive short-term prison sentences of six months or under. However, as those offenders constitute only a very small section of the prison population at any one time, the effects of diversion are minimal. In that respect, if alternatives to custody are to have any direct effect on the prison population they must be targeted at a higher level of the tariff system, thus diverting offenders who are given long sentences. This is, indirectly, a complementary policy of *reducing* the number of long-term prisoners and effectively keeping long sentences in check. Of course, this should not be interpreted as a policy favouring longer sentences in order to enable alternatives to be more successful. The aim should be a concurrent reduction in the length of sentences if any appreciable decrease in crowding is to be expected. Even there, unless care is taken to control the rate of incarceration and to prevent the emergence of a revolving-door policy, the benefits of diversion and a reduction in length of sentences will be hard to measure.

Resolving disparities in sentencing

As I have argued in Chapter 2, there are great disparities across the country in the way different courts use custody and alternatives to custody. No penal measure can claim consistency of operation and no criminal *justice* system can claim justice if inconsistencies in court practices can be allowed to exist at such an alarming level. Alternatives to custody cannot achieve their purpose of reducing the prison population if some courts persist in underusing or misusing them in preference to sending offenders to prison as a first resort.

Controlling malpractices in sentencing

Again, with regard to prison populations, there are various groups (such as untried and convicted but unsentenced prisoners, ethnic minority groups and women) who appear to be receiving unfavourable treatment by courts and whose rate of incarceration has been steadily climbing in the last few years. This does not only emphasise or exacerbate the possible existence of discriminatory practices within and outside courts but also helps to swell the prison population.

Additionally, 'collective forms of punishment', as they are practised in the community in the form of alternatives to custody, appear to be geared towards the young, white and unemployed male (cf. Box, 1987; Menzies and Vass, 1989; Parker et al., 1987; Vass and Menzies, 1989; Vass and Weston, 1990). This raises questions about the treatment afforded to older offenders, women, and members of ethnic minority groups. On a different level, the trend may also raise more general and structural questions about going beyond the criminal justice system (Box, 1987; Rutherford, 1984). Rutherford (1984: 175) summarises these structural issues thus: 'The reductionist approach to the prison system inevitably and necessarily overlaps with broader aspects of social and economic policy. In particular, policy and practice concerning education, mental health and the extent and distribution of poverty impinge upon directions set for the prison system.'

Structuring sentencing practices
The above issues bring to light the crucial problem of the judiciary and magistracy (hereafter judiciary). Many commentators have suggested that there is a need for the establishment of a commission or other authority with the legal powers of coordinating and determining sentencing guidelines. It is argued that 'an authoritative "supra-agency" statement of objectives and principles, applicable in practice, so that the experience of law enforcement and the administration of justice is as coherent and consistent as it can be throughout the many jurisdictions in different parts of the country' should be established (Bottomley, 1986: 214; see also Ashworth, 1983; Box, 1987; Downes, 1988; Rutherford, 1984). The purpose of these guidelines would be to exercise restrictions on sentencers and create a coherent criminal justice policy which would structure sentencing choices and decisions so that imprisonment would be seen as the penalty of last resort and for very serious crimes – such as 'crimes against life and the person, drug-trafficking and robbery' (Downes, 1988: 200).

The *Guardian*, in a leader comment, 7 February 1984, challenged the government's lack of policy on prisons thus:

> If [the Home Secretary] wanted to ease the crisis . . . he would . . . set up a sentencing council to provide a policy framework for sentencing so that this country could finally begin to have a criminal justice policy instead of the Home Office saying one thing and the courts running in the opposite direction.

Four years later, the newspaper returned to the same theme. On 27 August 1988, the *Guardian* wrote:

> The chaos in British criminal justice policy proceeds apace . . . The fact is that there will be no coherent criminal justice policy as long as the

government fails to tackle the subversive role of the judiciary which . . . is daily sending more and more people to prison for longer and longer. Judges must of course remain independent from political pressure when they pass individual sentences; but there is no constitutional bar whatsoever to bringing them in to talk to other branches of the system so that they are aware of the crucial part they play in shaping policy. Anything less than that can only be the short-term management of a long-term crisis.

There is evidence to suggest that clear reductions in the prison population can indeed be achieved from changes in the decisions of the sentencers alone and without the need to expand provisions for non-custodial penal measures (cf. Smith et al., 1984: 53–5). When this finding is taken together with a proper and determined use of alternatives to custody as true alternatives, and shorter sentences, one can have few doubts about the effectiveness of such a combination of factors to reduce the prison population. Nonetheless, any attempt to introduce guidelines to coordinate and structure judiciary decisions is resisted on the grounds that such activity would be against the interests of democratic process, that is to say, it would jeopardise the 'independence' (but see Griffith, 1985) of the judiciary and would absorb them into the arena of party politics, patronage and favour. As Downes (1988: 201) suggests, this resistance by the judiciary is only part of the problem. He states:

> The problem in England . . . is even more intractable than the absence of a clear set of policy directives and strategy for their overall co-ordination. It is not so much a lack of means for the construction of such a policy. That could be the task of the Home Office acting as prime mover in setting up an inter-departmental and joint body with the senior judiciary to tackle the job. A National Criminal Policy Committee such as was suggested by the Home Affairs Committee in 1981, but rejected by the government, could also be established. The first main problem is that significant resistance to any such move is embodied in the judiciary, at least at senior levels. Criminal justice policy is seen almost as a contradiction in terms by the judiciary, since it is defined as encroaching on their own preserve. The second main problem is that, even if we had such a policy, we lack the framework for its implementation. We have no constitutional . . . [machinery] . . . with its multi-agency role enabling prosecutors to mediate policy from the minister accountable to Parliament through to the police, the local authorities, and the courts. Given the resistance of the judiciary on the one hand, and the policy framework vacuum on the other, it is hardly surprising that no very substantial attempt has been made to enunciate an overall criminal justice policy.

In many respects, this resistance by the judiciary and the belief that they are free of any political interference or intervention is quite inaccurate. First, their 'independence' is not compromised by governments' attempts to reduce, for example, the average length of prison sentences or limit the use of imprisonment in general. The judiciary are still able to apply the law as enacted by Parliament and are still 'left to conduct its own business of establishing guilt and handing down a just punishment "within the law" ' (Box, 1987: 211). Secondly, in previous chapters I offered examples of ways in which governments use executive powers to effectively reduce the prison population. Thus, following the analysis offered by Bottomley and Pease on sentencing trends, it is obvious, as the authors argue, that the prison population 'is rather less than half what it would be if it were not for the various forms of executive intervention'. They go on to add (Bottomley and Pease, 1986: 101):

> In this way, it can be concluded that the Home Office is about as important as the judiciary and the magistracy in determining how much imprisonment is suffered!
> The image we get, of a Department of State making spectacular reductions in effective sentence length and hence in prison population, is very much at odds with the rhetoric of the separation of powers between executive and judiciary.

Conclusion

In this book I have attempted to offer a critical analysis of alternatives to custody and their relationship to prison and its recurrent crises. It is obvious from the analysis and discussion that the assumptions that alternatives to custody have nothing much to offer to offenders; that they merely make things worse; and that they succeed in expanding surveillance and control in the community and as such they are complementary sanctions to prison, have yet to be demonstrated. There are many flaws in the dispersal of discipline thesis and the argument that alternatives do more harm than good. I attempted to show that although alternatives are enmeshed in rhetoric and occasional fantasy about their assumed achievements, they have, nonetheless, a contribution to make to the criminal justice process and to the creation of a criminal justice *policy*. However, even though improvements in their administration and enforcement can be engineered which can establish them as true alternatives to imprisonment, they alone cannot be expected to resolve the prison crisis which is a *policy crisis*. It is too easy to send someone to prison. The prison exists, as a convenient dumping ground, for all those people — whether deserving or undeserving — whom courts choose to eject and dispose of as part of the process of excluding and curtailing people's liberty. In that sense, alternatives to custody may not often work as effectively as they should because their powers of exercising any real control over the rate of incarceration and the prison population are curtailed and sabotaged by the judiciary; or because they are misused and downgraded by those making recommendations to courts; or because they are targeted at the wrong offenders. But these reasons, and others, are all part and parcel of the same national problem which is in some respects equivalent to a national scandal: the lack of a clear policy and direction with regard to the role of prison, and alternative methods of punishing offenders in the community. Once again, Downes's (1988: 206) conclusion to his comparisons of England and the Netherlands, is worth reproducing here at some length:

> For the simmering but largely hidden crisis in the British criminal justice system needs to be addressed in the same open fashion adopted by the Dutch in relation to theirs. Nor need the judiciary fear that some subversive constitutional movement is going on whenever anyone suggests the need for sentencing policy to be subject to analysis and discussion outside their ranks. As Ashworth has tirelessly pointed out, sentencing policy is not the preserve of the judiciary. Its discussion by other bodies is not some act of *lèse-majesté* but an essential part of the democratic process . . . There is . . . a clear need for a policy framework capable of formulating and guiding the implementation of criminal justice priorities . . . Some means has to be found for situating a much more sparing use of imprisonment within a reformed criminal justice system . . . [W]e would do so from a position of such grossly inflated use of custody that much can be cut without serious backlash. The Dutch judiciary have shown great courage in insisting on humane standards and the minimum use of pain in the dispensation of criminal justice . . . It is . . . to be hoped that we find sufficient nerve to follow their example.

If that courage is not found, the current prison crisis and the 'good intentions' of the government to offer 'punishment in the community' will remain, as on numerous previous occasions, an expression of impotence. What is unfortunate and at the same time a sorry affair is that current trends, with an emphasis on punishment, are left to steer themselves into action without the benefit of any clear and pragmatic policy about how to tackle the growing and taxing prison problem.

The lack of any such criminal justice policy to direct and at the same time monitor developments is the Achilles heel of efforts aimed at a reductionist policy. The system, in being allowed to remain direc-tionless and lacking in proper restraints, is merely expanding at an alarming rate without any real benefits. The signs are that no real efforts are being made to reverse that process and that the prison, far from experiencing reduction in physical and human capacity, will continue to thrive for years to come. In the meantime, maybe the government, or the judiciary in their divine knowledge, or perhaps the 'system' in general, may ponder for a few moments on 'Joan's' perplexity who asks what is the logic of the 'system'. Maybe they could come up with some rational answer — they always do — to enlighten

'Joan', who having 'done time' inside for fine default, still searches for meaning and understanding about what that 'system' is all about and what it is supposed to achieve. Maybe the answer could also help all the other 'Joans' who have experienced that 'system' to know what its objective is:

> Maybe i was thinking on the wrong line. What were the last eight days for? Fines Money? I didn't lose or gain eny and i don't know anyone else gaining eny. So that wasnt the answere. Was it for a punishment? I enjoyed the expirence and what i didn't enjoy i could soon adapt to. Maybe iv defined punishment wrong. To teach a lesson? All i learnt was i had a pile of unanswered questions and understood the system less. If it were peoples attitudes to life they were trying to change, no one spoke of it. My logic didn't fit in here eather and just sent me round in circles asking the same question. What were those eight days for? Then i decided to stop thinking about it and put it down to the way the system works. And maybe someday ill understand it all ('Joan', 1985: 13).

Notes

1 Since the completion of this book, the government has produced a Green Paper (Home Office, 1990a) on its intentions to modify the structure, roles and tasks of the probation service. These intentions do not contradict the analysis and predictions made in this book. In addition, the government has published a White Paper (Home Office, 1990b) which defines the legislative character of 'punishment in the community', as it was originally stated in *Punishment, Custody and the Community* (Home Office, 1988c).
2 For an explanation of this and how it works in a 'spiritual' way; and a detailed discussion of various concepts used here (e.g. 'mutual seduction' and 'publicisation'), see Vass and Menzies (1989).
3 I am indebted to L.F. O'Brien, Probation and Welfare Officer, for informing me about the application of this option in the Republic of Ireland; and for furnishing me with a copy of a community service order form, Rule 4 – Form 1.

References

Advisory Council on the Penal System (1970) *Non-custodial and Semi-custodial Penalties* (Wootton Committee). London: HMSO.

Advisory Council on the Penal System (1977) *Powers of the Courts Dependent on Imprisonment* (Chairperson: Baroness Serota). London: HMSO.

Advisory Council on the Penal System (1978) *Sentences of Imprisonment*. London: HMSO.

Advisory Council on the Treatment of Offenders (1957) *Alternatives to Short Terms of Imprisonment* (Chairperson: H. Studdy). London: HMSO.

Allen, H.E. and Simonsen, C.E. (1986) *Corrections in America*. New York: Macmillan.

Alper, B.S. (1973) 'Foreword', in Y. Bakal (ed.), *Closing Correctional Institutions: New Strategies for Youth Services*. Lexington, Mass: Lexington Books, pp. vii–x.

Andrews, J. (1982) *Alternatives to Custody: A Study of Social Inquiry Reports*. Manchester: Greater Manchester Probation and After-care Service Information Unit.

Angelos, C. and Jacobs, J.B. (1985) 'Prison overcrowding and the law', *Annals of the American Academy of Political and Social Science*, 478: 100–112.

Ascher, K. (1987) *The Politics of Privatisation*. London: Macmillan.

Ashworth, A. (1983) *Sentencing and Penal Policy*. London: Weidenfeld and Nicolson.

Audit Commission (1989) *The Probation Service: Promoting Value for Money*. London: HMSO.

Austin, J. and Krisberg, B. (1981) 'Wider, stronger and different nets: the dialectics of criminal justice reform', *Journal of Research in Crime and Delinquency*, January: 165–96.

Austin, J. and Krisberg, B. (1985) 'Incarceration in the United States: the extent and future of the problem', *Annals of the American Academy of Political and Social Science*, 478: 15–30.

Bailey, V. (ed.) (1981) *Policing and Punishment in Nineteenth Century Britain*. London: Croom Helm.

Baldock, P. (1974) *Community Work and Social Work*. London: Routledge and Kegan Paul.

Bale, D. (1987) 'Using a "risk of custody" scale', *Probation Journal*, 34: 127–31.

Ball, R.A. and Lilly, J.R. (1983) 'Home incarceration: an alternative to total incarceration', paper presented at the 9th International Congress on Criminology, Vienna.

Ball, R.A. and Lilly, J.R. (1988) 'Home incarceration with electronic monitoring', in J.E. Scott and T. Hirschi (eds), *Controversial Issues in Crime and Justice*. London: Sage Publications, pp. 147–65.

Ball, R.A., Huff, C.R. and Lilly, J.R. (1988) *House Arrest and Correctional Policy: Doing Time at Home*. London: Sage Publications.

Banister, P.A., Smith, F.V., Heskin, K.J. and Bolton, N. (1973) 'Psychological correlates of long-term imprisonment', *British Journal of Criminology*, 13: 312–23.

Bayer, R. (1981) 'Crime, punishment and the decline of liberal optimism', *Crime and Delinquency*, 27: 169–90.

Beavis, S. (1988) 'No, Minister . . .', *Guardian*, 22 December.

Benington, J. (1974) 'Strategies for change at a local level: some reflections', in D. Jones and M. Mayo (eds), *Community Work One*. London: Routledge and Kegan Paul, pp. 260–77.

Biles, D. (1983) 'Crime and imprisonment: a two decade comparison between England and Wales and Australia', *British Journal of Criminology*, 23: 166–72.

Blagg, H., Pearson, G., Sampson, A., Smith, D. and Stubbs, P. (1988) 'Inter-agency co-ordination: rhetoric and reality', in T. Hope and M. Shaw (eds), *Communities and Crime Prevention*. Home Office Research and Policy Unit, London: HMSO, pp. 204–20.

Borna, S. (1986) 'Free enterprise goes to prison', *British Journal of Criminology*, 26: 321–34.

Bottomley, A.K. (1986) 'Blue-prints for criminal justice: reflections on a policy plan for the Netherlands', *Howard Journal of Criminal Justice*, 25: 199–215.

Bottomley, A.K. and Pease, K. (1986) *Crime and Punishment: Interpreting the Data*. Milton Keynes: Open University Press.

Bottoms, A.E. (1981) 'The suspended sentence in England 1967–1978', *British Journal of Criminology*, 21: 1–26.

Bottoms, A.E. (1983) 'Neglected features of contemporary penal systems', in D. Garland and P. Young (eds), *The Power to Punish: Contemporary Penality and Social Analysis*. London: Heinemann.

Bottoms, A.E. (1987) 'Limiting prison use: experience in England and Wales', *Howard Journal of Criminal Justice*, 26: 177–202.

Bottoms, A.E. and Light, R. (eds) (1987) *Problems of Long-term Imprisonment*, Cambridge Studies in Criminology, LVIII. Cambridge: Institute of Criminology.

Boyson, R. (1971) *Down with the Poor*. London: Churchill Press.

Box, S. (1987) *Recession, Crime and Punishment*. London: Macmillan.

Box, S. and Hale, C. (1986) 'Unemployment, crime and imprisonment and the enduring problem of prison overcrowding', in R. Matthews and J. Young (eds), *Confronting Crime*. London: Sage Publications, pp. 72–96.

Broad, R.A. (1988) 'Community work and development in the probation service.' Unpublished PhD thesis, School of Social Work, Middlesex Polytechnic.

Brody, S.R. (1976) *The Effectiveness of Sentencing: A Review of the Literature*. Home Office Research Study No. 35, London: HMSO.

Bullock, W.F. and Tidesley, W.M.S. (1984) *Special Requirements in Probation and Supervision Orders: A Local Case Study*. Cambridge: Institute of Criminology, Occasional Papers No. 11.

Bureau of Justice Statistics (1985) *Prisoners in 1984*. Washington, DC: Department of Justice, April.

Burney, E. (1980) *A Chance to Change*. London: NACRO.

Cain, M. (1985) 'Beyond informal justice', *Contemporary Crisis*, 9: 335–75.

Callison, H.G. (1983) *Introduction to Community-based Corrections*. New York: McGraw-Hill.

Chan, J.B.L. and Ericson, R.V. (1981) *Decarceration and the Economy of Penal Reform*. Toronto: University of Toronto Centre for Criminology.

Children's Society Advisory Committee on Penal Custody and its Alternatives for Juveniles (1988) *Penal Custody for Juveniles – The Line of Least Resistance*. London: The Children's Society.

Clear, T.R. and O'Leary, V. (1983) *Controlling the Offender in the Community*. Lexington, Mass.: Lexington Books.

Clemmer, D. (1958) *The Prison Community* (2nd ed.), London: Holt, Rinehart and Winston (first published in 1940, Boston: Christopher Publishing House).

Cobb, A. Jr. (1985) 'Home truths about prison overcrowding', *Annals of the American Academy of Political and Social Science*, 478: 73–85.

Cohen, S. (1979a) 'Community control: a new utopia', *New Society*, 15 March: 609–11.

Cohen, S. (1979b) 'The punitive city: notes on the dispersal of social control', *Contemporary Crisis*, 3: 339–69.

Cohen, S. (1985) *Visions of Social Control: Crime, Punishment and Classification*. Cambridge: Polity Press.

Cohen, S. and Taylor, L. (1972) *Psychological Survival: The Experience of Long-term Imprisonment*. Harmondsworth: Penguin.

Cook, S. (1988a) 'Home Office gets cash for two new prisons', *Guardian*, 2 November.

Cook, S. (1988b) 'Courts crack down on serious crimes', *Guardian*, 26 October.

Cork, M. (1989) 'Getting in the way of history', *NAPO News*, No. 6: 4–5.

Cornish, D.B. and Clarke, R.V.G. (1975) *Residential Treatment and its Effects on Delinquency*. Home Office Research Study No. 32, London: HMSO.

Cory, B. and Gettinger, S. (1984) *Time to Build? The Realities of Prison Construction*. Edna McConnel Clark Foundation.

Council of Europe (1987) *Prison Information Bulletin*, No. 9, 1 February.

Cox, E.W. (1877) *The Principles of Punishment as Applied in the Administration of the Criminal Law by Judges and Magistrates*. London: Law Times.

Crow, I. (1987) 'Black people and criminal justice in the UK', *Howard Journal of Criminal Justice*, 26: 303–14.

Curtis, L.A. (ed.) (1987) *Policies to Prevent Crime: Neighbourhood, Family, and Employment Strategies*. Annals of the Academy of Political and Social Science, 494, London: Sage Publications.

DHSS (1972) *A Guide for the Regional Planning of New Forms of Treatment for Children in Trouble*. London: HMSO.

DHSS (1973) *Intermediate Treatment Project: An Account of a Project set up to Demonstrate Some Ways of Providing Intermediate Treatment*. London: HMSO.

D'Atri, D.A. (1975) 'Psychological responses to crowding', *Environment and Behavior*, 7: 237–52.

Davies, M. (1974) *Prisoners of Society*. London: Routledge and Kegan Paul.

Day, P. (1981) *Social Work and Social Control*. London: Tavistock.

De Haan, W. (1987) 'Abolitionism, and the Politics of "Bad Conscience"', *Howard Journal of Criminal Justice*, 26: 15–32.

del Carmen, R.V. and Trook-White, E. (1986) *Liability Issues in Community Service Sanctions*. US Department of Justice: National Institute of Corrections.

Devon Probation and After-care Service (1980) *Community Service by Offenders Scheme 1979*. Exeter: Probation and After-care Service.

Ditchfield, J. and Duncan, D. (1987) 'The prison disciplinary system: perceptions of its fairness and adequacy by inmates, staff and members of Board Visitors', *Howard Journal of Criminal Justice*, 26: 122–38.

Doig, J.W. (ed.) (1983) *Community Corrections: Ideas and Realities*. Lexington, Mass.: Lexington Books.

Doleschall, E. (1977) 'Rate and length of imprisonment: how does the United States compare with the Netherlands, Denmark and Sweden?', *Crime and Delinquency*, 23: 51–6.

Dominelli, L. (1984) 'Differential justice: domestic labour, community service and female offenders', *Probation Journal*, 31: 100–103.

Donnison, D. (1975) 'Policies for social deprivation', in R. Holman and E. Butterworth (eds), *Social Welfare in Modern Britain*. Glasgow: Fontana/Collins, pp. 420–25.

Downes, D. (1979) 'Praxis makes perfect: a critique of critical criminology', in

D. Downes and P. Rock (eds), *Deviant Interpretations: Problems in Criminological Theory*. Oxford: Martin Robertson, pp. 1–16.

Downes, D. (1982) 'The origins and consequences of Dutch penal policy since 1945: a preliminary analysis', *British Journal of Criminology*, 22: 325–57.

Downes, D. (1986) Review, *Visions of Social Control: Crime, Punishment, and Classification*, Cambridge: Polity Press.

Downes, D. (1988) *Contrasts in Tolerance: Post-war Penal Policy in the Netherlands and England and Wales*. Oxford: Clarendon Press.

Drakeford, M. (1983) 'Probation: containment or liberty?', *Probation Journal*, 30: 7–10.

Durham County Probation and After-care Service (1975) *Community Service Orders: An Evaluation Report of Two Years of Community Service by Offenders in Durham County*. Durham: Probation and After-care Service.

Earnshaw, L. and Normandeau, A. (1987) 'Privatization in corrections: the Canadian situation', *Crimcare*, 3: 21–31.

Edwards, C. (1987) 'Retaining values without becoming marginal', *Probation Journal*, 34: 82.

Ellis, D., Grasmick, H. and Gilman, B. (1974) 'Violence in prisons: a sociological analysis', *American Journal of Sociology*, 80: 16–34.

Ely, P., Swift, A. and Clifton, M. (1983) 'The Medway Close Support Unit: an alternative to custody for juveniles', *Home Office Research Bulletin*, No. 16: 42–4.

Ely, P., Swift, A. and Sunderland, A. (1987) *Control without Custody? Non-custodial Control of Juvenile Offenders*. Edinburgh: Scottish Academic Press.

Empey, L.T. (1978) *American Delinquency: Its Meaning and Construction*. Homewood, Ill.: Dorsey.

Empey, L.T. (1980) 'Revolution and counterrevolution: current trends in juvenile justice', in D. Schichor and D.H. Kelley (eds), *Critical Issues in Juvenile Delinquency*. Lexington, Mass.: Lexington Books, pp. 157–81.

Empey, L.T. and Erickson, M.L. (1972) *The Provo Experiment: Evaluating Community Control of Delinquency*. Lexington, Mass.: Lexington Books.

Erickson, M.L. and Gibbs, J.P. (1980) 'Punishment, deterrence, and juvenile justice', in D. Shichor and D.H. Kelley (eds), *Critical Issues in Juvenile Delinquency*. Lexington, Mass.: Lexington Books, pp. 183–202.

Ericson, R.V., McMahon, M.W. and Evans, D.G. (1987) 'Punishing for profit: reflections of privatization in corrections', *Canadian Criminology*, 29: 355–87.

European Committee on Crime Prevention (1980) *Report on Decriminalization*. Strasbourg: Council of Europe.

Evans Skovron, S. (1988) 'Prison crowding: the dimensions of the problem and strategies of population control', in J. Scott and T. Hirschi (eds), *Controversial Issues in Crime and Justice*. London: Sage Publications, pp. 183–98.

Fairhead, S. and Wilkinson-Grey, J. (1981) *Day Centres and Probation*. Home Office Research Unit Paper 4, London: Home Office.

Fielding, N. (1984) *Probation Practice: Client Support under Social Control*. Aldershot: Gower.

Fielding, N. (1986) 'Social control and the community', *Howard Journal of Criminal Justice*, 25: 172–89.

Fitzmaurice, C. and Pease, K. (1982) 'Prison sentences and population: a comparison of some European countries', *Justice of the Peace*, 146: 575–9.

Flegg, D. (1976) *Community Service: Consumer Survey 1973–6*. Nottingham: Nottingham Probation and After-care Service.

Flynn, L.E. (1986) 'House arrest: Florida's alternative eases crowding and tight budgets', *Corrections Today*, July: 64–8.

Folkard, M.S., Smith, D.E. and Smith, D.D. (1976) *IMPACT: Intensive Matched Probation and After-care Treatment: Volume II: The Results of the Experiment.* Home Office Research Study No. 36, London: HMSO.

Foucault, M. (1977) *Discipline and Punish: The Birth of the Prison.* Harmondsworth: Penguin (translated by Alan Sheridan).

Funke, G.S. (1985) 'The economies of prison crowding', *Annals of the American Academy of Political and Social Science*, 478: 86–99.

Gans, H. (1970) 'The juvenile problem in Levittown', in P. Lerman (ed.), *Delinquency and Social Policy.* London: Praeger Publications, pp. 382–90.

Garland, D. (1985) *Punishment and Welfare: A History of Penal Strategies.* Aldershot: Gower.

Gibbons, D. (1970) 'Differential treatment of delinquents and interpersonal majority levels theory: a critique', *Social Service Review*, 44: 23–33.

Goffman, E. (1961) *Asylums: Essays on the Social Situation of Mental Patients, and Other Inmates.* Harmondsworth: Penguin.

Griffith, J.A.G. (1985) *The Politics of the Judiciary* (3rd ed.). London: Fontana Press.

Griffiths, R. (1988) *Community Care: Agenda for Action: A Report to the Secretary of State for Social Services.* London: HMSO.

Griffiths, W.A. (1982) 'Supervision in the community', *Justice of the Peace*, 146: 514–15.

Grygier, T., Nease, B. and Anderson, C.S. (1970) 'An exploratory study of halfway houses', *Crime and Delinquency*, 16: 280–91.

Guardian (1988a) 'Prisons at the limits', 16 May.

Guardian (1988b) 'Figures hide homeless', 29 December.

Guardian (1988c) 'Tags or slop pots?', 23 February.

Handler, J. (1973) *The Coercive Social Worker: British Lessons for American Social Services.* Chicago: Rand McNally.

Harris, K.M. (1985) 'Reducing prison crowding and nonprison penalties', *Annals of the American Academy of Political and Social Science*, 478: 150–60.

Henderson, P. (1986) 'Community work and the probation service', *Home Office Research Bulletin*, No. 20: 13–16.

Hil, R. (1982) 'Probation day care provision: a case study', *Home Office Research Bulletin*, No. 4: 38–40.

Hil, R. (1986) 'Centre 81: clients' and officers' views on the Southampton day centre', in J. Ponting (ed.), *Alternatives to Custody.* Oxford: Basil Blackwell, pp. 71–91.

Holman, R. (1973) 'Poverty: consensus and alternatives', *British Journal of Social Work*, 3(4); reprinted in R. Holman and E. Butterworth (eds) (1975) *Social Welfare in Modern Britain.* Glasgow: Fontana/Collins, pp. 403–19.

Holt, J. (1985) *No Holiday Camps: Custody, Juvenile Justice and the Politics of Law and Order.* Leicester: Association of Juvenile Justice.

Home Office (1968) *Report of the Committee on Local Authority and Allied Personal Social Services* (Seebohm Committee). London: HMSO.

Home Office (1977) *Review of Criminal Justice Policy 1976.* London: HMSO.

Home Office (1978) *The Sentence of the Court: A Handbook for Courts on the Treatment of Offenders* (3rd ed.). London: HMSO.

Home Office (1979) *Statistics of the Criminal Justice System England and Wales 1968–78.* London: HMSO.

Home Office (1982) *Probation and After-care Statistics England and Wales 1981.* Statistics Department, Tolworth Tower, Surbiton, Surrey: Home Office.

Home Office (1984a) *Criminal Justice: A Working Paper.* London: Home Office.

Home Office (1984b) *Statement of National Objectives and Priorities.* London: Home Office.

Home Office (1986) *Sentence of the Court: A Handbook for Courts on the Treatment of Offenders* (2nd ed.). London: HMSO.

Home Office (1987a) *Criminal Statistics England and Wales 1986*. London: HMSO.

Home Office (1987b) *Prison Statistics England and Wales 1986*. London: HMSO.

Home Office (1988a) 'Home Secretary's statement on prisons', circular ref. 2A MVAA, 5 April. London: Home Office.

Home Office (1988b) *Private Sector Involvement in the Remand System*. London: HMSO.

Home Office (1988c) *Punishment, Custody and the Community*. London: HMSO.

Home Office (1988d) *Tackling Offending: An Action Plan*. London: Home Office.

Home Office (1988e) *Report on the Work of the Prison Service April 1987–March 1988*. London: HMSO.

Home Office (1988f) *Criminal Statistics England and Wales 1987*. London: HMSO.

Home Office (1988g) 'Draft circular', ref. J.14(PD), 6 October. London: Home Office.

Home Office (1988h) *Criminal Statistics England and Wales: Supplementary Tables*, Vol. 4. London: Government Statistical Service.

Home Office (1988i) *Statutory Instruments: 1988: Criminal Law, England and Wales: The Community Service Rules 1988*. 1 November. London: Home Office.

Home Office (1990a) *Supervision & Punishment in the Community: A Framework for Action*. London: HMSO.

Home Office (1990b) *Crime, Justice and Protecting the Public: The Government's Proposals for Legislation*. London: HMSO.

Hope, T. and Shaw, M. (eds) (1988) *Communities and Criminal Reduction*. London: HMSO.

Hopkins, A., Schick, A. and White, S. (1977) 'A prison for the Australian Capital territory?', *Australian & New Zealand Journal of Criminology*, 10: 205–15.

Horton, J. (1981) 'The rise of the right: a global view', *Crime and Social Justice*, Summer: 7–17.

Hudson, B. (1984) 'The rising use of imprisonment: the impact of "decarceration" policies', *Critical Social Policy*, Winter, No. 2: 46–58.

Hylton, J. (1981a) *Reintegrating the Offender: Assessing the Impact of Community Corrections*. Washington: University Press of America.

Hylton, J. (1981b) 'The growth of punishment: imprisonment and community corrections in Canada', *Crime and Social Justice*, Summer: 18–28.

Hylton, J. (1982) 'Rhetoric and reality: a critical appraisal of community correctional programs', *Crime and Delinquency*, 28: 341–73.

Ignatieff, M. (1978) *A Just Measure of Pain*. New York: Columbia University Press.

Ignatieff, M. (1983) 'State, civil society and total institutions: a critique of recent social histories of punishment', in S. Cohen and A. Scull (eds), *Social Control and the State*. Oxford: Basil Blackwell.

Inner London Probation and After-care Service (1975) *Community Service by Offenders: A Progress Report of the First Two Years' Operation of the Scheme in Inner London*. London: Inner London Probation and After-care Service.

Inner London Probation Service (1989) *Response to the Green Paper. 'Punishment, Custody and the Community'*. London: Inner London Probation Service.

Jenkin, P. (1981) 'Trumpet volunteers', *Guardian*, 21 January.

'Joan' (1985) 'Eight days in the system', *Probation Journal*, 32: 11–13.

Johnson, A. (1989) 'Race bias fear may keep tagging out of London', *Guardian*, 13 February.

Jones, D. and Mayo, M. (eds) (1974) *Community Work One*. London: Routledge and Kegan Paul.

Jordan, B. (1983) 'Criminal justice and probation in the 1980s', *Probation Journal*, 30: 83–8.

Joseph, K. (1972) 'The cycle of deprivation'. Speech given at a conference organised by the Pre-school Playgroup Association, 29 June; reprinted in E. Butterworth and R. Holman (eds) (1975), *Social Welfare in Modern Britain*. Glasgow: Fontana/Collins, pp. 387–93.

Junger-Tas, J. (1986a) 'Community service in the Netherlands', *Community Service Newsletter*, Part I (13): 4–10.

Junger-Tas, J. (1986b) 'Community service in the Netherlands', *Community Service Newsletter*, Part II (14): 2–5.

Justice of the Peace (1981) 'Editorial, the cost of prison', 143: 110.

Justice of the Peace (1982) 'Notes of the week', 146: 1–3.

Kent Probation Service (1983) *The Kent Probation Control Unit – The First Year of Operation January–December 1981*. Gillingham: Kent Probation Service.

King, R. (1983) 'The price of prison', *Probation Journal*, 30: 123–6.

Klapmuts, N. (1975) 'Community alternatives to prison', in C.R. Dodge (ed.), *A World without Prisons: Alternatives to Incarceration throughout the World*. Lexington, Mass.: Lexington Books, pp. 101–31.

Lacey, M., Pendleton, J. and Read, G. (1983) 'Supervision in the community — the rightings of wrongs', *Justice of the Peace*, 147: 120–23.

Langdon, J. (1982) 'Whitelaw eludes forces of law and order', *Guardian*, 7 October.

Lawson, C. (1978) *The Probation Officer as Prosecutor: A Study of Proceedings for Breach of Requirements in Probation*. Cambridge: Cambridge Institute of Criminology.

Le Grand, J. and Robinson, R. (eds) (1984) *Privatisation and the Welfare State*. London: Allen and Unwin.

Lerman, P. (1968) 'Evaluating the outcome of institutions for delinquents', *Social Work*, 13: 55–64.

Lerman, P. (ed.) (1970) *Delinquency and Social Policy*. London: Praeger Publications.

Lerman, P. (1975) *Community Treatment and Social Control: A Critical Analysis of Juvenile Correctional Policy*. Chicago: University of Chicago Press.

Lerman, P. (1982) *Deinstitutionalization and the Welfare State*. New Jersey: Rutgers University Press.

Lerman, P. (1984) 'Child welfare, the private sector and community-based corrections', *Crime and Delinquency*, 20: 5–38.

Lewis, H. and Mair, G. (1988) *Bail and Probation Work II: The Use of London Probation/Bail Hostels for Bailees*. Research and Planning Unit Paper 50, London: Home Office.

Lijphart, A. (1975) *The Politics of Accommodation (2nd ed.)*. Berkeley: University of California Press.

Lipton, D., Martinson, R. and Wilks, J. (1975) *Effectiveness of Correctional Treatment: A Survey of Treatment Evaluation Studies*. Springfield: Praeger Publications.

Longley, R. (1985) 'Halving the custody rate', *Community Care*, 5: 17–19.

McConville, S. (1988) 'When punishment breaks out of gaol', *Guardian*, 24 August.

McCormack, C. (1988) 'Specified activities: raft or bridge?', *Probation Journal*, 35: 115.

McDonald, D.C. (1986) *Punishment without Walls: Community Service Sentences in New York City*. New Jersey: Rutgers University Press.

McCain, G., Cox, V.C. and Paulus, P.B. (1980) *The Effect of Prison Crowding on Inmate Behavior*, Washington, DC: Department of Justice, National Institute of Justice.

McIntosh, M. (1971) 'Changes in the organization of thieving', in S. Cohen (ed.), *Images of Deviance*. Harmondsworth: Penguin, pp. 98–133.

McRae, H. (1988) 'It may seem far-fetched . . . but what if we could work from choice and not necessity?', *Guardian*, 22 December.

McWilliams, B. and Murphy, N. (1980) 'Breach of community service', in K. Pease and W. McWilliams (eds), *Community Service by Order*. Edinburgh: Scottish Academic Press, pp. 92–114.

Mair, G. (1986) 'Ethnic minorities, probation and the magistrates courts: a pilot study', *British Journal of Criminology*, 26: 652–8.

Mair, G. (1988) *Probation Day Centres*. Home Office Research and Planning Unit, London: HMSO.

Mair, G. and Brockington, N. (1988) 'Female offenders and the probation service', *Howard Journal of Criminal Justice*, 27: 117–26.

Mannheim, H. (1939) *The Dilemmas of Prison Reform*. London: George Allen and Unwin.

Martinson, R. (1972) 'The paradox of prison reform', *New Republic*, 166(14): 23–5; 166(15): 13–15; 166(16): 17–19; 166(17): 21–3.

Martinson, R. (1974) 'What works? Questions and answers about prison reform', *The Public Interest*, Spring, No. 35: 22–54.

Martinson, R. (1979) 'New findings, new views: a note of caution regarding sentencing reform', *Holfstra Law Review*, 7(2): 243 ff.

Marx, G.T. (1985) 'I'll be watching you', *Dissent*, 30: 26–34.

Mathiesen, T. (1974) *The Politics of Abolition*. London: Martin Robertson.

Mathiesen, T. (1981) 'The view from Scandinavia', *Crime and Social Justice*, Summer: 57–8.

Mathiesen, T. (1983) 'The future of control systems', in D. Garland and P. Young (eds), *The Power to Punish: Contemporary Penality and Social Analysis*. London: Heinemann.

Matthews, R. (1987) 'Decarceration and social control: fantasies and realities', *International Journal of the Sociology of Law*, 15: 39–60.

Matthews, R. (ed.) (1988) *Informal Justice?* London: Sage Publications.

Mayhew, H. and Binney, J. (1862) *The Criminal Prisons of London and Scenes of Prison Life*. London: Griffin, Bohn.

Megargee, E.I. (1977) 'The association of population density, reduced space, and uncomfortable temperatures with misconduct in a prison community', *American Journal of Community Psychology*, 5: 289–98.

Menzies, K. and Vass, A.A. (1989) 'The impact of historical, legal and administrative differences on a sanction: community service orders in England and Ontario', *Howard Journal of Criminal Justice*, 28: 204–17.

Miller, W.B. (1970) 'Inter-institutional conflict and delinquency prevention', in P. Lerman (ed.), *Delinquency and Social Policy*. London: Praeger Publications, pp. 407–13.

Millham, S. (1975) *After Grace-Teeth: A Comparative Study of Residential Experience of Boys in Approved Schools*. London: Chaucer.

Moos, R.H. (1975) *Evaluating Correctional and Community Settings*. New York: John Wiley & Sons.

Morgan, R. (1982) *How Resources are used in the Prison System*. London: NACRO.

Morris, N. (1965) 'Prison evolution', in T. Grygier, H. Jones and J.C. Spencer (eds), *Criminology in Transition: Essays in Honour of Hermann Mannheim*. London: Tavistock Publications, pp. 267–94.

Morris, T.P. (1965) 'The sociology of the prison', in T. Grygier, H. Jones and J.C. Spencer (eds), *Criminology in Transition: Essays in Honour of Hermann Mannheim*. London: Tavistock Publications, pp. 69–87.

Morris, T.P. and Morris, P. (1963) *Pentonville: A Sociological Study of an English Prison*. London: Routledge and Kegan Paul.

Morrison, G. (1985) 'Small is beautiful? Observations on the Dutch penal scene', *Prison Service Journal*, 59: 2–7.

Mullen, J. (1985) 'Prison crowding and the evolution of public policy', *Annals of the American Academy of Political and Social Science*, 478: 31–46.

Murphy, N. (1979) 'Community service — whither?', *Justice of the Peace*, 143: 391.

Murray, P. (1986) 'The close support unit: an intermediate treatment provision for those at risk of removal from the community', in J. Pointing (ed.), *Alternatives to Custody*. Oxford: Basil Blackwell, pp. 39–54.

Musheno, M. (1982) 'Criminal diversion and social control', *Social Science Quarterly*, 63: 280–92.

NACRO (1982) *News Digest*. February, London: National Association for the Care and Resettlement of Offenders.

NACRO (1988) *Some Facts and Findings about Black People in the Criminal Justice System*. Briefing, June, London: National Association for the Care and Resettlement of Offenders.

Nagel, W. (1973) *The New Red Barn: A Critical Look at the Modern American Prison*. New York: Walker.

NAPO (1988a) *Supervision in the Community: Probation Working*. London: National Association of Probation Officers.

NAPO (1988b) *Punishment, Custody and the Community*. London: National Association of Probation Officers.

NAPO News (1988a) 'Untried persons (custody)', No. 1: 10–11.

NAPO News (1988b) 'Sentencing policy', No. 2: 4.

NAPO News (1989a) 'Prison population', No. 6: 18.

NAPO News (1989b) 'Black people and the criminal justice system', No. 6: 8–10.

NAPO News (1989c) 'NAPO interview', No. 6: 6–7.

National Executive Committee (1988) *Tackling Offending: An Action Plan: Guidelines for Branches*. NEC.96/88, 6 October, London: National Association of Probation Officers.

Nicholls, G. (1898) *A History of English Poor Law*, Vol. 2. London: Frank Cass.

Nimmer, R.T. (1974) *Diversion: The Search for Alternative Forms of Prosecution*. Chicago: American Bar Association.

Nuttall, C.P., Barnard, E.E., Fowles, A.J., Frost, A., Hammond, W.H., Mayhew, P., Pease, K., Tarling, R. and Weatheritt, M.J. (1977) *Parole in England and Wales*. Home Office Research Study No. 38, London: HMSO.

Oatham, E. and Simon, F. (1972) 'Are suspended sentences working?', *New Society*, 3 August: 233–5.

Palmer, T.B. (1971) 'California's community treatment program for delinquent adolescents', *Journal of Research in Crime and Delinquency*, 8: 74–92.

Palmer, T.B. (1973) 'Matching worker and client in corrections', *Social Work*, 18: 95–103.

Palmer, T.B. (1975) 'Martinson revisited', *Journal of Research on Crime and Delinquency*, 12: 133–52.

Parker, H., Jarvis, G. and Sumner, M. (1987) 'Under new orders: the redefinition of social work with young offenders', *British Journal of Social Work*, 17: 21–43.

Parker, T. (1973) *The Man Inside*. London: Michael Joseph.

Payne, D. (1977) 'Day training centres', *Home Office Research Bulletin*, No. 4: 5–7.

Pearson, G. (1983) *Hooligan: A History of Respectable Fears*. London: Macmillan.

Pease, K. (1980) 'Community service and prison: are they alternatives?', in K. Pease and

W. McWilliams (eds), *Community Service by Order*. Edinburgh: Scottish Academic Press, pp. 27–42.

Pease, K. (1983) 'Penal innovations', in J. Lishman (ed.), *Social Work with Adult Offenders*. Aberdeen: University of Aberdeen Press.

Pease, K. (1986) 'Community service as an alternative to custody', *Community Service Newsletter*, Part I (15): 15–18; Part II (16): 3–6.

Pease, K., Durkin, P., Earnshaw, I., Payne, D. and Thorpe, J. (1975) *Community Service Orders*. Home Office Research Studies No. 29, London: HMSO.

Pease, K., Billingham, S. and Earnshaw, I. (1977) *Community Service Assessed in 1976*. Home Office Research Study No. 39, London: HMSO.

Petersilia, J. (1988) 'Probation reform', in J.E. Scott and T.Hirschi (eds), *Controversial Issues in Crime and Justice*. London: Sage Publications, pp. 166–80.

Philips, D. (1977) *Crime and Authority in Victorian England: The Black Country 1835–1860*. London: Croom Helm.

Phillpotts, G.J.O. and Lancucki, L.B. (1979) *Previous Convictions, Sentence and Reconviction*. Home Office Research Study No. 53, London: HMSO.

Pitts, J. (1988) *The Politics of Juvenile Crime*. London: Sage Publications.

Plant, R. (1974) *Community and Ideology: An Essay in Applied Social Philosophy*. London: Routledge and Kegan Paul.

Platt, T. and Takagi, P. (1981) 'Law and order in the 1980s', *Crime and Social Justice*, Summer: 1–6.

Polonoski, M. (1981) *The Community Service Order Program in Ontario 4: Summary*. Toronto: MCS.

Pratt, J. (1986) 'Diversion from the juvenile court', *British Journal of Criminology*, 26: 212–33.

Priestley, P. (1970) *The Problem of the Short-term Prisoner*. London: National Association for the Care and Resettlement of Offenders.

Quay, H. and Love, C. (1977) 'The effect of juvenile diversion programs or rearrests', *Criminal Justice and Behavior*, 4: 377–96.

Raban, T. (1984) 'Searching for the pot of gold', reviews, *Social Work Today*, 16: 20.

Radzinowicz, L. (1968) *A History of English Criminal Law and its Administration from 1750: Grappling for Control*, Vol. 4. London: Stevens & Sons.

Ralphs, R. (1986) 'The evolution of control', *Justice of the Peace*, 150: 154–6.

Raynor, P. (1988) *Probation as an Alternative to Custody: A Case Study*. Aldershot: Gower.

Reckless, W.C. and Sindwani, K.L. (1974) 'Efforts to measure impact of institutional stay', *British Journal of Criminology*, 14: 369–75.

Rhys, M., Faulder, P., Hogarth, L., Parker, I., Raft, C., Turner, J. and Green, A. (1989) *Demonstration Unit*. London: Inner London Probation Service.

Richards, B. (1978) 'The experience of long-term imprisonment', *British Journal of Criminology*, 18: 162–9.

Richards, N.G. (1979) 'Letters', *Justice of the Peace*, 143: 509.

Rock, P. (1973) *Making People Pay*. London: Routledge and Kegan Paul.

Rodger, J.J. (1988) 'Social work as social control re-examined: beyond the dispersal of discipline thesis', *Sociology*, 22: 563–81.

Roethlisberger, F.J. (1945) 'The foreman: master and victim of "double talk"', *Harvard Business Review*, XXIII: 285–94; reprinted in R. Dubin (ed.) (1961) *Human Relations in Administration* (2nd ed.). Englewood Cliffs, NJ: Prentice-Hall, pp. 269–317.

Roll, E. (ed.) (1982) *The Mixed Economy*. London: Macmillan.

Rothman, D. (1971) *The Discovery of the Asylum: Social Order and Disorder in the New Republic*. Boston: Little, Brown.

Rothman, D. (1974) 'Prisons and the failure model', *Nation*, 21 December: 641–50.

Rusche, G. (1980) 'Labor market and penal sanctions: thoughts on the sociology of criminal justice', in T. Platt and P. Takagi (eds), *Punishment and Penal Discipline*. San Francisco: Crime and Social Justice Association.

Rutherford, A. (1984) *Prisons and the Process of Justice: The Reductionist Challenge*. London: Heinemann. Published in 1986 as an Oxford University Press Paperback. All quotations from the 1986 edition.

Rutherford, A. (1986) *Growing Out of Crime: Society and Young People in Trouble*. Harmondsworth: Penguin.

Rutherford, A. and McDermott, R. (1976) *Juvenile Diversion*. Washington, DC: National Institute of Law Enforcement and Criminal Justice.

Sapsford, R.J. (1978) 'Life sentence prisoners: psychological changes during sentence', *British Journal of Criminology*, 18: 128–45.

Sarason, S.B. (1974) *The Psychological Sense of Community: Prospects for a Community Psychology*. San Francisco: Jossey-Bass.

Scarborough, J., Geraghty, J. and Loffangen (1987) 'Day centres and voluntarism', *Probation Journal*, 34: 47–50.

Schulberg, H.C. (1973) 'From institutions to human services', in Y. Bakal (ed.), *Closing Correctional Institutions: New Strategies for Youth Services*. Lexington. Mass.: Lexington Books, pp. 39–48.

Scott, D. *et al.* (eds) (1985) *Going Local in Probation*. Norwich: University of East Anglia.

Scull, A.T. (1977) *Decarceration: Community Treatment and the Deviant: A Radical View*. Englewood Cliffs, NJ: Prentice-Hall.

Scull, A.T. (1984) *Decarceration: Community Treatment and the Deviant: A Radical View* (2nd ed.). Cambridge: Basil Blackwell/Polity Press.

Sharrock, D. (1989) 'Probation "increases risk of jail"', *Guardian*, 6 April.

Sheppard, B. (1980) 'Research into aspects of probation', *Home Office Research Bulletin*, No. 19.

Shichor, D. and Kelley, D.H. (eds) (1980) *Critical Issues in Juvenile Delinquency*. Lexington, Mass.: Lexington Books.

Smith, C., Farrant, M. and Marchant, H. (1972) *The Wincroft Youth Project*. London: Tavistock.

Smith, D. (1987) 'The limits of positivism in social work research', *British Journal of Social Work*, 17: 401–11.

Smith, D., Sheppard, B., Mair, G. and Williams, K. (1984) *Reducing the Prison Population: An Exploratory Study in Hampshire*. Research and Planning Unit Paper 23, London: Home Office.

Smith, L.J.F. (1982) 'Day training centres', *Home Office Research Bulletin*, No. 14: 34–7.

Smith, P. (1984) 'If it can happen here: reflections on the Dutch system', *Prison Journal*, 58: 847–50.

Solicitor General Canada (1982) *International Conference on Alternatives to Imprisonment Report, Toronto, June 8–11, 1980*. Ottawa: Communications Division Solicitor General Canada.

South West London Probation and After-care Service (1981) *Community Service in South West London 1975–1980*. London: Probation and After-care Service.

Sparks, R.F. (1971) 'The use of suspended sentences', *Criminal Law Review*, July: 384–401.

Spencer, N. and Edwards, P. (1986) 'The rise and fall of the Kent Control Unit: a local perspective', *Probation Journal*, 33: 91–4.

Stanley, D. (1976) *Prisoners among Us: The Problem of Parole*. Washington DC: The Brookings Institution.

Stephenson, J. (1979) *Popular Disturbances in England 1700–1870*. London: Longman.

Sussex, J. (1974) *Community Service by Offenders: Year One in Kent*. Chichester: Barry Rose Publishers.

Taggart, R. (1972) *The Prison Unemployment: Manpower Prisons for Offenders*. London: Johns Hopkins University Press.

Takagi, P.T. (1969) 'The effect of parole agents' judgements on recidivism rates', *Psychiatry*, 32: 192–9.

Takagi, P.T. and Robinson, J. (1969) 'The parole violator: an organisational reject', *Journal of Research in Crime and Delinquency*, 6: 78–86.

Tholfensen, T.R. (1976) *Working Class Radicalism in Mid-Victorian England*. London: Croom Helm.

Thomas, D.A. (1979) *Princples of Sentencing* (2nd ed.) London: Heinemann.

Thorvaldson, S.A. (1978) 'The effects of community service on the attitudes of offenders'. Unpublished PhD thesis, University of Cambridge.

Tomlinson, M.H. (1981) 'Penal servitude 1846–1865: a system in evolution', in V. Bailey (ed.), *Policing and Punishment in Nineteenth Century Britain*. London: Croom Helm, pp. 126–49.

Townsend, P. (1970) *The Fifth Social Service: A Critical Analysis of the Seebohm Report*. London: Fabian Society.

Van Krieken, R. (1986) 'Social theory and child welfare: beyond social control', *Theory and Society*, 15: 401–29.

Vanstone, M. (1985) 'Moving away from help? Policy and practice in probation Day Centres', *Howard Journal of Criminal Justice*, 24: 20–28.

Vanstone, M. (1986) 'The Pontypridd Day Training Centre: diversion from prison in action', in J. Pointing (ed.), *Alternatives to Custody*. Oxford: Basil Blackwell, pp. 92–105.

Vanstone, M. and Raynor, P. (1981) 'Diversion from prison — a partial success and a missed opportunity', *Probation Journal*, 28: 85–9.

Varah, M. (1987) 'Probation and community service', in J. Harding (ed.), *Probation and the Community*. London: Tavistock Publications, pp. 83–99.

Varne, S. (1976) 'Saturday work: a real alternative?', *Australian & New Zealand Journal of Criminology*, 9: 95–108.

Vass, A.A. (1979) 'The myth of a radical trend in British community work: a comparison of statutory and voluntary projects', *Community Development Journal*, 14: 3–13.

Vass, A.A. (1980) 'Law enforcement in community service: probation, defence or prosecution?', *Probation Journal*, 27: 114–17.

Vass, A.A. (1981) 'Community service for juveniles? A critical comment', *Probation Journal*, 28: 44–9.

Vass, A.A. (1982a) 'The probation service in a state of turmoil', *Justice of the Peace*, 146: 788–93.

Vass, A.A. (1982b) 'The enforcement of community service orders in one area of Southern England'. PhD thesis, University of London.

Vass, A.A. (1984) *Sentenced to Labour: Close Encounters with a Prison Substitute*. St Ives: Venus Academica.

Vass, A.A. (1985) 'The changing functions of social work in Britain'. Paper delivered at the 22nd International Congress of the Schools of Social Work, Montreal, July–August.

Vass, A.A. (1986a) 'Community service: areas of concern and suggestions for change', *Howard Journal of Criminal Justice*, 25: 100–111.

Vass, A.A. (1986b) Review, 'No holiday camps: Custody: juvenile justice and the politics of law and order', J. Holt, *British Journal of Criminology*, 26: 402–4.

Vass, A.A. (1988a) 'The marginality of community service and the threat of privatisation', *Probation Journal*, 35: 48–51.

Vass, A.A. (1988b) 'The effectiveness of social work interventions', *Eklogy*, No. 79: 180–94.

Vass, A.A. (1989) 'Tagging: Spiderman looks at the web of electronic tags', *Social Work Today*, 20: 20–21.

Vass, A.A. and Menzies, K. (1989) 'The community service order as a public and private enterprise: a comparative account of practices in England and Ontario, Canada', *British Journal of Criminology*, 29: 255–72.

Vass, A.A. and Weston, A. (1990) 'Probation day centres as an alternative to custody: a "Trojan horse" examined', *British Journal of Criminology* 30: 189–206.

Walker, D. (1987) 'Are day centres "alternative probation?"', *Social Work Today*, 26 January, 12–13.

Walker, H. and Beaumont, B. (1981) *Probation Work: Critical Theory and Social Practice*. Oxford: Basil Blackwell.

Walker, H. and Beaumont, B. (1985) *Working with Offenders*. London: Macmillan.

Walker, N. (1983a) 'Side effects of incarceration', *British Journal of Criminology*, 23: 61–71.

Walker, N. (1983b) 'The effectiveness of probation', *Probation Journal*, 30: 99–103.

Walker, N. (1983c) 'Probation and just deserts', *Probation Journal*, 30: 17–21.

Walker, N. (1985) *Sentencing: Theory, Law and Practice*. London: Butterworth.

Warren, C. (1981) 'New forms of social control: the myth of deinstitutionalization', *American Behavioral Scientist*, 24: 724–40.

Warren, M.Q. (1972) 'Correctional treatment in community settings: A report of mental health'. Paper prepared for the 6th International Congress in Criminology, Madrid, 21–27 September 1970.

White, S. (1973) 'Suspended imprisonment', *Criminal Law Review*, January: 7–11.

Williams, D. (1981) 'The view from New Zealand', *Crime and Social Justice*, Summer: 59–60.

Willis, A. (1977) 'Community service as an alternative to imprisonment: a cautionary view', *Probation Journal*, 24: 120–26.

Willis, A. (1979) 'Displacement from custody: a review of the day training centre experiment', quoted in M. Vanstone (1986) 'The Pontypridd day training centre: diversion from prison in action', in J. Pointing (ed.), *Alternatives to Custody*. Oxford: Basil Blackwell, pp. 92–105.

Willis, A. (1983) 'The balance between care and control in probation: a research note', *British Journal of Social Work*, 13: 339–46.

Willis, P.E. (1977) *Learning to Labour: How Working Class Kids Get Working Class Jobs*. Aldershot: Gower.

Winstour, P. (1989) 'Minister starts row on juvenile crime', *Guardian*, 31 March.

Wright, M. and Galaway, B. (eds) (1989) *Mediation and Criminal Justice: Victims, Offenders and Community*. London: Sage Publications.

Working Party (1982) *Social Workers: Their Role & Tasks* (Chairperson: P.M. Barclay). London: National Institute for Social Work/Bedford Square Press/NCVO.

Young, W. (1979) *Community Service Orders: The Development and Use of a New Penal Measure*. London: Heinemann.

Index